The Children Act Now

The Children Act Now

Messages from Research

Prepared for the Department of Health by

Jane Aldgate, Professor of Social Care, The Open University
and
June Statham, Senior Research Officer, Thomas Coram Research Unit,
Institute of Education, University of London

STUDIES IN EVALUATING THE CHILDREN ACT 1989

London: The Stationery Office

First published 2001

ISBN 0 11 322263 7

Published by The Stationery Office and available from:

The Stationery Office
(mail, telephone and fax orders only)
PO Box 29, Norwich NR3 1GN
General enquiries/Telephone orders 0870 600 5522
Fax orders 0870 600 5533

www.thestationeryoffice.com

The Stationery Office Bookshops
123 Kingsway, London WC2B 6PQ
020 7242 6393 Fax 020 7242 6394
68–69 Bull Street, Birmingham B4 6AD
0121 236 9696 Fax 0121 236 9699
33 Wine Street, Bristol BS1 2BQ
0117 926 4306 Fax 0117 929 4515
9–21 Princess Street, Manchester M60 8AS
0161 834 7201 Fax 0161 833 0634
16 Arthur Street, Belfast BT1 4GD
028 9023 8451 Fax 028 9023 5401
The Stationery Office Oriel Bookshop
18–19, High Street, Cardiff CF1 2BZ
029 2039 5548 Fax 029 2038 4347
71 Lothian Road, Edinburgh EH3 9AZ
0870 606 5566 Fax 0870 606 5588

The Stationery Office's Accredited Agents
(see Yellow Pages)

and through good booksellers

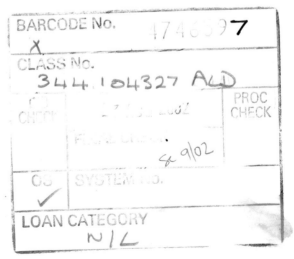

Printed in the United Kingdom for The Stationery Office
TN007646 07/01 C100 9385 15316

Contents

B. Reports and studies   243

Section III: References   257

Figures and tables

Figures

Tables

Foreword

The Children Act 1989 has generally been regarded as a major piece of reforming legislation for children. Because of the scale of its reforms, it has been essential to find out how the Act is being implemented in practice and whether it is making the difference that the legislators intended. A substantial programme of research has been commissioned by the Department of Health over the last decade to inform us about how the Act is working in England and Wales.

The findings of 24 studies have been brought together in this volume. They contain important messages. They highlight the nature of children's needs and the help that families value. They reveal the complexity of deciding when and how to intervene to protect and promote children's well-being. They emphasise that effective intervention depends on interagency working and partnerships between local council services, health, the family justice system and the voluntary sector. A key message is that many families see Social Services as the agency to which they would first turn for help. However, services are only effective if professionals and families learn from each other and if children and young people are fully involved in taking decisions about their lives. The findings point to the importance of the need to have an effectively integrated children's system for assessment and care planning, better management information, competent professional staff and a smooth interface between children's services and the court system. Heeding of the messages from these studies is essential for the improvement of our services for children in need and their families.

I am grateful to Professor Jane Aldgate and Dr June Statham who have brought to the challenging task of reviewing this wealth of material their clear expertise and experience of research and practice in England and Wales.

Professor Sir John Pattison
Director of Research, Analysis and Information

Acknowledgements

There are many people to thank for help with the preparation of this overview, especially the Advisory Group. This group had a broad membership, representing managers, academics and practitioners from different agencies and policy-makers from the Department of Health. Their expertise, enthusiasm, wisdom and tenacity kept the project going. The authors would like to express gratitude for their support.

There was also a range of individuals whose commitment, time and whole-hearted support was deeply valued. The authors wish to thank the Department of Health for supporting the project. In particular, the authors would like to express thanks to Dr Carolyn Davies of the Department of Health for her inspiration and management of this overview and the research programme on which it is based. We are also grateful to Caroline Thomas for seeing the project through to publication. Special thanks are also due to Jenny Gray, Helen Jones and Peter Smith, who spent some of their precious time with the authors to guide them on new policy initiatives, and to Jonathan Corbett for his advice on Welsh perspectives. Additionally, thanks go to others within the Department of Health who took time to look at the drafts: Bruce Clark, Chris Corrigan, Barbara Herts, Andrea Hickman, Tom Jeffery, Steve Kingdom, Arran Poyser, John Rowlands, Jennifer Ruddick, Chris Sealey and Ann Stephenson.

Thanks go to the authors of the projects, who gave unequivocal support throughout and provided us with invaluable comments on the text. We are also indebted to Janet Seden, Jeremy Roche and Peter Aggleton for their help.

The project would have foundered without the administrative support of Julie Stock at The Open University, Christina Cazelet at the University of Leicester and Heather Thorn at the Department of Health. We would also like to thank our own institutions for their support: the School of Health and Social Welfare at The Open University; the Thomas Coram Research Unit, Institute of Education, University of London, and the University of Leicester.

Finally, our knowledge of the Children Act 1989 was greatly enhanced by the support of Rupert Hughes CBE, who steered the Act to receive its Royal Assent, and of Wendy Rose, without whom the Children Act 1989 would never have achieved such an impact in the first years of its implementation.

The Advisory Group

Chair: Dr Carolyn Davies, Senior Principal Research Officer, Department of Health

David Allan, Strategic Planning Officer, Warwickshire Social Services

Celia Atherton, Director, Research in Practice, Dartington

Clare Chamberlain, Assistant Chief Social Services Officer, Islington Social Services

Jonathan Corbett, Social Services Inspector, National Assembly for Wales

Di Dallyn, Senior Social Worker, Leicester City Social Services

Ruth Forrester, Operations Manager, Powys Social Services

Moira Gibb, Director, Kensington and Chelsea Social Services

Rose Griffiths, Foster parent and Lecturer in Education, School of Education, University of Leicester

Anna Gupta, Lecturer, University of London, Royal Holloway College

Andrea Hickman, Social Services Inspector, Birmingham

David Morgan, County Solicitor, Leicestershire County Council

Trish Mylan, Principal Social Services Officer, Ely Family Centre, Cardiff

Sara Noakes, Senior Policy Advisor, Central Council for Education and Training in Social Work

Arran Poyser, Social Services Inspector, Department of Health

Clair Pyper, Principal Officer, Children's Social Services, Suffolk Social Services

Marilyn Revell, Guardian ad litem, Kent

Tony Rex, Principal Officer, Monmouthshire Social Services

Ian Rush, Director, Trafford Social Services

Dr Ruth Sinclair, Research Director, National Children's Bureau

Aston Smith, Deputy Manager, Charwood Care Services for Young People, London

Peter Smith, Social Services Inspector, Department of Health

Dr Roger Smith, Senior Policy Advisor, The Children's Society

Steve Tanner, Operational Services Manager, Coventry Social Services

Caroline Thomas, Principal Research Officer, Department of Health

Dr Tara Weeramanthri, Consultant Child and Adolescent Psychiatrist, Camberwell Child and Adolescent Service

Jenny Weinstein, Senior Policy Advisor, Central Council for Education and Training in Social Work

Jo Williams, Director, Cheshire Social Services

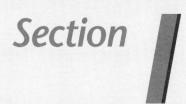

An overview of findings of the 24 Children Act studies

Section I draws out the messages from the individual studies for policy and practice. The findings are presented in the following eight chapters.

EDITORIAL NOTE:

Titles enumerated in the list of references in Section III are referred to throughout this book by their corresponding numbers (shown as superscripts in square brackets). The 24 titles in the Children Act research series are more specifically indicated by the use of a bold font.

1 The Children Act 1989

The Children Act 1989 within a broader child welfare context

Children are growing up in a context of rapid change. Neither they nor their parents can always expect a job for life and at least one-third are unlikely to stay in the same family unit for the duration of their childhood. Such changes are likely to affect the daily lives of children and families. The upbringing of its children is one of the significant activities for any country. The United Nations World Summit for Children suggested in 1990:

> that the lives and normal development of children should have first call on society's capacities and that children should be able to depend on that commitment in good times and bad.[101]

In most societies the preparation of children for adult citizenship is entrusted to families, with the recognition that families will require a system of support from the state to assist them in their task. The roles and tasks of the families and the state at any one time are circumscribed by social policies enacted in law, including income support, health, environment, the education of children and welfare services to safeguard children from harm and promote their well-being.

Countries differ on how they define the boundaries between the obligations of the state and those of the family. Nevertheless, there are some common themes that have been prominent in child welfare policy.

The first is the duty of any state to nurture its children, to promote their best interests. This theme subscribes to the view that children's development is multi-faceted. The principles of the 1989 UN Convention on the Rights of the Child, for example, support the view that concerted attention should be given by families and the state to various aspects of children's lives, including education, care, recreation, culture and health, and children's social behaviour.[100]

The second theme, which has gained credibility over the last two decades, is that children have a status as child citizens. This theme emphasises children's right to have their voices heard and to participate in any decisions affecting their lives.

The third theme relates to the protection of children from harm. This theme is open to differences in interpretation in what constitutes harm and at what level a state should intervene. How far protection of children is exclusively the domain of children's families or whether, and at what point, the state should intervene to support family responsibility differs between countries in Europe and elsewhere. Nevertheless, most European countries attempt to reconcile the right of children to be protected from harm with the responsibilities of adults to safeguard children and attend to their welfare.

Where countries place the boundaries for intervention to protect children from harm will influence the ways in which they provide welfare services for children and families. This overview is concerned with the most up-to-date embodiment of the relationship between the family and the state in relation to the care and upbringing of children in England and Wales – the Children Act 1989.

The Children Act 1989 and the overview

The Children Act 1989, a major piece of reforming legislation, was implemented in 1991, in the same year that the UN Convention on the Rights of the Child was ratified by the United Kingdom.

When the Children Bill came before Parliament in 1988, it was heralded as a significant new piece of legislation. At the time of its second reading in the House of Lords on 6 December 1988, the Lord Chancellor told the House:

> The Bill in my view, represents the most comprehensive and far reaching reform of child care law which has come before Parliament in living memory.[86]

Because of the significance ascribed to the reforms, it was important to watch carefully how the Children Act was being implemented and whether it was achieving the intentions of the legislators. Accordingly, the Department of Health commissioned a series of research studies that addressed several of the key aspects of the Act. These would provide information about how the Act was working.

This overview summarises the key findings from those studies and identifies emerging themes and trends. It relates the findings of the studies to the contemporary context in which services to children in need are being provided.

There are messages about key areas of practice. These include safeguarding and promoting children's welfare simultaneously; working with parents; listening to children; strengthening interagency planning and provision of services; and providing effective services.

The messages from the Children Act research studies are relevant for a wide range of professionals working with children at different levels. It is hoped that the messages will resonate with social work practitioners and their managers.

There are messages for planners and for those working in the courts. Those working in the field of social care and looking after children on a daily basis or for longer periods will also find some useful material. The principles of consulting children and working with parents apply as much in the health, education, youth justice and community development contexts as they do in the social care field. If optimal outcomes are to be achieved for children in need, simultaneous attention to health, education, social care and environment are all salient issues that need a co-ordinated response from different agencies and from central and local government.

The context that led to the Children Act 1989

The changes enacted by the Children Act 1989 need to be understood in the light of a century of child welfare legislation in England and Wales. From the first Acts of the 1890s, which introduced powers to intervene and to rescue children from cruel parents, to the compulsory supervision and Care Orders of the Children and Young Persons Acts of 1933 and 1969, the protection of children has been at the forefront of child welfare law. A second theme has been the promotion of children's welfare. The Children Act 1989 has its roots in the post-war Children Act 1948, which introduced the provision of regulated care for children deprived of a normal family life. The balance between the roles of family and state are also present. The Children Act 1989 built on the concept of prevention introduced in the 1960s in the Children and Young Persons Act 1963 and addressed more coherently the issues dealing with children subject to private law. The Children Act 1989 also took into account family proceedings legislation, including the guardianship legislation enacted between 1923 and 1973 and wardship legislation, which has an even longer history in England and Wales. Finally, the Children Act strengthened the rights of children as citizens by building on the parts of the Children Act 1975 and the statutory instruments governing the review processes for children in care that emphasised the rights of children to be heard in decision-making.

Although it is possible to see some continuity over time in successive child welfare legislation prior to 1989, there were also many contradictions, resulting from separate and piecemeal developments. Consequently, by the early 1980s, the law concerning the upbringing of children was, at best, complex and confused and, at worst, contradictory. The extent of the problem is shown by the fact that the Children Act 1989 finally repealed over 50 pieces of legislation relating to children's welfare.

In response to the contradictions, in 1983 the House of Commons Social Services Committee, headed by Renée Short, undertook a review of children in care. The Committee reported in 1984, recommending that the government should establish a review of child care law.[88] This was completed remarkably quickly by 1985.[84] At the same time, parallel concern emanated from the Lord Chancellor's Office about children's welfare in court cases in private law.[90] From here, the Children Act 1989 began to take shape. The White Paper that preceded the Act, published in 1987, outlined the principles upon which the new Children Act would be based.[85]

There were other sources of information and ideas that reinforced the thinking of the House of Commons Social Services Committee and the Child Care Law Review. Notable among these were reports and research studies commissioned by government and other funding bodies. These included the publication by the Department of Health and Social Security in 1985 of the first overview of research studies on children in the care of local authorities, *Social Work Decisions in Child Care*.[50] This volume, which was widely disseminated and became known as 'the pink book', provided research evidence about the value of working in partnership with parents, about the deficiencies of the care system, the poor planning and decision-making that took place and the cumbersome bureaucratic arrangements and inadequacies of post-qualifying training that hampered both the practice and management of social work with children and families.

Research had also drawn attention to rigid practice in adoption and fostering. An influential study by Thoburn and her colleagues for the Department of Health and Social Security showed that permanence for older children could be achieved in a variety of ways, including adoption with contact and permanent foster care.[99]

Much-publicised deaths of children from abuse and neglect in the 1980s – for example, Jasmine Beckford, Tyra Henry and Kimberly Carlile – and the removal to care of over 100 children alleged to have been sexually abused in Cleveland were also a major cause of political, public and professional concern.[98] There were concerns that social workers did not have the appropriate power to act swiftly to protect children in emergencies. On the other hand, the law had allowed social workers to be heavy-handed and remove children on flimsy evidence for unwarranted periods. Either way, assessment of the impact of abuse on children's development was faulty. The absence of good interagency working had also led to some vital omissions of information. Even where there was information recorded on files, sometimes its significance in safeguarding children's welfare went unrecognised. Too often, the focus was on the parents and their circumstances rather than on the impact of harm to the child in question. This culminated in the recognition in the 1988 Cleveland Report that:

> the child is a person and not the object of our concern.[62]

Although, in relation to child maltreatment, it had been said that sometimes there was too much emphasis on the rights of parents, pressure groups concerned with the parents of children looked after argued the opposite. Concern about children had caused parents to be neglected, resulting in loss of contact with their children. Instrumental in this approach was the work of the Family Rights Group. A successful challenge to the European Court by an English parent to regain access to her children in care led to the production in 1983 by the Department of Health and Social Security of a Code of Practice on access,[83] which aimed to redress the balance. This more balanced view underpinned the subsequent legislation and regulation about contact.

The principles of the Children Act 1989

The Children Act 1989 was different from previous legislation in that it provided a unifying framework for most aspects of the law relating to the care and upbringing of children.[45] It was concerned with defining the framework of the legal and organisational responses to achieve the most helpful decisions in court cases and with the provision of services best suited to promote the welfare of children in need.

In the White Paper of January 1987 the government's approach to the new legislation was guided by a clear set of principles.[85, para. 5]

Principles underpinning the Children Act 1989

- The primary responsibility for the upbringing of children rests with parents; the state should be ready to help parents to discharge that responsibility especially where doing so lessens the risk of family breakdown.

- Services to families in need of help should be arranged in a voluntary partnership with the parents. Where such services include looking after the child away from home, close contact should be maintained so that the children can continue their relationships with their families and where appropriate be reunited with them as soon as possible.

- The transfer to the local authority of parents' legal powers and responsibilities for caring for the child should only be done with a full court hearing following due legal processes. Such a transfer must rest on establishing that there is harm to a child who is not receiving adequate parental care or is beyond parental control and that a court order is the best method of safeguarding his interests.

- Court processes affecting the child must recognise that, though the interests of the child are the primary concern, the parents' legal status in relation to the child is at issue. Parents should be properly represented and it follows that they should be full parties to such court proceedings in addition to the child.

- The application of emergency powers to remove a child at serious immediate risk, which necessarily cannot be preceded by a full court hearing, should be of short duration and subject to court review if the parent or child wishes to challenge it.

- Where local authorities are caring for a child away from home their legal responsibilities should be clear, as should the powers and responsibilities of parents in these circumstances.

Making the principles operational through *Guidance and Regulations*

Extensive guidance and regulations accompanied the Children Act 1989. The nine volumes of *Guidance and Regulations*[49] and accompanying index volume were, and still remain, very important in helping those implementing the Act to understand the thinking behind it. Over and above this, they continue to provide detailed information that practitioners can use to effect the best possible practice with children and families. Most of the *Guidance* remains robust. Some additions have been made to respond to developments in policy and practice, such as the introduction of Children's Services Planning,[78] which makes explicit the intentions of the Children Act 1989. Other amendments have been made to strengthen the safeguarding of children. For instance, changes resulted from the 1997 *Report of the Review of Safeguards for Children Living Away from Home*.[103] Critics of the volumes of *Guidance and Regulations* have complained they leave little room for professional judgement. Those who support them say they provide a firm foundation for professional judgement. Wherever one stands, there is no doubt that the *Guidance and Regulations* continue to be important tools in the translation of the Children Act 1989 into practice.

The operational principles that were embedded in the *Guidance and Regulations* were made transparent for the first time in child welfare law in England and Wales and published by the Department of Health in 1990 as *The Care of Children: Principles and Practice in Regulations and Guidance*.[46] They provided a coherent framework for the detail of the collected volumes of *Guidance and Regulations*. The operational principles were intended 'to assist practitioners and supervisors to relate law to practice and to understand the context in which Regulations and Guidance were issued'.[46, p. iii] Some of the key operational principles are as follows:

Key operational principles

- Children and young people and their parents should all be considered as individuals with particular needs and potentialities.

- Although some basic needs are universal, there can be a variety of ways of meeting them.

- Children are entitled to protection from abuse, neglect and exploitation.

- A child's age, sex, health, personality, race, culture and life experiences are all relevant to any consideration of needs and vulnerability and have to be taken into account when planning or providing help.

- There are unique advantages for children in experiencing normal family life in their own birth families and every effort should be made to preserve the child's home and family links.

- The development of a working partnership with parents is usually the most effective route to providing supplementary or substitute care for their children.

- Parents should be expected and enabled to retain their responsibilities and to remain as closely involved as is consistent with their child's welfare, even if that child cannot live at home either temporarily or permanently.

- Wider families matter as well as parents – especially siblings and grandparents.

- Continuity of relationships is important and attachments should be respected, sustained and developed.

- Time is a crucial element in child care and should be reckoned in days and months rather than years.

- Account should be taken of children's wishes and feelings both in the courts and in any decisions affecting their lives. This duty applies especially if children are to be looked after by the local authority.

Challenges for service provision

The main principles underpinning the Children Act 1989, together with the operational principles embedded in *Guidance and Regulations* and some sections of the Act itself, presented many challenges for service provision.

There was, for example, a new definition of children in need, which attempted to relate services to children's developmental and welfare needs. There was also a broader definition of family support related to service provision for children in need. This embraced a range of services, including placements away from home in accommodation.

There is, in the Children Act 1989, an expectation that social services and other departments in the local authority will co-operate to identify, safeguard and promote the welfare of children in need in their area.

The Children Act 1989 provides the opportunity for working in partnership with children and families. Although such an approach was not new in child welfare practice, its universal application, in both voluntary and compulsory cases, was a major challenge for many practitioners.

The Act places an emphasis on the importance of professional judgement and balance. While the paramountcy of a child's welfare is clear in court cases, in the offering of services to children and their families a balance has to be found between responding to the needs of a particular child and those of his or her parents, siblings and other immediate family members to ensure that the child's long-term welfare is promoted. This requires careful, evidence-based, professional judgement.

There was a further challenge to effective implementation – the introduction in 1992 of the National Health Service and Community Care Act 1990. Implementing this legislation at the same time as the Children Act 1989 put a serious strain on management capacity in local authorities. There were also major differences in philosophy between the two pieces of legislation. The community care legislation emphasised a purchaser/provider ethos to under-pin the delivery of services and the introduction of quasi-markets within and between welfare agencies. As the Audit Commission pointed out in 1994, the purchaser/provider organisation of services put impediments in the way of providing an easily accessed continuum of services for parents who needed services in their own right, such as those with mental health problems that affected their capacity to respond effectively to their children's needs.[58]

The Children Act 1989 came into force on 14 October 1991. Its early imple-mentation was accompanied by an extensive national training programme that was targeted at all agencies who would come within its remit. Accepting and acting on the messages from the training was in itself a major challenge for practitioners.

The Children Act 1989 in the context of contemporary English and Welsh child welfare policies

Like all legislation, the Children Act 1989 has been subject to some amend-ments over the last five years. None has undermined the integrity of the legislation; rather they have strengthened the original intentions of the Act and made them more explicit.[44]

First, changes have strengthened existing powers to respond to growing social problems affecting children. For example, new powers add Exclusion Orders to Interim Care Orders where domestic violence is an issue, thus allowing for the child to remain at home but for the violent person to be removed.

Second, during the first decade of the Children Act's implementation there have also been several important government initiatives that have 'had a significant impact upon how the expectations of the Children Act 1989 are delivered'.[44, para. 1.3] These include:

Measures to protect children from abuse and poor care

These measures have been introduced through a series of initiatives against a background of continuing concern about the effectiveness of child protection arrangements as shown in a number of inquiry reports and other important documents. An example is the revised guide to interagency working to safeguard and promote the welfare of children: *Working Together to Safeguard Children*.[80]

The introduction of Children's Services Planning

An order made under the Children Act 1989, and which came into force in 1996,[78, 104] strengthened the requirements on local authorities to plan for children's services in order to secure a better range of services and better outcomes for children, both locally and nationally. These requirements have been the subject of consultation in 2000 to establish how further guidance could strengthen and develop Children's Services Planning.[77] The draft consultation document suggests how planning for children could be rationalised so that there is better co-ordination and coherence between plans. It also aims to ensure that the planning process as a whole is more effective and demonstrably delivers better outcomes for children in need.

Setting clear objectives for those providing children's services through *Quality Protects* and *Children First*

The intention of *Quality Protects* [69] in England and *Children First* [106] in Wales is to improve the management and delivery of children's services. The objectives in these programmes for local authorities and in The Government's Objectives for Children's Social Services[73] develop further the requirements of safeguarding and promoting children's welfare in the Children Act 1989 and strengthen the strategic planning that has been put in place since the implementation of the Act. Links between these objectives and the research findings are explored throughout the overview and in more detail in Chapter 8.

The agenda for children of the National Assembly for Wales

Devolution has begun to impact on the provision and delivery of children's services in Wales. The National Assembly for Wales has a clear agenda for taking forward children's services. This includes the creation of a post of Children's Commissioner and plans to develop a Children's Strategy for Wales. The Welsh concern with the rights of children to be seen as child citizens may well shape a very distinctive agenda in child welfare in Wales over the next decade, building on the foundation for children's participation that has been laid in the Children Act 1989.

The overview

At one level the research studies in the overview are more concerned with the implementation of the main thrust of the Act – 'the practices and procedures when courts and local authorities intervene in the lives of children and their families with a view to safeguarding and promoting children's welfare'.[44, para. 1.15] In this respect the overview serves as a chronicle of the implementation of some of the fundamental and operational principles of the Children Act 1989 over the last decade.

At another level, precisely because the studies in the overview consider these processes and practice, they provide valuable evidence on how some of the government's objectives for children's social services[73] and those in *Quality Protects* [69] and *Children First* [106] can be accomplished and on the pitfalls to be avoided.

The issues for the overview

The Children Act 1989 brought about significant changes in the law. However, the legislation can only be the framework for change; actual change comes through implementation of the law. In this respect the implementation of the Children Act is rather like a theatrical production. The director sets the aims and tenor of the production and steers the actors towards the vision of the play that is in his/her mind. On the night it is up to the actors to carry forward that vision. Their performance will depend on many factors, including the dynamics between them and their rapport with the audience. So it was with implementation of the Children Act 1989. The policy-makers wrote the script, rehearsed the players through a national implementation training programme and launched them on to the stage of social care services. The audience of children and families, eager to participate in the production, as promised in the programme, waited in anticipation. From then on it was in the hands of the players and the audience to take the vision forward together. How far they succeeded in doing this, and the tensions they encountered on the way, are major themes of the overview. At the end of the first run of the play, which has been almost a decade, we are left with an evaluation of its success. The main aim of the overview has been to consider these key questions:

Key questions for the overview

- How far can changing the law influence changes in attitudes and practice?

- How robust were the main principles of the Children Act?

- What can current policy and practice learn about the Children Act 1989 from the research?

- What should be consolidated, what has not worked and where can further changes be made?

- Above all, has the Children Act 1989 made a difference to the lives of children and families?

The scope of the studies

There are 24 studies in the overview, all of which were commissioned by the Department of Health over the first eight years of implementation. These studies can be broadly grouped into five administrative areas:

- children, parents and the courts, including the role of guardians ad litem and expert witnesses; the implementation of the 'no order' and 'no delay' principles and the making and carrying out of Care Orders;

- safeguarding children at risk of maltreatment and the use of protective and supportive services for children in the community;

- services for children in need, covering early and later national implementation and specific areas of practice, such as family centres, day care, services for disabled children; family support services, including the use of accommodation;

- the care of children looked after by local authorities, including processes to assess and measure outcomes for children, care planning, the implementation of working in partnership with parents of looked after children; consulting children about their wishes and feelings; contact between children and families and the impact of changes in the law on the welfare of young people leaving care; and

- the impact of the law on influencing interagency co-operation and a mixed economy of services.

These areas were chosen primarily because they could offer information on how the principles underpinning the Act were being implemented in the public law domain. Of particular concern at the time was the provision and delivery of services and the strengthening of the regulatory strategy.

Complementing other overviews

A parallel series of sixteen studies on child protection was commissioned slightly earlier than the bulk of the Children Act studies. Many of these evaluated the organisational and practice context of child protection. Some were undertaken around the time of implementation. These studies were presented in the Department of Health's overview *Child Protection: Messages from Research*, published in 1995,[52] and make complementary reading to the studies in the current volume. An overview of studies of the care of children in residential care, *Caring for Children Away from Home: Messages from Research*,[54] and another on teenagers, including young people looked after by the local authority, *Focus on Teenagers: Research into Practice*,[53] are also complementary to the content of the Children Act studies, while the overview of studies on adoption, *Adoption Now: Messages from Research*,[55] explores in more detail a service that was the outcome for some children in the court studies in this overview.

Any research programme is necessarily selective and cannot cover every aspect. The topics chosen within the scope of the 24 studies represent a fair spread of the major areas that necessitated significant changes in policy and practice. Some areas are not included because the work was taken forward elsewhere, although several studies in the overview touch on areas in other projects. There was, for example, work funded by the Rowntree Foundation on disabled children[95] and the study funded by the Lord Chancellor's Office on court processes in the private law domain.[59]

Some areas of practice were not included because they were not sufficiently developed at the time the studies were commissioned. This included the implementation of the regulatory strategy for children living away from home in boarding schools and hospitals.

There was concern in the Children Act programme to gain more information about services for black and minority ethnic families. Consequently, black and Asian children are more in evidence in the 24 studies than in earlier research, and there are some examples of services that are helpful to these families.

Taking account of the programmes elsewhere and the state of services, the Children Act studies represent a fair range of the practice and procedures affecting the children in need and their families who are in receipt of services from Social Services or voluntary child care organisations, and who have come to the attention of the family proceedings courts because of serious concerns about children's welfare.

The character of the studies

All the studies took as their focus the implementation of one or more aspect of the Children Act 1989. They were targeted on key questions:

Key questions for the Children Act studies

- Did the court system protect children in need in the way the Act intended?

- How did local authorities interpret children in need and family support services?

- Did the new definition of family support break down the barriers between children being in and out of care?

- How was accommodation and contact between children and their families working?

- How far had the ideal of working in partnership with parents been achieved?

- Did children have a voice in decision-making?

- How far were agencies working together?

- Was there evidence of improved planning, service provision and delivery under the Children Act 1989?

The main features of the studies

Table 1 describes the main features of the 24 studies and provides a short title for each study to be used as a point of reference in the text.

Some research issues

This overview is deliberately focused on children in need who live at home or who are looked after by local authorities. Within this remit there are a variety of studies that bring different styles and methodologies to bear on a range of issues. This has to be borne in mind when the findings of the studies are being discussed. There are several issues:

Conducting the research in different parts of the country

The organisation of social services departments leaves a great deal of discretion to individual authorities with respect to how they deliver their services. Similarly, different courts will organise their business to suit local need. Geography will also influence service delivery. A rural department may have different priorities from an urban one. This diversity inevitably influences the findings from the different studies. Although some studies have tried to account for this by drawing their samples from different parts of the country, there will be some idiosyncrasies. This has to be borne in mind when the findings are used to make general conclusions.

Table 1 *Brief descriptions of the 24 studies*

1 *Short title* **Implementing Section 17**
 Authors Aldgate and Tunstill (1995)
 Description An early snapshot of how English local authorities were implementing section 17 of the Children Act.
 Sample and methods Postal survey of all English social services departments, interviews with managers in ten authorities.
 Fieldwork dates Autumn 1992–93

2 *Short title* **Short-term Fostering**
 Authors Aldgate and Bradley (1999)
 Description A 'before and after' study of children receiving planned short-term accommodation under section 20 of the Children Act.
 Sample and methods Sixty children and their families in four authorities. Interviews with parents, children and social workers before service offered and six to nine months later; interviews with foster carers; standardised tests.
 Fieldwork dates 1994–96

3 *Short title* **Moving On**
 Authors Biehal, Clayden, Stein and Wade (1995)
 Description A study of care leavers' experiences of transition to the community and the contribution made by leaving care schemes.
 Sample and methods Four leaving care schemes in three authorities. Survey of 183 young people leaving care (through postal questionnaire to social workers); interviews with 74 young people, their social workers and leaving care workers with follow-up at 18–24 months.
 Fieldwork dates 1991–94

4 *Short title* **Safeguarding Children**
 Authors Brandon, Lewis, Thoburn and Way (1999)
 Description A study tracking the progress and interim outcomes of children newly identified as suffering or likely to suffer significant harm in the early years of implementing the Children Act.
 Sample and methods Four authorities including rural and urban areas and high proportion of minority ethnic families. Tracked progress of 105 children over a year. Analysis of case files; interviews with social workers and other professionals; interviews with parents and children in 51 families.
 Fieldwork dates 1993–95

5 *Short title* **Expert Evidence**
 Authors Brophy, Bates, Brown, Cohen, Radcliffe and Wale (1999)
 Description Investigated use of experts during child care proceedings.
 Sample and methods National postal survey of guardians in England and Wales including analysis of 557 cases; court-based study in one authority tracking 65 cases (114 children); interviews with 35 guardians from 3 panels; in-depth interviews with 17 child and adolescent psychiatrists.
 Fieldwork dates 1992–96

6 *Short title* **Day Care Services (England)**
 Authors Candappa, Bull, Cameron, Moss and Owen (1996)
 Description Examined the implementation of the Children Act as it affects day care services for young children.
 Sample and methods Stratified random sample of eighteen English authorities. Document analysis; interviews with key officers in statutory and voluntary organisations; interview survey of over 400 day care providers; case studies on particular themes.
 Fieldwork dates 1992–95

7 *Short title* **Fostering Family Contact**
 Author Cleaver (2000)
 Description Explored impact of the Children Act on contact between foster children and their families.
 Sample and methods Retrospective survey of 152 case files; prospective study of 33 foster children aged 5–12 who were expected to be looked after for at least four months. Interviews with children, key family members, foster carers and social workers six weeks after placement and twelve months later.
 Fieldwork dates 1995–98

8 *Short title* **Children in Need (Wales)**
 Authors Colton, Drury and Williams (1995)
 Description Examined the provision of services for children in need and their families under Part III of the Children Act, primarily in Wales.
 Sample and methods Document analysis and interviews with social services department child care managers in all Welsh authorities and postal questionnaire to other agencies; in-depth study of practice in two authorities involving interviews with social workers, managers and over 120 parents and children on social worker case loads.
 Fieldwork dates 1992–94

9 *Short title* **Parental Perspectives**
 Authors Freeman and Hunt (1998)
 Description Documented the views and feelings of the parents in Study 12 whose children were involved in care proceedings.
 Sample and methods In-depth interviews with 35 adults in 25 families (44% from a minority ethnic group).
 Fieldwork dates 1992–94

10 *Short title* **Planning to Care**
 Authors Grimshaw and Sinclair (1997)
 Description Evaluated the effectiveness of the regulatory framework introduced by the Children Act for planning and reviewing the care of individual young people looked after by local authorities.
 Sample and methods National survey of local authority planning and review documents; examination of 180 cases in three authorities using case file analysis; observation of review meetings; interviews with practitioners; interviews with a small number of children and parents; focus groups of young people.
 Fieldwork dates 1993–95

11 *Short title* **Making Care Orders Work**
 Authors Harwin, Owen, Locke and Forrester (forthcoming)
 Description Investigated the influence of court care plans on case management by Social Services and on outcomes for children.
 Sample and methods One hundred children in 57 families who were made subject to Care Orders in 1997 in five authorities. Analysis of court files and interviews with social workers, guardians ad litem and local solicitors at the start point. Phase II interviews with social workers and analysis of social services files after 21 months. Interviews at end point with 18 birth parents, 44 current carers and 26 children aged 7 or over.
 Fieldwork dates 1997–99

12 *Short title* **The Last Resort**
 Authors Hunt, Macleod, Freeman and Thomas (1999)
 Description Investigated the impact of the Children Act on the use of compulsory intervention in child protection cases and their management by the courts by comparing cases brought before and after the Act.
 Sample and methods Three authorities. 105 pre-Act cases compared with 83 brought before the courts in the first two years of the Children Act. Analysis of social work files and court records; interviews with practitioners and parents (see Study 9); observation of court hearings in 30 post-Act cases.
 Fieldwork dates 1991–94

13 *Short title* **Best-Laid Plans**
Authors Hunt and Macleod (1999)
Description Follow up to Study 12, investigating the outcome of orders made by the courts.
Sample and methods Compared the plans made for 131 children in 81 families with outcomes eighteen months to four years later. Analysis of case files; postal questionnaire and interviews with practitioners; interviews with nineteen family members.
Fieldwork dates 1996–97

14 *Short title* **Leaving Care in Partnership**
Authors Marsh and Peel (1999)
Description Explored how family members could support young people leaving care, and how social workers, young people and their families felt about this.
Sample and methods Three authorities. File review of 160 young people leaving care; questionnaire to social workers on 87 of these; interviews with 43 young people (21 followed up) and 34 key family members.
Fieldwork dates 1995–97

15 *Short title* **From Care to Accommodation**
Authors Packman and Hall (1998)
Description Examined the provision of full-time care (accommodation) for children on the basis of agreement with their families, under section 20 of the Children Act.
Sample and methods 177 admissions to accommodation in two authorities between October 1992 and May 1993. Follow-up at six months and two years after admission. File analysis; interviews with social workers and a sample of parents, children and carers; observation of 29 planning meetings.
Fieldwork dates 1992–95

16 *Short title* **Play and Care Out of School**
Authors Petrie, Poland and Wayne (1994)
Description An early baseline study to describe and classify out-of-school play and care services.
Sample and methods Case studies based on visits to fifteen different out-of-school services in England and Wales; postal survey of 120 services in eighteen English and two Welsh authorities.
Fieldwork dates 1991–92

17 *Short title* **Out-of-school Services**
Authors Petrie, Egharevba, Oliver and Poland (2000)
Description Explored parents' and children's perspectives on out-of-school services for particular groups: 10 to 13-year-olds, disabled children and children from minority ethnic families.
Sample and methods Ethnographic fieldwork in 33 out-of-school services; interviews with parents and children in 93 families; telephone survey of 187 parents.
Fieldwork dates 1996–98

18 *Short title* **Services to Disabled Children**
Authors Robinson, Weston and Minkes (1995)
Description An action research project evaluating the quality of two types of service for disabled children: residential homes offering short-term care and specialist day care services for under-fives.
Sample and methods Five settings of each type evaluated twice with development work in between; interviews with managers and staff; questionnaire to parents; observation; guided discussion with children (aged 10+) using specially designed materials.
Fieldwork dates 1991–93

19 *Short title* **Family Centres**
Author Smith (1996)
Description Study of six family centres run or supported by the Children's Society, with a particular focus on users' views.
Sample and methods In-depth interviews with 125 parents (mainly mothers) using the centres over one week; observation in centres; interviews with staff; analysis of records.
Fieldwork dates 1988–92

20 *Short title* **Day Care Services (Wales)**
Author Statham (1996)
Description Linked to Study 6 in England, with additional focus on rural areas and Welsh language issues.
Sample and methods All Welsh authorities. Document analysis; interviews with key officers in statutory and voluntary organisations; interview survey of 200 day care providers; attendance at Children and Family Forum meetings.
Fieldwork dates 1992–95

21 *Short title* **Sponsored Day Care**
Authors Statham, Dillion and Moss (forthcoming)
Description Study of local authority purchase of places in independent day care services to support the families of children in need.
Sample and methods National postal survey of English social services departments; interviews with key officers and postal survey of day care providers in twelve authorities; study of referral and allocation process in two authorities; case studies of a small number of placements including interviews with parents, child-minders and referrers and observation of the quality of care provided.
Fieldwork dates 1996–99

22 *Short title* **Family Support and Maltreatment**
Authors Thoburn, Wilding and Watson (2000)
Description Study of families with child under 8 who were referred to social services departments because of concerns about emotional maltreatment or neglect. Includes comparison with families requesting or referred for a family support service.
Sample and methods Three authorities (rural and urban). Analysis of 555 referrals; file study of 180 families; intensive study of 122 families involving interview with parent and data on children's health/development from school nurses and health visitors, repeated after a year; group interviews with social workers and managers.
Fieldwork dates 1994–97

23 *Short title* **Services for Children in Need**
Authors Tunstill and Aldgate (2000)
Description Study of the services offered to families under section 17 of the Children Act; initial focus on children aged 7–12.
Sample and methods Seven authorities; 93 children, half aged 7–12. Interviews with main parent/carer at time of referral and six months later; questionnaire to social workers.
Fieldwork dates 1995–97

24 *Short title* **Looking After Children**
Authors Ward and the 'Looking After Children' research team (1995)
Description A research and development project testing the assessment and action schedules developed as part of the Looking After Children (LAC) project, before their final implementation.
Sample and methods Assessment of 379 children in the community using LAC materials; consultation with social workers and managers in five authorities; analysis of use of the records for 204 looked after children.
Fieldwork dates 1993–94

Measuring effectiveness

It has to be remembered that, at the time the studies were commissioned, the concerns were focused on the processes of implementation of new areas of practice. Issues such as performance assessment were only beginning to be identified in agencies. Similarly, the costs of services were less of an issue. These factors are the subject of later research initiatives by the Department of Health, such as those on parenting support and costs and effectiveness. Nevertheless, this overview can, and does, examine how things worked out for service users in different ways. Change is sometimes measured through the application of standardised research instruments at different points in time. There are also self-evaluations of services by service users and professionals at different points in time before and after services were delivered.

Comparing practice before and after the Act

Because all the studies were commissioned after the Children Act came into force there was little opportunity for the researchers to compare practice and processes pre- and post-Children Act, with the exception of the care to accommodation study[15] and, to some extent, the last resort study.[12] The care to accommodation study replicated an earlier one and was able to make comparisons with practice in the same local authorities that had been in operation before the Act. However, some of the children studied were at different stages of their welfare careers.

The studies covered different stages of implementation

Overall, the studies include research carried out for nearly a decade from 1991. This had the advantage of seeing progress over time, as in the studies on the use of Care Orders[11, 13] and family support.[1, 23] In the later family support studies[21, 22, 23] it was also interesting to see the impact on practice of the Department of Health's refocusing initiative in the latter half of the 1990s.[68]

The ongoing impact of the research on policy

Some of the earlier studies had already had an impact on policy before the later studies were completed. For example, the recommendations of the day care studies[6, 20] for an integrated interagency approach had come to fruition in the late 1990s with the national childcare strategies in England and Wales.[64, 105] One or two of the later studies were funded to follow up on the findings of those completed by the mid-1990s, such as those on care proceedings. Several of the studies have provided evidence for government and other reports, especially those on children looked after by local authorities[89] and have informed new legislation, such as the Children (Leaving Care) Act 2000.

Cumulative messages

As in previous overviews, there are cumulative messages from the research which add considerable weight to the findings of individual studies. These cumulative messages are strengthened by the fact that there are several studies in similar areas of service provision. The cumulative messages from the 24 studies are also reinforced by the inclusion of significant Social Services Inspectorate national inspection reports and a series of short studies commissioned by the Social Services Inspectorate on various aspects of the working of the courts.

The structure of the overview

The overview is in three parts. Section I is the main text and reviews the studies; Section II includes summaries of the studies and other relevant documents; Section III provides a comprehensive list of references.

To make sense of the wealth of detail in the 24 studies the overview has necessarily had to be selective, but it should be seen as an accompaniment to the series of books on which it is based. Issues of safeguarding and promoting children's welfare in different parts of the Act are addressed. There is a strong focus on the views of the children in need and their families whose lives have been affected by the Children Act 1989. This is appropriate in view of the Act's intentions to listen to children and work with parents to safeguard and promote children's welfare. How services are organised and delivered will also have an impact on the outcomes for children and families. The overview therefore looks at service provision, identifies changes that may improve the organisation and delivery of services and gives some examples of good practice. The final chapter summarises the findings and links them to contemporary policies for children in need.

The structure of the overview

Section I describes the context of the overview, presents findings of the studies across seven key areas and links the findings to contemporary policy initiatives.

Chapter 1 sets the Children Act 1989 in a broader child welfare context.

Chapter 2 explores the definition of children in need and gives some insight into the lives of children in need and their families.

Chapter 3 addresses the underpinning dimensions of safeguarding and promoting children's welfare in different settings.

Chapter 4 is concerned with the implementation of the Children Act from the perspective of parents and families.

Chapter 5 evaluates the children's views on their experiences of the Act, looking particularly at how children are consulted and are included in decision-making.

Chapter 6 explores the beginnings of interagency collaboration and includes some examples of innovative practice.

Chapter 7 discusses service delivery, exploring whether the Children Act has made a difference to practice.

Chapter 8 makes links between the findings from the overview and current policy initiatives.

Section II has two parts: The first (A) summarises the 24 studies; the second (B) presents summaries of findings from some important national Social Services Inspectorate inspections relating to the Children Act 1989 and from a selection of relevant court order studies conducted by the Social Services Inspectorate in the early stages of implementation.

Section III provides a comprehensive reference list. It gives the full references for the books on which the overview is based and presents a list of publications referred to in the main text of Sections I and II. These are numbered throughout Section I to provide easy referencing without detracting from the text.

2 The children in need and their families

This chapter is about the children in need and their families whose contacts with public child welfare services are chronicled in the 24 studies by the researchers. Four main approaches were taken by the research studies to describe children in need:

- exploring different ways of counting and interpreting who are children in need;

- describing the circumstances of the families of the children in the studies;

- formulating a typology of families; and

- recounting the children's own perspectives of what it means to be a child in need.

All the children described in the overview come within the Children Act definition of children in need. This definition is a key element of the Children Act 1989. It marked a change from previous child welfare legislation in England and Wales in three areas:

- it moved from concern about an undifferentiated group of vulnerable children to specific groups;

- it defined this specific group in the context of children's development; and

- it linked children in need to the provision of services.

According to section 17 of the Children Act 1989, a child is in need if:

(a) he is unlikely to achieve or maintain, or have the opportunity of achieving or maintaining, a reasonable standard of health or development without the provision for him of services by a local authority;

(b) his health or development is likely to be significantly impaired or further impaired without the provision for him of such services;

(c) he is disabled. (Children Act 1989, section 17(10))

Section 17 defined local authorities' responsibilities towards children more broadly than the definition of prevention in previous legislation. Disabled children were considered to be a special case in their own right, and their inclusion in section 17 was made in recognition of their special developmental needs. Within the other two categories of need, the intention of the Act was to move consciously from identification of risk of harm, including child maltreatment, to the assessment of the impact of that risk of harm on a child's development and the *impact* of no service provision on that child's health and development. This move embraced the idea of simultaneously safeguarding and promoting children's welfare and of going further than merely identifying impact of harm to providing services. Given the breadth of issues affecting children in need and their families, it followed that a broad range of services would be necessary to respond to those needs.

Setting the definition of children in need within the context of child development indicated clearly that negative impacts on children's health and development could arise from a variety of circumstances. Therefore, as Volume 2 of *Guidance and Regulations* suggests, it would not be legal for the local authority to confine its services only to children at risk of child maltreatment:

> The definition of need . . . is deliberately wide to reinforce the emphasis on preventive support to families. It has three categories: a reasonable standard of health or development; significant impairment of health or development; and disablement. It would not be acceptable for an authority to exclude any of these three – for example, by confining services to children at risk of significant harm which attracts the duty to investigate under section 47 [para. 2.4].[47]

Some problems of interpreting who are children in need

The implementation process demanded that each local authority identified children in need in its area and, on the basis of that identification, provided an appropriate range of services to meet their needs.

This section of the Act has been poorly understood, resulting in many problems in its implementation. For example, the studies on implementing section 17 show, both in Wales and in England, that local authorities had generally inconsistent understandings of 'reasonable standard of health and development' and 'significant impairment'. Nor did they understand that both sections 17 and 47 (enquiries to ascertain if a child is suffering significant harm) can be used as gateways to gain access to services specified in the Act.

The studies conclude that problems of interpretation were linked to three factors:

- a failure to understand that duties in relation to section 17 of the Children Act are statutory;

- a continuing emphasis on linking interpretations of 'in need' with eligibility criteria based on risk; and

- concern that moving to a broader definition of children in need, as the Act intended, would open the floodgates to a demand for services that could not be met.

As the study on children in need in Wales suggests, the outcome was an absence of consistency of interpretation of definition across many social services:

> The deliberately broad definition of need means, in practice, that the services provided by any local authority to a particular child or to any category of children will depend almost entirely on how the authority defines and prioritises the concept of need.[8]

The issue was by no means confined to Wales but was also widespread in England.[1] With local authorities taking such an individual approach to the interpretation of who were children in need in their area, it is not surprising that it has been difficult over the first eight years of implementation to ascertain nationally, both in England and in Wales, the extent and characteristics of children in need within the Children Act definition. Several of the studies on family support services show clearly that in some cases that had been 'closed' by Social Services the children could be identified as 'in need' within the Children Act definition.[21, 22, 23] The problem is compounded by the fact that there were also children in need who were vulnerable but did not come forward for services. Others were offered services but refused them. Counting children in need as being only those receiving services from the local authority was also problematic as many of the children in need might be receiving services from voluntary agencies.[23]

The extent of the children in need

The complexities of counting children in need are recognised in a contemporary approach to looking at the extent of need in England that comes from the *Framework for the Assessment of Children in Need and Their Families*, published in 2000 by the Department of Health, the Department for Education and Employment and the Home Office.[79] A companion volume in Wales was published under the same title.[92]

As can be seen from Figure 1, children may be defined as in need in many different circumstances. There are around 11 million children in England, of whom around 4 million are deemed to be vulnerable, living in families with less than half the average household income, and are disadvantaged children who would benefit from extra help from public agencies in order to make the best of their life chances. The information on how many children are known to Social Services is not available nationally, but current estimates suggest between 3–400,000 children are known to Social Services at any one time. About 53,000 children are looked after by the local authority at any one time, excluding disabled children receiving respite care. Approximately 32,000

Figure 1
*Representation of
extent of children
in need in England
at any one time*

Source: *Framework for the
Assessment of Children in
Need and Their Families* [79]

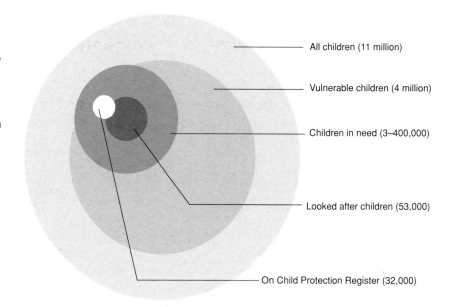

All children (11 million)

Vulnerable children (4 million)

Children in need (3–400,000)

Looked after children (53,000)

On Child Protection Register (32,000)

children's names are on a Child Protection Register at any one time because they require a child protection plan.[79]

The extent of children in need in Wales is calculated in a similar way. In Wales, out of a total child population of 674,000, around one-third (240,000) are considered to be vulnerable children living in households with less than half the average household income.[92] An estimate of the numbers of children in need known to Social Services has not been made in Wales, but if the same proportion of the child population (3%) were in need as in England, this would amount to some 20,000 children. On 31 March 1998, around 3,400 children were looked after by local authorities and some 2,500 were on Child Protection Registers.[110]

Characteristics of children in need under the Children Act 1989

The studies in the overview have been bedevilled by the same problems of counting the numbers of children in need that have exercised the government statisticians. What can be confirmed is that children in need in all the studies are either in contact with Social Services or are in receipt of services under Part III of the Children Act 1989.

Several of the studies grappled with the problem of categorising and describing why children were in need of services, and they developed broad groups of reasons for children being in need, several drawing on the 1997 work of Sinclair and Carr-Hill[97] who explored different ways of grouping reasons for children being in need:

Broad groups of reasons for children being in need

Three broad groups of reasons emerge from the studies:

- the intrinsic health and development of the child (e.g. the child's impairment, mental health problems, substance misuse);

- the child's family circumstances (e.g. child suffering as a result of family stress or conflict, abuse by parents and living in social deprivation); and

- the child not meeting the expectations of the wider community (e.g. child's anti-social behaviour, delinquency, truancy, linguistic or cultural difficulties, refugee status).

Across the family support studies the most common reason for children to be in need was within the second group, with a subgroup of the child suffering because of family stress, followed closely by children living in conditions of social disadvantage or poverty.[8, 22, 23] Children looked after span all the groups.[3, 13, 15]

It would be misleading to think that all children had only one problem that led to their being in need. The three groups are not mutually exclusive, and many children were living in circumstances where different factors interacted. What is of note is that the children who are the subject of care proceedings are often those from families who have experienced long-standing, complex circumstances of multiple disadvantage that have had an impact on children's behaviour, health and educational attainment.[12, 13] Such findings resonate with the guidance on assessment in England and Wales.[79, 92]

The families referred to or seeking help from Social Services will have dif[ferent] levels of need. Many will be helped by personal advice or practical servi[ces] short-term intervention. A smaller proportion will have problems of suc[h] complexity and seriousness that they require more detailed assessment, involving other agencies in the process, leading to appropriate plans and interventions.[79, para. 1.7]

The main points

- There are not yet reliable statistical data on children in need under the Children Act 1989.

- It is estimated that at any one time there may be around 3–400,000 children in need known to Social Services in England, and possibly around 20,000 in Wales.

- There is a broad range of reasons why children may be in need which requires an equally broad range of services to be provided by different agencies.

The circumstances in which children in need live

The second approach to understanding children in need adopted by the studies is to place the children in the context of their families' circumstances. Although the studies of children in need in the community, and those looked after, used varying sampling techniques and included children who were at different points in their care careers, there are striking consistencies about the general issues that affect their families' lives. There are, however, differences between individual families in the level and scope of problems they experience.

Single- or two-parent households

About a third to half of the families across at least eight of the studies were headed by a lone parent. Around half had also experienced recent changes to the family structure.[4, 22, 23] Although many children had the stability of one parent, the presence of changing stepparents was noticeable. In the study on services for children in need nearly half the parents cited separation from a partner as a factor contributing to the children's behavioural problems.[22]

Race and ethnicity

Most of the family support studies had chosen some research areas with a strong multi-racial mix. Families from the minority ethnic groups represented in the studies were characterised by their diversity. The same number of children were from dual-heritage families as were from families where both parents were black. Families of African and Afro–Caribbean origin were more likely to be represented than families originating from the Indian sub-continent.[22, 23]

Minority ethnic families were far more in evidence in urban as opposed to rural sites. In two of the later family support studies black and minority ethnic families were better represented than they had been hitherto, and there was clear evidence of black families referring themselves to Social Services for help.[22, 23]

Poverty

Financial problems and low income permeate the circumstances of families in many of the studies. Ninety-eight per cent of the families whose children were at risk of suffering emotional maltreatment or neglect were characterised by the extreme poverty of their material environment.[22] About half of the families in the study on section 17 services for children in need[23] and in the short-term fostering study[2] were similarly living in poverty, defined in terms of income in relation to state benefits. Families with younger children were more affected than those with older children. There was little difference in the impact of poverty between one- and two-parent families, mainly because there were very few families overall with high income earners. A frequent pattern was for one or both parents to aggregate their income from a series of unskilled and part-time jobs.

An exception to the pervasive picture of families struggling to survive financially was a minority of families whose children were at risk of suffering significant harm through physical or sexual abuse.[4]

Housing

The housing needs of families across the family support studies varied from those where it was not an issue[2] to those where half the parents felt they were living in overcrowded conditions.[23] The majority of families lived in rented accommodation, but whether this was public housing or privately rented varied according to area. Housing problems were associated with a plethora of other problems and, not surprisingly, were more prevalent in families who were living on very low incomes, irrespective of whether they were one- or two-parent households.[22]

Families were characterised by their high mobility: over one-third of the families in three studies had moved in the previous year but often within the same location.[4, 22, 23]

Social isolation

Six of the studies draw attention to the importance of social support and social networks in providing a cushion against adversity, particularly the onset of depression in mothers.[2, 3, 4, 19, 22, 23]

In two of the family support studies lack of emotional support was the factor that tipped the balance, turning a previously manageable situation into one that was untenable. The absence of practical support in terms of child care or help with a child with behavioural problems was also a major factor that led families to seek help from professionals.[2, 21, 23]

There are two notable absences in sources of support:

- extended family; and

- neighbourhood facilities.

Geographical proximity of kin is generally held to be an important factor in identifying the presence of kinship support. The studies on family support revealed that the problem was more complex. In one study, although extended kin lived within a half-hour's access by public transport, families had become distant through falling out or because it cost too much to travel. Some parents were ashamed to admit to their kin that they had problems. Others had been demoralised by unsupportive parents whom they had rejected in adulthood.[2, 4]

The role of the extended family was altogether more positive for care leavers. Here, although contact had been lost with parents, extended kin provided ports of call for youngsters and offered a sense of belonging even if they were short on practical support.[14]

Some families lived in hostile neighbourhoods and feared to venture out. With the exception of day care, community resources were under-used.[22] Problems related to distance, cost or stigma of using services, or simply that the effort of finding out what was there outweighed the possible gains. Where families had managed to find positive supportive services, such as the family centres, these were highly valued and proved invaluable in strengthening parenting capacity.[19] Similarly, as will be shown later in the overview, the input of social workers, health visitors and general practitioners was a structured source of support that could lead to the enhancement of self-esteem.

Health problems

The continuing ill health of parents was a consistent theme throughout all the studies. Many parents were unwell, some over a considerable period of their children's lives. Over a quarter of the parents in three studies had been an in-patient in hospital in the previous year.[2, 4, 23] Although ill health was a problem shared by many families, there were three particular types of problems:

- chronic physical health or disability;

- acute physical health problems; and

- mental health problems.

The ill health of parents had an impact on children in three ways:

- parental inability to carry out household tasks;

- parental inability to care for children; and

- the necessity for children to act as carers of their parents and siblings.

Chronic physical health or disability

Chronic health problems were present in about one-third of the families across the family support studies.[4, 21, 22, 23] These included serious degenerating illnesses, such as multiple sclerosis, Crohns disease or heart disease, and serious disabilities, such as hearing impairment or loss of mobility. Being socially isolated and unable to afford domestic help or child care placed a strain on both parents and children.

Many parents had niggling illnesses or suffered pain in their heads or stomachs that made them feel debilitated. Ironically, it was only when intervention had helped them feel stronger emotionally that parents were able to seek medical help to resolve some of these long-standing ailments.[2, 4, 23]

Almost a quarter of the families in the study on making Care Orders work had one parent with a learning disability,[11] although there were a minority in other studies.[2, 22] Those who came to the attention of Social Services did so because of concern about their children's physical or emotional well-being. The critical protective factor for children was the presence of support from others in the household.[22]

Acute physical health

Acute physical health problems beset about a quarter of the parents across the studies. This included the outcome of injuries that limited mobility or problems pre- or post-hospitalisation. It also included parents with chronic problems whose conditions worsened suddenly. A good example was a single mother whose family was in Australia. She suffered from constant anxiety about the care of her children if she died. This was very real and distressing.[23]

Mental health issues

Over three-quarters of the parents in the significant harm study were rated depressed on a standardised test.[4] There was also an overwhelming sense of fatigue among parents in several studies.[2, 4, 22, 23] The stress of living in poverty, sometimes exacerbated by difficult family relationships or, worse, domestic violence, took its toll on families. It was little wonder that some parents sought refuge in drugs or alcohol.

Problem drinking or drug misuse

One-third of the families in the emotional abuse and neglect study[22] and two-fifths of the parents in the study on making Care Orders work[11] had problems with the misuse of drugs or alcohol. As might be expected, the incapacity caused by parents' drug use placed considerable burden on the children. The potential for causing significant harm to children through neglect was worrying, but some older children were able to manage their lives through taking over the parental responsibility. Key factors in the impact on children were the age of the child and the presence or absence of a supportive adult within the household.[22]

Domestic violence

In the 1995 overview of research studies on child protection,[52] domestic violence was identified as an issue that was present in many families who were likely to maltreat their children. In the Children Act studies domestic violence was present in many families of children in need. It was particularly noticeable in families where children were at risk of suffering emotional harm or neglect but was also a source of stress for families in other studies.[4, 12, 23] Asking for help to escape from a violent partner was one reason that brought parents to Social Services. There was an association in the studies between abuse of drugs or alcohol and domestic violence.[22, 23]

Domestic violence was a factor associated with children being accommodated, either because the children themselves had asked to leave a home marked by arguments or because the children were so argumentative and uncontrollable that they had been rejected by parents.[15]

Relationship problems with partners

Not all problematic relationships between parents involved actual violence, but problems in relationships between adults brought one-third of the families with partners to Social Services in the short-term accommodation study[2] and were reported to exacerbate child behavioural problems in two other studies.[4, 23] Often social workers did not see intervention in relationship problems as part of their brief, a view that was not shared by the parents.[2]

Formulating a typology of families

The cumulative evidence from the studies is of families who are generally living in conditions of poverty. Housing varies from adequate to poor. Some neighbourhoods are hostile and unsafe; others are congenial with good facilities for families. Social support from kin and friends is sometimes absent. There is an impression of many families, in poor health, who are struggling to bring up their children in conditions of emotional and material adversity.

It would, however, be wrong to assume that all of the families of children in need are living in continuing adversity. There are some differences between families in the quantity and intensity of problems that bring them in contact with Social Services. The families whose children were the subject of care proceedings had similar problems to those whose children were receiving family support services. However, it was notable that the level and scope of the problems of the families in the court studies were deeper and wider, being multiple, long-standing and entrenched. These multiple and serious troubles had affected the parenting capacity of the families to such an extent that the children were likely to be suffering significant harm.[9, 11]

Several studies present a typology of the families of children in need derived from that developed in 1995 by Cleaver and Freeman.[63] This is useful because it helps to identify differences in the level and scope of the services needed, thus helping to plan the most effective differential interventions.[2, 4, 22, 23] The typology has three groups:

● families who need help with specific issues;

● acutely distressed families; and

● families with multiple and long-standing problems.

Families who need help with specific issues

These were by far the most likely families to refer themselves to Social Services for help. There was at least one parent who could usually provide adequate care, physically and emotionally, for the children but who was facing a new challenge at the time they made contact with Social Services. Examples are families who sought help because sudden illness or an increase in the misuse of drugs or alcohol had limited their coping skills, or refugees who managed their lives well in their countries of origin but were destabilised both by the events that forced them to leave and by having to adjust to a new country with different customs and a new language. Sudden withdrawal of support from extended family brought lone parents to Social Services to ask for help with child-minding over school holidays. Families in poverty asked for financial help with specific items such as cookers or clothes for their children. About half of these families had been known to Social Services previously, but many were new referrals. Dual-heritage families were likely to be in this group.[2, 4, 22, 23]

Acutely distressed families

These families were characterised by the fact that at the point they made contact with Social Services they were in a state of near or actual collapse.[23] Some had been struggling for months to contain their problems, particularly the management of a child's behaviour or domestic conflict. About half of the families who presented themselves for section 17 services or those whose child was considered to be at risk of suffering significant harm came into this category.[4, 22] Many families were socially isolated. Families where both parents were from ethnic minorities were more likely to be in this group than in the other two. There was a higher incidence of children at risk of suffering significant harm in this group than had been found in studies from previous overviews.[4, 22]

Families with multiple and long-standing problems

These families were usually well known to Social Services and had experienced chronic problems from a number of causes. They were likely to be families living in a climate of domestic violence. They were also more likely to be poor, living in inadequate housing in hostile neighbourhoods. Some families had engaged in criminal activities, especially drug dealing. They were beset by poor health, which was exacerbated by misuse of drugs and alcohol. Above all, their parenting capacities were impoverished, placing their children at risk of suffering significant harm from physical neglect. Two-fifths of the families whose children were at risk of significant harm or significant impairment were in this group,[4] and therefore, not surprisingly, so were many families whose children were the subject of care proceedings.[12] Minority ethnic families were less likely to be in this group than in either of the other two.[4]

The research suggests that, over time, families may move from one category to another. Most often single issues are likely to become enmeshed with other long-standing problems if there has been an inappropriate response from Social Services and other public services in the past. However, some of the studies show that some families who might have had multiple problems in a previous referral had managed to resolve enough of their problems to present a single issue at a later date. Child maltreatment is not necessarily associated with any one type of family.

The implications for practice from the findings on family circumstances are important. The studies strongly suggest that any assessment of parenting capacity has to be differential and take into account factors in the past and present that may identify families' past strengths, experiences of solving problems and potential for change at the present time.

The main points

- Many families of children in need are struggling to bring up their children in conditions of material and emotional adversity.

- Poor health and poverty are dominant themes in the studies for the majority of families.

- Domestic violence and drugs and alcohol misuse are present in families with more severe problems.

- There are differences in the level and scope of problems – families whose children are subject to care proceedings have more entrenched and long-standing multiple problems.

- Families of children in need can be grouped in three ways: those who need help with specific issues, acutely distressed families and families with multiple and long-standing problems.

- Families move from one category to another as problems improve or deteriorate.

The children's perspectives on their needs

The third way adopted by the studies of describing the lives of children in need was to give children's own accounts of their circumstances and the issues that were important to them. Like all children, children in need should be given the opportunity of voicing their concerns. One of the major principles of the Children Act 1989 is that children in need, as well as their parents, are to be seen as individuals with 'particular needs and potentialities'.[46]

A philosophy that purports to be child-centred must be rooted in listening to what is important to children. This will add to the knowledge of how children may best be helped to achieve their own individual optimal outcomes. As some of the studies in previous overviews have shown, children can sometimes have surprisingly different perceptions and preoccupations from adults. Acknowledging and responding appropriately to children's feelings and perspectives helps encourage confidence and self-esteem, both of which are essential building blocks of child development.

Several of the studies interviewed children in need in different circumstances, although most of the children represented the views of those looked after by local authorities. This was inevitable as the focus of children's views reflected the circumstances in which the Children Act requires their wishes and feelings to be sought. In spite of this bias, there are some themes shared by children of different ages who were living with their families or away from home.

Preoccupations and concerns of the children in need

The general impression from the studies in which children were interviewed is of troubled, anxious children who would undoubtedly benefit from services. They were sometimes physically malnourished and lacked psychological nurture. They were often anxious about themselves and others close to them. Some lived in fear of being maltreated. Others feared being abandoned by family or being moved to a new carer. Some had low self-esteem and were anxious about school and peers. A deep sense of sadness pervaded those who had been neglected or abused or who had been separated from their families for a long time. A minority of children were detached from both adults and other children and some serious concern was expressed by researchers about their well-being. To counteract these negatives, there is evidence of positive attachments to family and significant others, signs of experiences to counter adversity and examples of sound common-sense from children of all ages about themselves, their families and their circumstances.

The children's anxieties about themselves

Anxious about health

Both children living with their families and those looked after by the local authority had some serious concerns about their state of health. Three-quarters of the children in the significant harm study complained about aches and pains. More worryingly, over half of the children in this study showed some signs of depression that did not diminish over time.[4]

Children who were looked after were also worried about themselves. The anxiety sometimes manifested itself in belligerent behaviour at reviews. These children were continually worried about the future.[3, 15]

School – a source of anxiety or sanctuary

Children told the researchers of their worries about educational attainment. Some children were aware that circumstances at home were placing their educational attainment at risk. Fifteen-year-old Joe said:

> I worry about the SATs [Standard Attainment Tests] – all of them. I always try
> my hardest but I worry I won't get a good job. At the moment because of all
> the bother people expect less of me – they don't expect me to do good work so
> I have to work extra hard.[4]

Some children felt they were not liked by their teachers and the fact that their parents had argued with the teachers had made things worse.[8] Teachers' insensitivity to the poverty of the children's home circumstances was sometimes a problem. Children found it upsetting and shaming to cope with the stigma of being reprimanded for not having a swimming costume or gym shoes.

School also held fears of being bullied or teased. Several children across the family support studies reported their experiences, and in one study over half of the children at risk of suffering significant harm were likely to be bullied at school.[4] More worryingly, almost half of the children interviewed in that study were to some extent bullies themselves.

Racism had also been a problem for some children and had seriously disrupted their educational development:

> Like the children would wipe their fingers on me and that to see if my colour'd
> come off and call me milky bar and blackies and things like that, it was terrible
> ... they didn't like me and I was the only black child in the school. I hated to go
> to school so in the end I never used to go, me mum used to teach me at home.
> I never really went to a primary school.[3]

Children who were accommodated did not want others to know of their circumstances. It was clear that the stigma of being 'in public care' had not been eradicated entirely by a change of name from care to accommodation. Reactions varied. Some youngsters in short-term accommodation felt ashamed of having to go away from home and feared they would be teased. Others thought friends might be jealous of their good fortune of a weekend away with another family.[2] Older children in accommodation felt the stigma more and occasionally resorted to taking revenge on those who were seen to have betrayed their circumstances to their peers:

> *Interviewer:* Did your school friends know you were [in accommodation]?
> *Girl, aged 10:* No, but one of them heard 'cos another girl told her, and she
> spread it round the school I think.
> *Interviewer:* Were you unhappy about that?
> *Girl:* Yeah. I beat her up.[15]

It is worth noting that, in time, some children in short-term accommodation did talk to their peers about their placements and found them receptive and accepting. These children had enjoyed their time spent away from home.[2]

It was clear from the research that the children's behaviour at school could be an indicator of their well-being. Insensitive responses to behaviour – such as the 14-year-old who was suspended from school, in spite of the protests of her grandmother, the day before she was to make a video about an alleged rape – were unsupportive to children.[8]

Not all of the children were anxious about school. Indeed, school was a place where three-quarters of the children in the safeguarding study said they 'often had fun'. Teachers were seen as the children's best helping person in one-third of the cases.[4] But this result is tempered by the experiences of those children who rated teachers poorly as actual or potential confidants because of their negative experiences of school.[15]

Removal to a new school could have positive effects. The skilled teaching and attention given to a child in a special placement improved performance and enthusiasm for learning, but it also raised anxieties about an impending return to a former school at which the child had performed badly.

Unexpected changes, sometimes linked to changes in placements for looked after children added to the children's difficulties with educational progress and making friends.[4] Worst of all was the example from an accommodated youngster whose residential placement was far from home and who had missed an essential school year:

> *Interviewer:* So what did you do all day?
> *Young man:* Be bored. There was only certain times you had the TV room open. You weren't allowed to go out in school time either. If the staff weren't busy they'd sometimes sit down and play cards with you . . . Eventually, they got me into a tuition centre. She was giving English and Maths that I'd done in middle school.[15]

The outcome of such neglect of education was poignantly expressed by care leavers:

> I can't see much future . . . sometimes I get depressed, I think there's no future for me.[3]

The significance of school in children's lives

The Children Act studies emphasise the significance of school in children's lives, not only as a source of educational progress but, just as importantly, as a source of emotional support and self-esteem. Understanding children's feelings and perceptions about positive and negative experiences of school is a necessary part of responding to and enhancing their potential for educational attainment.

The importance of family

For good or ill, children universally gave the same message to researchers: their families were very important to them. This applied as much to children who were looked after by the local authority and had lost contact with parents as to those living with their families, and included children whose personal safety had been put at risk by parents.[2, 4, 8, 15, 22, 23]

There was a complex matrix of views. Families were often a source of nurture, but they could also raise anxieties in a child and, at worst, be threatening and unsupportive. However, to a care leaver, any family was better than no family.[3, 14]

Several key issues reveal children's perspectives on their families:

Attachments and trust

There was a wide range of family styles and problems, which, in turn, had an impact on children in different ways. Children who were least at risk of suffering serious impairment tended to come from families where a single issue or acute distress had brought them to Social Services. These children were well attached to their families, felt safe at home and saw home as a place of physical nurture and love. This was evidenced by the trust the children had in their parents and their coping skills in managing the transition between home and accommodation:

> *6-year-old:* I'm not sure really what will happen. It will be alright. Ask my mum she knows.[2]

Some of the older children in these families had a remarkable sense of foresight. They were able to see that improving the situation for their parents would, in the long term, ensure their continued security at home. The children's stoical acceptance of the value of respite care to their parents was impressive.[2] However, as Mary's words show, her placement could be managed because Mary knew her home and her mother were constant:

> *Mary, aged 14:* I think my mum needs a break and then she feels a lot better. It's quite nice for me. I like them [carers] and I know she's [mum's] at home.[2]

Where families were supportive to children, the mothers, aunts and grand-mothers seemed to take the main credit.[2, 4, 13, 15] Attachments between siblings were also very important.[11] Fathers and stepfathers were less frequently cited as sources of support but, where they were, there was evidence of strong and positive attachments.[2, 23] Attachments were no less important between children and their carers in the studies on looked after children.[2, 11]

The presence of support from parents and wider kin provided positive research findings to endorse the value of a nurturing and protective family. It reinforces the view that early intervention may be productive in preventing family breakdown at a later stage. Even when Care Orders are necessary, there is a place for the extended family in providing placements for children.[4, 7, 10]

Not all of the families could provide that nurture. One of the disturbing findings from the studies, both of children living at home and of those looked after, was the reports of the minority of children who had no one to turn to. In the study on children in need in Wales, 8 out of 63 children said they could confide in no one.[8] Similarly, in the significant harm study, researchers were most concerned about the children who said there was no one they could turn to for support at home or at school.[4]

A minority of the looked after children were also detached and lonely, neither able to relate to their carers nor look forward to contact with their parents. In the fostering family contact study the research team stressed that foster and residential care could not be held entirely responsible for this detachment. Rather it was heavily influenced by the children's early experiences of inconsistency and rejection before they came into the care system.[7]

Living in an atmosphere of strife

The studies of children at risk of suffering significant harm or impairment revealed a permeating theme of children living in an atmosphere of family arguments and strife, frequently exposed to a climate of warring adults:

> From the children's responses, it would appear that for most conflict at home was happening around them rather than involving them directly. Since almost half of the children were living in families where there was violent conflict between parental figures . . . the harm stemming from this should not be underestimated.[4]

Older children became embroiled in this tense climate, finding themselves as targets of their parents' rows. Less than half of the children in the significant harm study 'got on' with their families. Rows with parents and siblings were common.[4]

Feeling unsafe at home

One of the most worrying issues reported to researchers in the safeguarding children and family support and emotional maltreatment studies was the children's fear about harm to themselves or harm to others in the family. In a minority of cases children were directly at risk of suffering maltreatment and clearly lived in an atmosphere of fear for their personal safety. Sometimes this was mitigated by a protective parent. Even when abusing parents were removed, the long-term effect on children's well-being was disturbing:[4, 22]

> When Nathan, aged 15, was asked what was the best thing that had happened since the recent problems emerged, he said his mother getting an injunction against his father. The worst thing was the temper he had developed himself, when his dad left home.[4]

However, the complexity of these abusive parent–child relationships has to be understood. The dilemmas of implementing the Children Act principles of safeguarding and promoting welfare are nowhere more evident than in the cases of children who were strongly attached to abusive parents.

> Yes, my dad has really hurt and upset me. He believes in different things and I believe in different things – so that's the reason we have arguments. I do love him though.[4]

Children as carers

Many children in the family support studies were worried about the well-being of their families. Sometimes this was borne out of the parents' ill health and fears that parents might die,[2, 3, 23] an anxiety experienced by many children in middle childhood as they become aware of the mortality of adults. For others, the fears went beyond normal anxieties. The tense atmosphere of a home beset by conflict and violence had led some children in at least three of the studies to take on a role of parental responsibility beyond their years.[2, 4, 23] Other children had taken on this role because of parental illness or, in some cases, parental incapacity as a result of misuse of drugs or alcohol. Others tried to safeguard a parent from abuse by another adult. These carer-children were fiercely protective of their parents and siblings. They had considerable anxiety about being absent from their families and felt they were responsible for keeping the family going. Hence when they were accommodated, their anxiety was translated into serious and inappropriate concerns about how their families would manage without them.[2] When foster carers took over the parenting role, young people who had previously been in charge of their families found this change of status very difficult:

> I don't think they quite realised how much I was doing on my own at the time and then automatically it was straight back down to being a kid again, from being like the adult in the family even though I was only 13. [11]

The significance of going away from home

Sometimes the arguments between parents and adolescents led to youngsters being accommodated. Although some teenagers told researchers they deliberately 'wound up' their parents, others had clearly been shocked that they had ended up in accommodation. They felt the situation had got out of their control and they had been abandoned by their parents:

> I knew we were having arguments but I didn't think it was that bad to have sent me away, if you know what I mean.[15]

Even in the best of circumstances, where children had been well prepared for accommodation, going away from home was a significant event in the children's lives. In the short-term fostering study over 90% of the children felt homesick, a feeling that took some time to diminish. Many of these children, along with those in the contact study, came to terms with their feelings by diversionary tactics. They rarely wanted to talk to their carers about their feelings. More often they wanted to be alone or to lose themselves in a television programme. An important finding was the children's need for emotional and physical space in which to come to terms with being away from home.[2, 7]

The exceptions to sadness about being away from home were the minority of teenagers for whom accommodation was a positive and safe haven. For these young people separation had provided a useful gap in which a new pattern of relationships could be established. Along with others who had re-established contact with their families on leaving the care system, these youngsters were impressive in their grasp of the limits of what they might expect from their families:

> When I'm not at home and I go back for weekends, me and my mum get on really well.[15]

But in spite of the views of these teenagers, for many of the children the significance of accommodation was that it might hold a hidden agenda of permanent abandonment and rejection.

> At first I thought I would stay there for ever, do you know what I mean?[15]

Anxiety about separation was not confined to the initial admission to accommodation. Children who were looked after were constantly anxious about the next move – how long would they stay in one placement?

Fear of the unknown was a preoccupation for young people leaving care.[3, 14] While leaving care schemes have done much to prepare young people for independent living, the fears of managing life in isolation and without any real emotional support were very real:

> I don't know, it's just my family seems so close and everything and I'm just far apart, just drifting on a raft somewhere . . . I feel everyone's gone and left me basically.[3]

> I can imagine me and my brother sat under a Christmas tree with no one there, 'cause there isn't anyone, is there?[14]

The importance of maintaining family links

The children and young people in all of the studies were in no doubt that their families mattered. For looked after children and care leavers,[7, 11, 15] the maintenance of connections retained the same significance as it had done in the 1985 overview.[50] However, the studies of young people leaving care in this overview suggest that what has changed for the better because of the Children Act 1989 is the maintenance of links with families.

In contrast to the 1985 overview of research studies, in which young people described their total severance of links with their families on leaving care, it was heartening to learn that most young people in the study on leaving care in partnership could cite at least 20 family members to whom they felt connected.[14] Similarly, while many young people in the moving on study could not return to their families, they valued family links with siblings, grandparents and other members of their extended family, as did those in the Care Orders study.[3, 11] However, an important finding was that if young people felt links had diminished to the extent that they had no meaning, these relatives were no longer counted as family. The leaving care in partnership study also noted that black teenagers leaving care had fewer relatives with whom they were in contact.[14]

In spite of improvements since 1985, there were still some young people who did not have kin. They tended to adopt honorary family members of two kinds: those, such as long-term foster carers, who were seen as replacement 'kin' and those who were transient, such as adults in charge of supervised lodgings.

On balance, those who had retained family links, even with some ambivalence, seemed better able to make sense of their lives. Even where relationships were poor, maintaining family links 'offered a symbolic reassurance to young people and engendered a sense of belonging'.[3]

The main points

- Children in need say they feel anxious about the health and well-being of their families and their progress at school.

- Families are extremely important to all of the children, whether they are at home or are looked after.

- Many children are securely attached to and well nurtured by their families; others feel unsafe or alone.

- Children are upset by having to live in an atmosphere of strife.

- Some children are being forced to take on parental responsibilities beyond their years.

- School can be a haven or a source of stress.

3 Safeguarding and promoting children's welfare – balance and judgement

Safeguarding and promoting children's welfare are intertwined principles that underpin the structure and philosophy of the Children Act 1989. Before describing the research findings, a short exploration of these two principles may be useful to provide a context for the research findings. The studies explore the implementation of safeguarding and promoting welfare in three domains:

- when children are living with their families;

- when children are looked after by the local authority; and

- when children come before the family proceedings courts.

The elements of safeguarding and promoting welfare

Within the Children Act 1989 safeguarding has two elements:

- a duty to protect children from maltreatment; and

- a duty to prevent impairment of development.

The duty to protect children from maltreatment or to make sure their development is not impaired demands a knowledge and understanding of child development. Prevention from impairment is only part of what is needed to ensure that children have maximum chances of developing to an optimal level. Actions will be needed by parents and others to ensure that children's welfare is actively promoted. This is why the promotion of welfare, as well as the need to safeguard, is the legal basis for any decision-making and intervention.

The promotion of welfare within the Children Act also has several elements:

- understanding and helping to provide the necessary building blocks of optimal child development for a particular child;

- understanding the importance of children's families to their development;

- understanding how the environment in which a child is growing up can positively or negatively influence development; and

- understanding that the quality of experience in childhood will contribute to outcomes and life chances in adulthood.

The tensions of implementing the safeguarding and promoting of welfare

Most parents wish to create opportunities for their children to grow up in circumstances that are consistent with the provision of safe and effective care. In practice, safeguarding and promoting the welfare of children is bound to bring inherent tensions between families and professionals. There is a balance to be struck between encouraging families to be independent and offering timely and effective services when children are in need of them. There is also an uneasy balance between compulsion and voluntariness. As early guidance on the Act suggested:

> The Act seeks to protect children both from the harm which can arise from failures or abuse within the family and from the harm which can be caused by unwarranted intervention in their family life. There is a tension between these objectives which the Act seeks to regulate so as to optimise the overall protection provided for children in general. [45, para. 1.31]

There are dilemmas in the real world that social workers and other professionals working with children face every day, and there are complex decisions that have to be made. When should families with children living at home be supported and when should children be removed from these families? When should children be returned home and when should alternative families be sought to provide children with the optimal chances of attaining best outcomes? What are the circumstances in which removal should be voluntary or compulsory? And, most difficult, what are the factors to be weighed in giving parents 'one more chance' or in grasping the nettle and deciding which children will be best served by growing up in another family who can give them a safe and nurturing childhood to maximise their life chances in adulthood?

Such questions are not easy to answer and are, in the end, matters of professional judgement. What the Children Act 1989 does is to provide a framework in which those decisions can be made and carried out. In particular, it spells out the circumstances in which, on the one hand, families should be supported in bringing up their children and, on the other, the state considers the risk of harm to individual children to be so serious that it may authorise the removal of those children from their families. Any of these decisions are grounded in the intertwining principles of safeguarding and promoting children's welfare.

Safeguarding and promoting welfare now

The philosophy of the Children Act to safeguard and promote children's welfare has been strengthened by recent government initiatives and by guidance to professionals. The *Quality Protects* programme in England[69] and *Children First* in Wales[106] build on the Children Act by emphasising that every child should have the opportunity of achieving optimal outcomes in his or her development. Further, the opportunities placed before children at crucial stages of their development will contribute significantly to achieving the goal of optimal development. Positive opportunities for physical, emotional, social and intellectual development in childhood will in themselves then become sound foundations for maximising life chances in adulthood.

Safeguarding children has always, rightly, been at the forefront of child welfare policy and practice, but it has not always been intertwined with promoting welfare. The recent guidance, *Working Together to Safeguard Children*, reaffirms the Children Act philosophy of an integrated approach to safeguarding and promoting welfare:

> Effective measures to safeguard children cannot be seen in isolation from the wider range of support and services available to meet the needs of children and families.[80, para. 1.9]

It also emphasises how this is facilitated by an interagency approach:

> Promoting children's well-being and safeguarding them from significant harm, depends crucially on effective information sharing, collaboration and understanding between agencies and professionals.[80, para. 1.10]

There has also been some updating of guidance on care proceedings and Care Orders.[70] This reiterates the importance of avoiding delay and of good collaboration between professionals in the courts.

Achieving the balance between compulsion and voluntariness through making informed and discriminating assessments is one of the aims of the Department of Health et al.'s *Framework for the Assessment of Children in Need and Their Families*.[79] The Children Act studies have messages about the balance that supports the use of the assessment framework.

The research messages on implementing the principles of safeguarding and promoting welfare

Safeguarding and promoting the welfare of children in need is linked in the Act to the provision of services. Indeed, the definition of 'in need' is about children who require services in order to develop properly and reach their potential. Where parents are, for whatever reason, unable to provide safe and effective care, and their children are 'in need', the intention of the Children Act is that services should be provided through section 17. Some children, however, do not receive services until they have been the subject of section 47 enquiries to establish whether they are at risk of significant harm or have been through court proceedings.

The relationship between safeguarding, children's needs and the provision of services is spelt out in early guidance accompanying the Act in relation to section 47 enquiries:

> The aim of an enquiry should be to establish whether the authority need to
> exercise any of their powers under the Act with respect to the child (47(3)).
> They may decide that an application should be made to a court, for example
> for a care or supervision order, or they may decide to offer services to the child
> or his family under Part III of the Act.[45, para. 6.5]

The *Guidance* accompanying the Act is very clear about the need for a broad tranche of family support services:

> The definition of in need is deliberately wide to reinforce the emphasis on
> preventive support and services to families.[47, para. 2.4]

Care plans that spell out the needs of children and link them to expected outcomes are also concerned with the provision of services. Families will continue to need services if their children are subject to Care Orders and are looked after by the local authority, whether the plan is to return them home or to seek alternative permanent families for the children. It is, for example, quite possible that a young child who is subject to a Care Order may benefit from day care. Many parents will need services in order to change the family relationships and to maintain appropriate contact in preparation for reunification. A minority will need help to relinquish their children.

Safeguarding and promoting the welfare of children living with their families

The balance between compulsion and voluntariness exercised the minds of planners, managers and practitioners in the early stages of implementation. In Chapter 2 we saw how authorities struggled towards interpreting the definition of children in need and wished initially to confine their understanding to the categories of children at risk that were in operation before the Children Act 1989, in spite of instructions to the contrary.

The research studies on both sections 17 and 47 reveal just how difficult it has been for authorities to shift their views. Consequently, in well over half of the authorities in England, in the first four years of the Act, child protection concerns continued to be 'the gateway to support services'.[4] Social workers and families were still trying to get round narrow eligibility criteria set by individual social services departments by 'interpreting concerns about impairment as borderline concerns about possible significant harm'.[4] Significantly, it was *only* if there was evidence of potential significant harm that access to family support services could be gained in some authorities.

In the study on implementing section 17,[1] over three-quarters of the authorities in England prioritised services where they considered children were at risk of suffering abuse. This contrasted markedly with just over one-tenth who considered that children were priority cases for services when they were living in households with no gas, water or electricity. In spite of long-standing cumulative research that associates children's physical environment with severe health and social problems,[60, 102] there remained a remarkable unwillingness to equate need with anything other than identification of serious child maltreatment.

This is an important finding, both from the studies on the implementation of services through section 17 and the studies on the use of section 47 enquiries. In the opinion of the researchers in the family support and maltreatment study, an exclusive focus on identification of whether maltreatment has occurred can be 'deleterious to child welfare, by allowing needs to go unnoticed, allowing problems to recur, or by dealing with cases via a section 47 investigation that do not warrant it'.[22]

In most child protection conferences the safeguarding children study also noted:

> what appeared to be an unconscious avoidance of discussion of the nature of 'significant harm' to the child in question, in favour of discussion of specific acts of abuse or neglect and categories for registration.[4]

The safeguarding children study suggested that, several years into implementation of the Act, child protection conferences still concentrated on measures to counteract specific acts of maltreatment and tended to produce protection plans that ignored important causes of harm or impairment to the child within the family.[4] The Children Act research studies suggest that families who are 'high on criticism and low on warmth'[52] may be displaying only one of the many patterns of parental behaviour that are likely to place children at risk of suffering impairment or significant harm. Domestic violence was present in nearly half of the cases in the safeguarding children study but was rarely mentioned in child protection plans. The safeguarding children study, for example, was at pains to point out that there are factors within individual children, such as temperament or behaviour, that need to be taken into account:

> Individual children will respond differently to similar events and lifestyles. What is significantly harmful to one child may not damage another.[4]

The value of studies that cover a long period of implementation was revealed in the information from the later studies on family support, carried out in the mid- to late-1990s. These showed the beginnings of shifts in attitudes. There was evidence that the Department of Health's 1996 initiative on refocusing services[68] was beginning to take effect to the benefit of a broader group of children and families.[22, 23]

In the study on services for children in need, three out of the seven authorities 'had enthusiastically accepted the challenge of the policy change that encouraged them to put more of their resources into Part III services to meet the needs of a broader range of children in need and change the balance between section 47 enquiries and the provision of services'.[23] These same authorities had widened their prioritised groups of children in need from the time of the first study on section 17[1] to include families under stress and those with child behavioural problems at home and at school.[23]

The Children Act studies themselves support the refocusing argument. The two studies on safeguarding children[4, 22] dispel myths that working 'in partnership' with parents where child maltreatment is an issue is likely to place children at increased risk. In all four authorities in the safeguarding children study, the children's welfare and safeguarding was simultaneously given the highest priority alongside any work plan carried out with the parents.[4]

The studies on children living with their families suggest a more discerning approach is needed, with more emphasis on the matching of children's needs to appropriate services.[4, 8, 21, 22, 23] This includes keeping a watchful eye on children who *might be* at risk of significant harm. Whilst it was very encouraging that, with intervention, the well-being of more than two-thirds of the children in the safeguarding study had improved, 55% still had some problems.[4] Although there was protection for most of the children for whom suffering significant harm related to abuse, a group of older children, including some who were looked after children, were still held to be at risk of suffering significant harm because of their continuing acts of self-harm or risk-taking behaviour. Many children still needed services that were not being provided, a finding that resonates with the Social Services Inspectorate inspection of family support services in 1999.[35]

The balance between safeguarding and promoting welfare for children in need who are living with their families has not yet been achieved. It seems that families who require help where children are in need for reasons other than child maltreatment are not always getting access to services. The findings point towards the need for a wider system of assessment that could lead to differential and well-planned patterns of intervention. This is explored further in Chapters 7 and 8.

The main points

- The shift from an identification of children in need as those at risk of suffering harm to an identification based on the impact of factors on children's development has not yet been achieved.

- There is an urgent requirement for a common, interagency language of need that defines safeguarding more widely than child maltreatment.

- Some children are not being properly safeguarded; others are denied access to family support services.

- The refocusing debate has helped shift away from section 47 enquiries as the primary route to provision of services, but more matching of children's needs to Part III services is required.

Safeguarding and promoting the welfare of looked after children

Local authorities in England look after around 55,000 children at any one time and accept responsibility for about 88,000 in any one year.[74] The Children Act 1989 is very clear that looked after children should have the same attention paid to their safety and welfare as children in need in the community:

> The cornerstone duty is that a local authority must safeguard and promote the welfare of each child whom they look after [section 22(3)a] . . . The authority [is] required to make reasonable use (for the benefit of children who are looked after) of the services and facilities which are available to children cared for by their own parents.[45, para. 5.9]

To achieve these objectives several areas of activity were strengthened by the Act, including the introduction of a regulatory strategy, both for placements and for individual children. The impact of regulation on residential child care has been the subject of the Department of Health's overview *Caring for Children Away from Home* published in 1998.[54] The Children Act studies provide information on four areas, introduced to take forward the principles of safeguarding and promoting welfare for children who are looked after by the local authority.

- Accommodation was introduced as a Part III service to replace the old voluntary care system.

- The process of planning and reviewing the progress of children was strengthened.

- Contact between looked after children and their families was to be encouraged and supported wherever possible.

- The powers of the local authority with regard to children leaving the care system were strengthened under section 24.

Using accommodation to support children and their families

Research carried out in the 1980s and included in two previous overviews[50, 51] had raised concerns about the shrinking use of voluntary care and the concomitant expansion in the removal of children to care on court orders. Although the reduction in the use of voluntary care was influenced by the intention of preventing family breakdown, thus using care as a last resort, the same research had also suggested that voluntary care was valued as a service by many families in difficulties'.[15] Unless there were clear grounds for compulsory action, voluntary care could be used as a supportive service for children and families. The stress and costs of taking children through the courts did not justify extensive use of court orders if voluntary arrangements would achieve the same outcome of safeguarding and promoting children's welfare.[50]

Taking account of this research, and mindful of the Children Act philosophy that children are best brought up in their own families wherever possible, it was the intention of the Children Act that barriers should be broken down between services offered to children in need in their own homes and those offered when children are accommodated by the local authority. Indeed, accommodation, under section 20, is deliberately placed within Part III of the Act and near to section 17 in order to emphasise its relevance as a Part III service to children in need. As one of the studies says:

> At least four of the major principles on which the Act is based – the concept of enduring parental responsibility, the emphasis on partnership with parents, the shift in 'prevention' from the gateway of the care system to the door of the courtroom, and an increased attention to the voice of the child – are all firmly encapsulated in the provision of accommodation.[15]

The impact of working with parents, listening to children and improving the systems of planning for children are explored later in this overview (Chapters 4, 5 and 7). This chapter is concerned with the overarching issues surrounding accommodation that relate to the balance between voluntariness and compulsion.

The balance between compulsory care and voluntary accommodation

First, it is clear that the intention of the Act to alter the balance between Care Orders and voluntary arrangements did succeed in the first four years of implementation. The care to accommodation study was able to compare its findings with similar groups of children 'in care' ten years earlier, provide a 'before and after' look at arrangements and conclude with some confidence that the 'no order' principle is having considerable impact on practice.[15] The trend in this study is backed up by statistics on the workings of the Children Act 1989.[75]

However, as can be seen from Table 2, the last four years of implementation show the balance has moved back towards a steady increase in children looked

Table 2 *Numbers of looked after children in England at 31 March 1992–99, by legal status*

Legal status	Years							
	1992	**1993**	**1994**	**1995**	**1996**	**1997**	**1998**	**1999**
Care Orders	37,500	31,800	28,900	28,500	28,900	30,000	32,100	34,100
Section 20	17,100	18,500	18,800	19,500	19,900	19,200	19,100	18,900

Source: *Children Looked After by Local Authorities* [75]

after on Care Orders, with 64% of the children being looked after on Care Orders in 1999. Although accommodation has also risen with some fluctuations, there has been a growing decline in its use from 1996 onwards, which mirrors the rise in Care Orders. Nevertheless, accommodation remains an important resource for children looked after by the local authority.

One trend that poses a dilemma with respect to children's welfare is the steep rise in repeat admissions.[15] An important principle of the Act is to promote continuity for looked after children, in recognition of earlier research that reported the negative effects of unplanned separations on children, including the breakdown of placements.[51]

The care to accommodation study reported that more than half of the youngsters in this study had been admitted more than once within the space of two years, and a substantial minority had experienced several episodes. The researchers pose the question whether such repeat admissions could be managed so that children return to the same carers, and they raise practice issues that will be addressed in Chapter 7. Some of the issues they raise are addressed in what has emerged as the most promising use of accommodation – planned short-term arrangements.[2]

Family support and short-term accommodation

The most successful use of accommodation as a family support service has been the provision of planned short-term or respite arrangements. The regulation of these placements for both disabled children and others in need was unified and strengthened under the Act. Short-term accommodation has several features that distinguish it from the general definition of full-time accommodation in the Children Act 1989. In short-term accommodation all placements should be with the same carer; all placements should occur within a period that does not exceed one year; no single placement should be for a duration of more than four weeks; and the total duration of the placements should not exceed 90 days.

Several studies describe the burgeoning of this service for a range of children, including those about whom there are concerns of potential significant harm and adolescents who are in danger of becoming estranged from their families.[4, 15] Further, adequate safeguarding can be provided by a combination of short-term accommodation and other support services for the majority of children at risk of significant impairment.[2, 4] There are indications that short-term accommodation is a helpful service for other families under stress.

In the short-term accommodation study there were measurable benefits for the well-being of both parents and children.[2] Measures were taken at the beginning and end of the study along several dimensions. When other factors had been accounted for, the parents' sense of control over their lives showed a positive shift over the period of intervention, measured on a standardised test. Additionally, quantitative measures showed that, on the dimensions of a number of anticipated benefits, such as recuperation, feeling less lonely and coping better with everyday life, over 80% of expectations were met. Changing children's behaviour and improving relationships with partners over the few short months of the study were less successful, which suggests that these areas may need longer-term intervention. Finally, there were measurable changes in the families' support networks. Relationships with extended family had been improved and, through the carers, parents had made more contact with others in the community.

There was strong evidence that children benefited from the experience of planned short-term accommodation, provided they were well attached to families in the first place, were well prepared and were actively supported throughout the placements by parents, carers and social workers.[2] In the majority of cases the children's quality of life was enhanced by their accommodation experience. Working positively with parents helped increase parental self-esteem and strengthen the parenting capacity to respond to the children's needs.

Full-time accommodation as a Part III service

The use of full-time accommodation is, however, not so straightforward. Whilst the intention of the Act was that accommodation should be used as a voluntary service to support families, the studies suggest that 'voluntariness' may be open to different interpretations. This is best exemplified by three models of working with parents that were compiled from the findings of several studies.[2, 7, 12, 13, 15]

- Accommodation is the service of choice jointly agreed by the local authority, the child and the family and meets the needs of a child and family in difficulty.

- Accommodation is offered in a crisis within the context of 'the insistent family and the reluctant social worker'. This applies particularly to young people wishing to escape from violent families.

- Accommodation is arranged in the context of a negotiated partnership where children and parents are offered accommodation or going to court as the alternative. All concerned recognise that safeguarding issues must receive attention and the use of court proceedings in the future is not ruled out.

Accommodation and the 'no order' principle

The third type of accommodation arrangement tests the balance between compulsion and voluntariness. The Children Act studies suggest that the early use of accommodation can be explained in the context of the 'no order' principle.[12, 15] Although the no order principle applies mostly to the making of court orders, its influence has 'trickled down' to the use of accommodation. The no order principle seeks to use voluntary agreements rather than court orders where this is in the interest of promoting the children's welfare.

Clearly, the Children Act is saying that court orders should be avoided if other means can be employed, but in all cases safeguarding and promoting the children's welfare should drive any decisions.

Employing a voluntary approach does not assume that each case will have the same model of working with parents, as the studies on short-term accommodation and family support and maltreatment show.[2, 22] Take, for example, a capable parent who needs a hospital admission but has no family or friends who can look after the children. Her situation may be rather different from a parent about whom there are suspicions of emotional abuse. In this latter case, workers may have to invoke the positive use of authority to explain to the parent(s), openly and with precision, that the outcome of using accommodation arranged by negotiated formal agreement will depend on the parents keeping their side of the contract. Such an approach has inherent tensions. The authority role brings with it the need for workers and parents to recognise overtly the power imbalance between them. Sometimes this can work well, as examples from the family support and maltreatment study show.[22] By contrast, it is clear from the earlier court studies, that social workers, solicitors and guardians ad litem are concerned about issues of justice and fairness, as the view of one team leader suggests:

> The fact that we have to go for accommodation with a threat of an application if parents don't agree, that's a much more subtle use of power than actually putting it before the court. I would have thought it felt more oppressive. Best practice would ensure you use accommodation wherever possible but this is forcing accommodation.[12]

This quote reflects the findings from several studies, albeit in a minority of cases, which talk of 'enforced' or 'sham partnerships' between social workers and families. The findings from the research studies suggest that practice in relation to accommodation has been rather confused. In some cases social workers are misunderstanding the negotiated nature of accommodation. So, for example, in the fostering family contact study, there were cases of accommodated children having to be supervised during contact with parents.[7] In other cases, in this and other studies, accommodation seems to have been used when a Care Order would have been more appropriate to safeguard children at risk of suffering impairment or even on the margins of suffering significant harm.[7, 12, 13] In the early days of implementation there was a misunderstanding about the no order principle by some social workers and local authority solicitors, the mistaken view being that court proceedings should be avoided in all circumstances.[12] This contradicts the flexibility built into the Children Act 1989 to provide different routes to safeguard and promote children's welfare.

How has accommodation been used to safeguard and promote the welfare of children?

The research raises several questions about the implementation of the use of accommodation. How far have attitudes shifted to see accommodation as a possible first, rather than a last, resort to support families under stress? What is the attitude to using accommodation in cases of those children whose development may be at risk of being impaired? Where were the boundaries of the no order principle set in relation to accommodation and Care Orders? The evidence from the studies presents a complex picture but comes down on the side of accommodation being a helpful service, exemplified by this summing up from the care to accommodation study:

> Families and children who might previously have faced lengthy and expensive court proceedings are being offered support and protection without apparent detriment to their welfare. Promising respite arrangements for stressed parents and their children are beginning to develop, and should be encouraged and expanded . . . Offering a range of support services from within and outside social services departments, as a complement to accommodation is current practice.[15]

There were also positive indicators of purposeful planning and working with parents and children, which are explored later in the overview.

On the negative side, there were two main areas of concern: that court action is not being used soon enough in some cases and that courts are being used inappropriately when negotiated arrangements might have been more appropriate.

The consequences of the confused use of accommodation has meant that, in an important minority of cases, delays in seeking court orders have had a damaging effect on children's welfare.[12, 15] Where courts have been used inappropriately as a 'last resort', it is suggested that inappropriate use of accommodation caused delays to the processes of safeguarding children through court proceedings.[12, 15, 36]

There were also cases where Care Orders were inappropriate. One unexpected area of concern was where accommodation was being used as an alternative to family support services in the community for some minority ethnic children. This in itself was acceptable, even desirable, within the framework of the Children Act. However, because accommodation was seen in some areas as the main gateway to compulsory action, these children may have then been inappropriately catapulted into care proceedings. Concerns were expressed by the researchers that 'difficulties in providing a culturally sensitive response to child protection issues may be exposing such families to a higher level of intervention'.[12] Similarly, the safeguarding study also found that Care Orders were being taken unnecessarily in some cases where negotiated accommodation would have been more appropriate.[4] These were cases where a parent 'had a mental illness or an addiction or an alcohol problem'. The researchers in this study believed that more active use of kinship placements and earlier community-based family support services to help parents resolve their problems might have prevented care proceedings.[4]

These mixed findings suggest that the use of accommodation needs to be refined and to be used with more attention to the individual circumstances of the children in need. The increased use of accommodation as a family support service needs to be encouraged, but its use in safeguarding cases could benefit from a review of policy and practice. Accommodation will undoubtedly continue, rightly, to play an important part in safeguarding and promoting the welfare of what is a significant group of children in need in terms of size and vulnerability. There are, however, indications (Table 2) that use of accommodation is declining slightly and that Care Orders are being increasingly used for looked after children. That change may reflect the needs of individual children, but it will be important to keep an eye on that balance so that a return to the 1985 position of Care Orders being used excessively is avoided.

The message from the research is that more discriminating assessment is required to achieve a proper balance between compulsion and voluntariness, a balance that reflects responsiveness to the needs of individual children. With the evolution of better practice, underpinned by more careful assessment of children's needs and parents' capacities, the balance between using care and accommodation appropriately is more likely to be achieved.

The main points

- The balance between care and accommodation has fluctuated since implementation of the Children Act 1989, with a current trend towards an increased use of both accommodation and Care Orders.

- There are concerns about the increase in the repeated use of unplanned short periods of accommodation.

- Planned short-term accommodation can provide effective family support for many children.

- Full-time accommodation has provided a positive and cost-effective family support service for many families who might otherwise have faced lengthy and expensive court proceedings.

- A number of children might have been safeguarded more effectively at an earlier stage through use of the courts rather than accommodation.

- The increased use of accommodation as a family support service needs to be encouraged, but its use in safeguarding cases could benefit from a review of policy and practice.

Children within the courts

The focus on safeguarding and promoting children's welfare is nowhere more apparent than in court proceedings. Indeed the Children Act 1989 makes it clear in its very first section that, in decisions of the court, children's welfare is paramount. Paramountcy does not exclude the possibility of a voluntary solution if this is in the children's best interests. This is encapsulated in the 'no order' principle as applied in the court setting. The synergy between safeguarding and welfare is contained in the emphasis on 'no delay', in effecting decisions quickly to take account of children's developmental time-scales. *The Introduction to the Children Act 1989* sums up these principles:

> Section 1 sets out three principles which guide a court which makes decisions under the Act. The first is that the child's welfare is the paramount consideration when a court determines any question with respect to his upbringing (the welfare principle). The second is that the court should not make an order under the Act unless it considers that to do so would be better for the child than making no order at all. The third is that the court should have regard to the general principle that delay in determining a question with respect to the upbringing of a child is likely to prejudice his welfare.[45, para 3.13]

To help with these complex decision-making processes, the court is provided with a welfare checklist, which emphasises issues relevant to safeguarding and promoting children's welfare.

The family proceedings structure under the Act was redesigned to provide a forum for decisions that would support social workers and others charged with the responsibility of safeguarding and promoting the welfare of children subject to court orders.

A wider range of court orders was made available and there was a fairer and more transparent system in which the views of children and parents could be fairly represented, recognising that there may be tensions between them. Accordingly, a balance was sought to give parents and others holding parental responsibility the status of parties to the proceedings, while the role of the independent guardian ad litem was strengthened to represent the interests of children separately and to represent their wishes and feelings.

A more professional approach was introduced. This ensured access to significant documents for all involved in a court case. It also ensured that clear reasons for decisions were conveyed in writing to families and professionals.

There were many fears about the changes, especially that the abolition of wardship would reduce protection for children. However, the research is unequivocal in demonstrating that this has not happened. To some extent the loss of power to the judiciary has been compensated for by the opportunity extended to judges to scrutinise the care plan.[11] Indeed, the researchers conclude that, overall, the court system is working remarkably well in many aspects,[11, 12] and the Act 'has to be regarded as a substantial achievement which has had an enormous impact on practice'.[12] One set of criteria now governs state intervention in family life and this has had a positive impact on the courts:

> The concepts to which the conditions give expression are widely accepted as
> valid and providing a structured and more rigorous framework for decision-
> making, both in demonstrating the justification for and estimating the effects
> of intervention. Throughout the system practice is seen to have become more
> thoughtful and measured.[12]

The research reveals much about the interface between the child welfare system and the judicial processes and explores the impact of the Children Act 1989 on the use of the courts and the outcomes of court cases for children in need.

Raising the threshold for intervention

The research shows that the Act has achieved its purpose of raising the threshold for court intervention. The children who were being brought to court appropriately had very serious problems. Some had been in a programme of intervention of a voluntary nature for a considerable time. Others, appropriately, had come straight to court.[4, 12, 22]

The studies show that, in the majority of cases, court action was sought at an appropriate moment, when planned and purposeful intervention to support the children and their families had been tried and failed.[4] This provides an acute contrast to the findings of the research in the 1980s, prior to the Act – already discussed in the context of providing accommodation – where extensive and inappropriate use of compulsory measures was evident.[50] However, in the Children Act studies, in a minority of cases, the right balance may not have been struck between compulsion and voluntariness in relation to initiating care proceedings. A minority of children might have benefited from planned care proceedings being brought at an earlier stage.[12]

In spite of this caveat, the court studies show that one of the major aims of the Act has been achieved in that fewer care proceedings are instigated in a crisis. The studies found that families who came to court were more likely to have had children looked after or their children's names placed on the Child Protection Register for some time. Six out of ten children in the safeguarding study were living at home prior to coming to court. Because fewer cases came to court in a crisis, it was not surprising that in general, as the Act intended, Emergency Protection Orders were used sparingly and often reserved for the protection of infants. A solicitor in one study summed up the trend:

> What has changed with the whole of the Children Act thinking is that Social Services aren't likely to go for an Emergency Protection Order unless it's absolutely essential.[8]

The changes have brought about an improvement in the preparation of cases for court.[36, 38] Achieving this change has challenged practitioners who have responded positively. Local authority social workers, guardians ad litem and lawyers have had to adopt a careful, evidential approach to bringing cases to court.[5, 12] In summary:

- the new legal criteria themselves are clearer, more demanding and stricter;

- the evidence is subject to more rigorous scrutiny by the courts;

- legal departments are more involved in considering the strength of evidence before an application is made and are judged to adopt a cautious approach;

- best practice under the Children Act is seen to be about partnership, negotiation, voluntarism and the importance of maintaining family links; and

- all parties are now made accountable for their actions during proceedings and evidence is now timetabled.

Whilst there is evidence of careful and considered judgements being exercised in the preparation of evidence for care proceedings, there are some negative consequences of the new system. The careful approach has caused some delay in bringing cases to court. This may have had a detrimental effect on a minority of children who have been living in uncertainty,[11, 12] and it can ca further uncertainty at a later stage because of delays in finding adoptive c foster placements.[11]

A further source of delay within the court system is the time involved in deciding to transfer a case to a higher court. The expert evidence study found that transferring cases from the family proceedings courts to a care centre added just over three months to cases, whilst transfer to the High Court added over four and a half months to cases.[5]

The fact that the Children Act studies were conducted over several years also provides evidence that the achievement of the balance between voluntarism and compulsion has been a process rather than an event. Whilst, initially, the swing to trying to keep children out of the courts was very marked,[12] by the time of the later studies the evidence shows a settling process and a more balanced approach to deciding when proceedings were to be initiated.[11, 13] Nevertheless, the fact that the last resort study suggested that 22 out of 83 children had been further harmed or had been deprived of the security of a long-term permanent alternative home by inappropriate delay in bringing the case to court leaves no room for complacency. It has to be set alongside the other finding, cited above, that most children accommodated, even in situations of risk of suffering impairment, benefited from negotiated rather than court-mandated care. The need for continued monitoring of this complex balancing is indicated by these studies.

The research studies raise questions about interpretation of the concept of working 'in partnership' with parents. It was never the intention of the Act that partnership should be an end in itself, but rather that the participation of parents in decisions should be part of the process of promoting children's welfare at all levels, from participation in family centres to participation in the courts. As suggested earlier in this chapter, working with parents did not compromise safeguarding in child protection enquiries. Working with parents in the courts has equally demanded from social workers and their managers an ability to assess and manage the safeguarding of children. Decisions will sometimes have to be made about the inappropriateness of voluntary family support.

Questions remain about balance and judgement. It was clear that the ability to exercise professional judgement was inhibited by misinterpretation in the early implementation of the 'no order' principle in some instances. There was evidence that some workers had wished to bring cases to court at an earlier stage but had been advised against this by cautious legal departments.[12] Although, by the end of the later studies, there had been some changes in the balance, the research concludes that anxieties remain about whether some children might have been protected earlier.[13] It is also possible that, with a broader use of family support services, including placements with kin at an earlier stage, stresses on parents and children might have been reduced, thus avoiding the courts later on.[4, 13]

The courts as first resort and last resort

Two clear messages from the studies present a paradox.

First, the courts should be more of a *first resort* on occasions where it is clear that the children are suffering significant harm and that, even with informal and professional support, parenting cannot be improved to a level to safeguard and promote the children's welfare while they are living with their parents at home within time-scales that can meet the children's developmental needs.

More discriminating assessment and decision-making based on evidence of children's needs might better guard against depriving a minority of children of life chances through permanent alternative foster or adoptive placements. While children are out of their family, therapeutic work could be done to ascertain if they can return to their parents or if they need alternative longer-term placements. The development of such assessments are discussed in Chapter 8.

Second, and at the same time, the courts could be more of a *last resort* in relation to some children from families living in conditions of long-standing poverty and strife. This is another aspect to the story that permeates all the studies, from family support to accommodation and within the courts. There are insufficient, effective interagency support services available to many families at an early stage of their problems. The research was clear that there were occasions when court proceedings could have been avoided if appropriate interventions had been available to child or family at an earlier stage.[12, 13] This was of particular concern in relation to services for minority ethnic families. Court action was eventually taken because the accumulation of stresses and problems within the families had weakened parental capacity to the point that the children were at risk of suffering significant harm. An important implication of the research is that failure to offer support at an earlier stage may necessitate more trenchant, expensive and distressing interventions at a later date.

Safeguarding and promoting children's welfare through court processes

In the area of court processes, implementation of the Children Act 1989 seems to be generally successful. The best-laid plans study reports that the court framework has 'been transformed'.[13] The Act has succeeded in the following areas:

- Most remedies are available at all levels of court proceedings, and all child and family matters can be dealt with together. The bringing together of private and public law offers the degree of flexibility previously only available in wardship.

- Children are entitled to legal representation and, importantly, to representation of a type that can accommodate their rights and their needs.

- Anyone with a legitimate interest in children's welfare can participate in court proceedings.

- The tightening of rules of evidence and the use of written depositions and advance disclosure has provided for a fairer and more participatory system.

- Parents report a high level of satisfaction with the judiciary and appreciate the opportunity for a more informal approach.

- Throughout the system practice has improved, but all professionals have been challenged by the expansion of their roles.

There remain some substantive issues, but the research emphasises that these are seen as problems to be resolved in the evolution of the court system and the training of practitioners rather than as fundamental problems in the legislation. This view is endorsed by several of the court order studies undertaken by the Department of Health.[36–41]

One major recommendation is that there is scope for moving away from an adversarial model within cases of child welfare. Throughout several studies there is an emphasis on the need for all professionals to be knowledgeable about children's development and skilled in communicating with children and families. Whether this can be accomplished within the present system or whether steps should be taken towards a dedicated court for families is worthy of debate. In any event, to serve the interests of children in need there seems to be scope for:

> the establishment of a more dedicated magistracy, perhaps making greater use of those with relevant experience and restricted to those who have a particular commitment to and an aptitude for the work.[12]

Safeguarding and promoting welfare in the courts with no delay

The expertise of participants in the court arena may well be an important factor contributing to children's welfare. Another factor, also important in relation to children's development, is the account taken of children's time-scales by avoiding delay in decision-making in the courts. This principle is enshrined in section 1(2) of the Children Act 1989. However, the research reports that the Children Act has not achieved its aim and that delay continues to be a problem:[5, 11, 12]

> Only one in ten of the sample cases completed within the original 12-week target. Over a third took more than six months with the longest lasting for 78 weeks.[12]

It is a 'multi-factorial problem'. On average, three or four factors influenced a single case, but there could be more. Cases of longer duration were more likely to have multiple reasons for delay.

There was some association between the characteristics of the cases and their duration. Where cases were transferred between courts, this invariably caused delay. The use of experts also increased the duration of cases and caused delay,[37] but this has to be balanced against ensuring that the best decision is made to promote children's welfare in the long term.[5] Additionally, the court order studies report that some delays can be purposeful[37] and that time may be needed for a final hearing to be delayed, for example until a parent has completed a treatment programme. Case law has now established that section 1(2) of the Children Act 1989 should not be interpreted to mean that delay is always detrimental a child. Nevertheless, in spite of these caveats, the research suggests that unplanned delays do occur. These tend to be caused by processes within the courts or actions of the professionals or parents. Among the key reasons why delay occurred in the court studies are:

- cases not firm before coming to court;

- parents delaying their legal processes;

- lack of co-operation by parents;

- waiting for cases to start;

- lack of court time;

- the level of the court at which a hearing was heard;

- number of hearings;

- transferring cases between courts;

- guardians ad litem wishing to be assured care plans are sound;

- assessment by experts;

- local practice in the courts; and

- lack of judicial resources to make the system run smoothly.[5, 12, 13, 37]

The remedies for delay are as multi-faceted as the causes. More stringent monitoring of delay might throw more light on local area problems. Relocation of judicial resources might help, reducing the number of hearings and limiting evidence-in-chief could also be useful. The provision of evidence from experts in writing and in advance is also suggested.[5, 11, 12, 13] The finding of foster or adoptive placements might be speeded up by concurrent planning that ensures the necessary procedures, such as referral to adoption or foster panels, are initiated before the final order is made.[11]

The use of guardians ad litem, case management and experts

Guardians ad litem are appointed as independent professionals to safeguard and promote children's welfare in court proceedings and to act as advisors to the court. Most are experienced social workers. The presence of guardians in the court processes is generally reported positively in the research studies[5, 11, 12, 13] and in an additional study conducted in this area by Brophy.[61] The expert evidence study suggests that guardians regard themselves and are regarded by the court as experts on social work practice and child care matters.[5] In complex cases requiring experts, this study demonstrates that guardians have exacting standards. They wish to appoint highly qualified and experienced experts and are sometimes frustrated by not being able to draw on suitable experts from local child and adolescent mental health services. Additionally, guardians find it difficult to call on any clinical expertise to assist them in their assessments prior to court hearings.

Guardians exercised considerable control in ensuring that proceedings were not concluded without sound care plans. They also played an important role in mediating and negotiating with parties in the corridors of the courts to resolve disputes about the use and evidence of experts.

The key to successful case management was an ability to apply a high level of practice-based experience and analytical skills backed by sound training, along with an ability to maintain independence and flexibility during proceedings. The former skills were particularly important in highly complex cases that contained expert reports from more than one discipline.

Compared with the more limited responsibilities that were originally envisaged for guardians within the Children Act 1989, the expert evidence study suggests that guardians now occupy complex roles as negotiators, mediators and gatekeepers in care proceedings. Some of this important work is undertaken 'at the door of the court'.[5]

The Children Act 1989 has resulted in considerable use of expert evidence in family proceedings courts. Practices and procedures for obtaining this evidence have changed and improved over the course of several years of implementation. Experts are drawn from many sources but notably from child psychiatrists and psychologists.[5, 12] Some psychiatrists for children and adolescents make substantial efforts to meet the demands of Children Act proceedings. However, the current system of providing and funding experts is reported as contentious because experts are drawn from a relatively small pool. The expert evidence study suggests that 'current arrangements do not provide consistently high quality work for parties or the courts'.[5]

The experts themselves reported considerable improvements in their work resulting from the Children Act. However, criticisms of some practices were evident, including the loss of multidisciplinary teams in clinical practices generally. Consequently, the study recommends that there should be a review of the system of providing certain types of expert evidence, and also a new multidisciplinary approach to the use of experts that would result in multidisciplinary assessments.

A new approach should incorporate new and more radical principles to the acquisition of certain types of evidence. It should be based on a more therapeutically orientated model and within a framework in which child and adolescent mental health services are more integrated into the family justice system but also more accountable.[5]

Safeguarding children with a range of court orders

The last resort study showed that the majority of care proceedings still end in Care Orders, as they did prior to the Children Act 1989. Indeed, Care Orders are used more frequently than they were before the Act. However, there has also been a rise in the proportion of cases ending in no orders. The findings inspire some confidence that, although the 'no order' principle may have delayed some cases coming to court, once court proceedings begin, there has been a genuine shift in attitude towards consideration of the impact of an order on the child's welfare. The welfare checklist has evoked careful consideration of whether or not an order should be made. In this respect, the 'no order' principle in the courts may be working. Here the balance between compulsion and voluntariness may have been achieved in the way the Act intended.

The fact that Care Orders are now granted more frequently than before the Act still requires some explanation. This evidence is complex. On the one hand, there are clear indications that local authorities are only bringing cases that will have a chance of success. On the other hand, as the last resort study suggests, the increase in Care Orders may signal that the menu of orders introduced under the Act is not being used as widely as it might have been. Supervision Orders, for example, have been little used.

There is conflicting evidence from the research about the use of Supervision Orders, with some indications that, early in the implementation, Supervision Orders were rarely used. The last resort study, for example, suggests that the kinds of less serious cases formerly used for Supervision Orders no longer reach court because of the swing towards voluntariness. Additionally, a major reason for care proceedings is often the non-co-operation of parents.[12] If parents are working in partnership with the authority, a written agreement may be just as effective as a Care Order. The later studies on family support and care proceedings show that Supervision Orders can be used effectively.[11, 22] The studies suggest that Family Assistance Orders have been little used as a positive alternative to Supervision Orders to help strengthen parenting capacity. The Crime and Disorder Act 1998 has introduced Parenting Orders. Though aimed at families where children's behaviour is causing concern, whether these new orders will have an impact on the use of Supervision Orders and Family Assistance Orders, within the framework of the Children Act 1989, remains to be seen.

The grounds for making Care Orders appear to be generally satisfactory. Any complaints from practitioners are related more to the tensions that have arisen from the changes made in the Children Act to separate out the court's role in decision-making from the implementation of those decisions by the local authority. Thus, the local authority social services department has been given the full mantle of responsibility for the safeguarding and promotion of the welfare of children subject to Care Orders. How much that service has succeeded in safeguarding and promoting children's welfare is explored in Chapter 7.

Overall, the choice and use of compulsory orders seems to be working reasonably well. The last resort study concludes that the range of orders:

- is an improvement on those previously available under the Children and Young Persons Act 1969, even if it does not quite provide the flexibility of wardship;

- offers increased scope for ingenuity in matching remedies to needs if not the tailor-made packages that appeared to be promised; and

- covers most situations adequately if not every situation perfectly.[12]

The main points

- One of the major aims of the Act has been achieved in that fewer care proceedings are instigated in a crisis.

- There is evidence of careful preparation of cases for court by social workers and lawyers.

- Guardians ad litem make an important contribution to safeguarding children through their reports and through mediation with other professionals.

- In some cases the balance between court orders and voluntariness has not yet been achieved: delays in bringing cases to court may have further damaged some children, but unnecessary use of court proceedings may have harmed others.

- The Children Act 'no delay' principle has not solved the problems of delays in court processes.

- The 'no order' principle is generally working well in relation to the balance between voluntary and compulsory outcomes from care proceedings.

- There have been substantial improvements in court practices and the use of experts, but the current system of providing and funding this evidence is in need of review.

- The range of orders has not been used as effectively as the Children Act intended and needs further consideration.

- There needs to be a more discriminating approach to using the courts as a first or a last resort.

4 *Working with parents*

As shown in Chapter 2, children in need, like all children, hold the view that their families matter. Recognition of the significance families have for children is incorporated into the principles of the Children Act 1989, but the Act takes a definition of 'family' that is deliberately wide, recognising the part played by significant others, especially where children are not brought up by two birth parents. Adoptive families, reconstituted families and, in some cases, foster parents and extended family can all hold parental responsibility for the upbringing of children. Indeed, the diversity of family life in England and Wales at the beginning of the 21st century is firmly recognised in the Children Act 1989:

> Although some basic needs are universal, there can be a variety of ways of meeting them. Patterns of family life differ according to culture, class and community and these differences should be respected and accepted . There is no one perfect way to bring up children and care must be taken to avoid value judgements and stereotyping.[46, p. 7]

The relevance of working with parents now

The importance of working with parents of children in need is as relevant to safeguarding and promoting children's welfare as it was when the Children Act was implemented. The concept of working in partnership has proved credible and has been made explicit in the *Framework for the Assessment of Children in Need and Their Families* published in 2000 by the Department of Health, Department for Education and Employment and the Home Office[79] and by the framework issued by the National Assembly for Wales.[92] Both sets of guidance about assessment believe it is important to build on parents' strengths. The valuing of parents' capacities lies at the heart of any assessment of children's needs and the services that might meet those needs:

> The majority of parents want to do the best for their children. Whatever their circumstances or deficiencies, the concept of partnership between the State and the family, in situations where families are in need of assistance to bring up their children, lies at the heart of child care legislation . . . In the process of finding out what is happening to a child, it will be critical to develop a co-operative working relationship, so that parents or caregivers feel respected and informed, that staff are being open and honest with them, and that they in turn are confident about providing vital information about their child, themselves and their circumstances.

Working with family members is not an end in itself; the objective must always be to safeguard and promote the welfare of the child.[79, paras 1.44–45]

Parents and the Children Act 1989

The objectives for working with parents in the assessment framework are at one with the philosophy of the Children Act 1989. Any rights that parents or others acting in a parental role might have, under the Children Act 1989, flow from their duties towards their children. They are not vested in a priori or automatic rights that follow from their status as parents. It is both a complex and a common-sense principle. It is not a matter of parents' rights versus children's rights but rather that the children's welfare comes first.

All those who are engaged in the upbringing of children have duties and responsibilities for their welfare. The Children Act 1989 seeks to recognise these in its concept of parental responsibility:

> The Act uses the phrase parental responsibility to sum up the collection of duties, rights and authority which a parent has in respect of this child. That choice of words emphasises that the duty to care for the child and raise him to moral, physical and emotional health is the fundamental task of parenthood and the only justification for the authority it confers.[45, para. 1.4]

Supporting parents to provide a nurturing environment is a logical consequence of the philosophy of valuing what families mean to children. There are two important points here, spelt out by the operational principles accompanying the *Regulations and Guidance*.[46] Firstly, extended family and close links with other significant adults may have a part to play in preserving families for children:

> If young people cannot remain at home placement with relatives and friends should be explored before other forms of placement are considered.[46, p. 8]

Secondly, where children are separated from their families, parents should continue to exercise their responsibilities towards their children:

> Parents should be expected and enabled to retain their responsibilities and to remain as closely involved as is consistent with their child's welfare, even if that child cannot live at home either temporarily or permanently.[46, p. 12]

Thus the parental responsibility of absent parents is not extinguished when children live in reconstituted families. Its continuation is also encouraged when children are looked after by local authorities, even in cases where children are on Care Orders. It is only extinguished by adoption. The retention of parental responsibility following care proceedings marked a radical change from previous law, which allowed for the removal of parental rights to the local authority. The Children Act 1989 recognises that the birth family holds a symbolic and important place in the lives of individual children. Although children's wishes and feelings will be brought into the equation, the studies suggest that the retention of links is important for many children.[11, 14] Therefore, working with parents is an integral part of any services for children in need.

The context of the Children Act 1989 helps to explain the principles of working in partnership with parents. The importance of working with parents was part of the thinking of the mid-1980s. The first overview of research studies, *Social Work Decisions in Child Care*,[50] suggested that many parents whose children were in public care prior to the Children Act had felt that their legitimate interests had been denied and their links with their children had been wittingly or unwittingly severed. Child protection research had also drawn attention to the fact that the outcome for children's welfare was often better when parents participated in decision-making.[52] The research from both these quarters recommended a more participatory approach towards parents. Parents should be actively involved in decision-making about their children. This approach came to be known as working 'in partnership' with parents. The rationale for such an approach is summarised in a 1995 guide on working in partnership by the Social Services Inspectorate:

> The fact that they can take part in decision-making helps build up their self-esteem and encourages adults and children to feel more in control of their lives. Professional practice which reduces a family's sense of powerlessness, and helps them feel and function more competently, is likely to improve the well being of both parents and children.[81, p. 11]

With hindsight, the term partnership was perhaps unfortunate, subject to much variation in interpretation and did not reflect the tensions that surround social work intervention in cases of child maltreatment. It is worthy of note that nowhere in the Children Act 1989 does the term partnership appear. Participation might have had a more precise and measurable meaning. However, the intention was clear: to include parents in decision-making about their children.

'Partnership' with parents in the Children Act studies

Thirteen of the 24 Children Act studies reported the views of parents on their contact with social workers or the courts. One or two studies attempted to define the nature of partnership.[4, 22] It is clear that whether parents are in court, receiving family support services or participating in their children's accommodation or care by the local authority, there are common themes. Overarching is the view that partnership is a *process* not an *event*. In most cases, the desired outcome will be the strengthening of parental responsibility, but helping parents relinquish their children may also be an outcome in a minority of cases.

The studies provide evidence on some of the key features of successful 'partnership' with parents:

Successful features of partnership with parents

- a shared commitment to negotiation and actions about how best to safeguard and promote children's welfare;

- mutual respect for the other's point of view;

- recognising the unequal nature of power between parents and professionals;

- recognising parents have their own needs which should be addressed;

- good communication skills by professionals;

- the establishment of trust between all parties;

- integrity and accountability on the part of both parents and professionals;

- shared decision-making;

- joint recognition of constraints on services offered; and

- recognition that partnership is not an end in itself.

Several of the studies that interviewed parents argued that the outcomes of working in a participatory manner justify the effort needed to make it work, especially where compulsory action is warranted.[2, 4, 9, 19, 22, 23]

Working in 'partnership' with parents is not without its tensions. It is important to recognise that, in cases where Social Services take steps of legal enforcement through the courts, the position of the social workers *vis-à-vis* the parents will be one of authority and power. Attempts to deny this reality will appear to the parents to be tokenistic or patronising, as the parents reported to the researchers.

This section of the overview explores how the parents in the studies experienced working with professionals, within the Children Act framework, in a range of circumstances:

- through family support services;

- where their children were looked after; and

- in the courts.

Many of the themes that emerged from the studies are common to all three domains and add to the strength of the research messages. In the following it is pointed out if an issue relates to only one of these settings.

The messages for professionals from the parents' experiences fall into two main areas:

- recognising that parents have their own perspectives; and

- strategies for enhancing parental participation.

Recognising the parents' perspectives

The trials and tribulations of parenthood

All parents know that it is hard to bring up children, even in optimal circumstances. As shown in Chapter 2, the parents of the children in need in the studies were often facing their parenting tasks in situations of multiple adversity. They unanimously valued recognition of this fact by the professionals. This view transcended all the different settings. In the safeguarding study, one parent said:

> What impressed us most was that three specialists spent time on him and they met and put it together and they actually told us what it was like to parent Eric. It was the first time in 12 years that anyone had told us what it was like to live with him.[4]

In the family support studies,[2, 22, 23] there were many examples of the relief of parents that their stress was recognised and understood, as exemplified by this mother:

> She listened to my problems. I thought she'd think I was hopeless but she didn't. She said she'd helped lots of parents like me.[2]

Foster carers also played their part in showing empathy for parents. Non-judgemental carers who appreciated the stresses of parenting in difficult circumstances did much to de-stigmatise the experience of having children looked after:

> They were so understanding, told me all about the time they had been in difficulties. That made me feel not so bad, you know as if they knew what it was like.

> I was so relieved someone was going to help me, I cried. I kept apologising. They said they would cry too if they had coped with what I'd coped with.[2]

On the negative side, some parents felt that the focus of intervention was on the family, to the exclusion of their needs. A common complaint across several studies was that social workers saw a problem in terms of family relations, not the child's behaviour.[2, 15, 23] This might have been an accurate assessment from the professional perspective, but not recognising the parents' perspectives left parents feeling angry and alienated.

Children's behaviour had often led parents to the door of Social Services to ask for help. What mattered to parents was to improve their children's behaviour. An approach that recognised this position made more progress than one that blamed parents.

> We went to [family therapy] . . . everything was directed at me. He was just drawing a picture. It was a waste of time. I had better things to do.[9]

The value of taking parents seriously was summed up by one parent:

> If a family comes to you and says we are having a problem, you should look at that – all families are different. You should take what parents say seriously because they know the child better than anyone else. All statements should be looked at without prejudice and without personal opinions.[22]

Respecting difference

The importance of responding to different styles of parenting and respecting cultural norms was highlighted by minority ethnic parents. In the study on parental perspectives on care proceedings:

> a number of interviewees from ethnic minority groups commented that social workers sometimes failed to appreciate the extent to which the exposure of their parenting difficulties left them vulnerable to stigmatisation within their own communities.[9]

Conversely, a black mother, with a child of dual heritage, felt she had been deprived of the short-term accommodation she desperately needed because the social services department demanded a placement of the same dual-heritage match. The mother had been willing to accept a placement with a white, black or dual-heritage family, so long as the carers supported the child's heritage and her parenting. They also had to live near enough to be reached by public transport. In the end, after several months of persistence on the part of the parent, the child was placed with white carers in the same neighbourhood as the family, a decision that was totally acceptable to the parent.[2]

A further issue was parenting styles in relation to sanctions on children's behaviour. Parents in the care to accommodation study were outraged that their children were allowed to smoke and stay out late in residential care, behaviour that would not have been condoned at home.[15]

These examples serve to reinforce the Children Act principle of accepting differences in parenting styles, providing safeguarding issues have been considered. They also illustrate the value of listening to parents' wishes and responding to the needs of the particular child and family.

Recognising parents have needs of their own

It was easy for social workers to respond to parents who were experiencing a crisis that temporarily inhibited their parenting capacities. Where difficulties of parenting in poverty were compounded by mental illness or problems with drugs and alcohol, the balance between strengthening parental capacity and protecting children was difficult to achieve.[7, 9] In cases where parental limitations had led to care proceedings, as these three examples from the study on parental perspectives in care proceedings show, parents often felt that they were 'prejudged and condemned', and that there was little recognition of the stresses they were under or their desire to contribute as much as they could to their children's lives:

> They don't give you a chance. I mean if you are ill it is obvious you can't take care of yourself and you can't guarantee you are not going to be ill.

> The social worker made me feel like a junkie and that there was no hope for me and the children. She wrote me off.

> Because I was in prison they didn't consider me. Just forget about him, he's a criminal.[9]

What parents wanted in these circumstances was recognition of their own emotional needs and circumstances, rather than the narrow focus on alleged abuse to the child. They would have welcomed more attention being paid to the practical difficulties in their lives. Domestic violence was a particular issue that surfaced across several studies but was not given enough prominence from the parents' perspectives:[2, 4, 9, 22, 23]

> They just don't understand when violence is in the home. I needed much more support and help from them, not being ignored.[9]

It is important in this discussion not to minimise the limitations in parenting skills that were evident in some families. The tensions of safeguarding children and supporting parents were very real. The studies are helpful in explaining why families may react badly to what they see as threats to their role as parents. Those who are most under threat are those who feel accused. They will react most strongly, denying the problem or placing the blame on others.[9] However, as the care to accommodation study exemplified, parents across all the studies were:

> not merely describing what had happened to them, but attempting to provide a justifiable and morally adequate version of their circumstances. In particular the parents resisted being categorised by Social Services, and emphasised their unique circumstances.[15]

Recognition of each family's individual biography is the foundation of working in partnership with parents.

Recognising the power differential

The power of Social Services to offer or withhold help, to remove children and influence court action and to retain control over decision-making once children were looked after was a factor that permeated many of the studies.[4, 7, 8, 9, 12, 15, 22]

Parents felt particularly powerless in the court studies, 'both to resist an all-powerful agency and to avert a train of events which in retrospect was seen as somehow inevitable, even pre-planned':

> They just wanted my baby, that was it, I know it was like that.[9]

In Chapter 3 the tensions between compulsion and voluntariness in the use of accommodation were discussed. From the perspective of the parents, there were some examples of what the researchers called 'sham' or 'enforced' partnerships. Take the study on parental perspectives in care proceedings, for example. Here, parents:

> felt under pressure to comply, to be negotiating from a weak and powerless position which left them little option . . . to be threatened with court action if they did not agree.[9]

Similar issues were raised in the fostering family contact study. As one parent said:

> I had to agree. With the social worker at the door I'd no choice. I either agreed or they'd slap a Care Order on us.[7]

Such findings go to the heart of the difficulties social workers face and reveal how important are skills of negotiation in situations where the balance between compulsion and voluntariness is to be made. It may be that explaining the subtleties of the 'no order' principle of the Children Act 1989 represents an impossible challenge for social workers.

It may also be that some social workers were not so skilled at explaining to parents the tensions and dilemmas that face professionals in these circumstances. Social workers can undertake this complex work to good effect. There is good evidence from the child protection overview that parents were able to emerge from child protection enquiries saying that they did not like the intrusion of social workers but they had been on the receiving end of a job well done.[52] The Children Act studies point to the need for the transfer of such skills to the interface between family support and looked after children.

The value of an approach that treats parents with dignity

One issue that emerges from the Children Act studies is the importance of treating parents with dignity. This is especially important in the courts, where parents need access to the same quality of legal representation as the professional parties.[5] Where the power differential is most visible, such as in the courts, parents place an exceptionally high price on being treated with dignity:

> I wish they had treated me more as a person.[9]

There were examples from the study on parental participation in care proceedings, for example, that demonstrated the importance of an empathic approach. A response from legal representatives that displayed warmth, understanding and humour was much appreciated.[9, 11] Little gestures of kindness from the judiciary were also much appreciated, such as the judge who took time to look at a family album in a care proceedings case and a solicitor who took a sympathetic interest in family life.[9]

Parents had recommendations to make about the physical surroundings in the court. They felt strongly that improvements could be made to the environment of the court waiting rooms, including facilities for refreshments, smoking and adequate heating. These comments may well be a reflection of the inadequacy of many old court buildings on a national basis. The juxtaposition of criminal and civil proceedings in the same building also added to stresses:

> It would help to treat people like human beings and not like they are dirt all the time.[9]

Recognising the stigma of having children looked after

The further erosion of often fragile parental self-esteem by handing over the care of children to others, however positive arrangements may be, was evident in both the short-term fostering and the fostering family contact studies.[2, 7] Even without the tensions of compulsion and voluntariness discussed earlier, there is a long way to go before accommodation is seen by parents as a family support service. The stigma of the public care system is not yet dead. Where children were accommodated, recognition of the power differential was a highly sensitive area: 'They're in charge of your kids'.[15] As the fostering family contact study suggested:

> Whatever the good intentions of professionals, the fact that parents are seeking help for themselves and accommodation for their child, or . . . having social workers' attentions thrust upon them, places parents at a disadvantage.[7]

In addition, the feelings of filial deprivation in parents who are separated from their children in care or accommodation remains as strong as it was in the 1970s.[56] The fostering family contact study reported that, although a few parents felt relief when their child was accommodated, most felt distressed.[7] Parents had few resources to cope with the distress of separation:

> I don't know if it were a good idea 'cos I broke me heart when I came out.

> I took the easy way out because I couldn't face taking her.[7]

Working directly with parents to rebuild their self-esteem early in the placement also remains a factor associated with the successful maintenance of contact and the reunification of children.[7]

Foster carers were significant players in strengthening or inhibiting parental responses to their children who were looked after. The findings from the Children Act studies serve to reinforce the importance of carers' attitudes towards parents in contributing to parental participation in the placement. The gratitude displayed to carers who offered parents what might be considered normal courtesies serves to emphasise the fragility of parents' self-respect:

> The foster mum is alright. She asked if I minded Jane's ears being pierced. I thought it was very nice of her.[9]

Carers in the short-term fostering study were held in high regard by parents.[2] Their attitudes towards working in partnership were much influenced by the fact that many were based in the same neighbourhood and had been appointed from a child-minding background, both factors that helped to prevent any potential tensions of rivalry. As one scheme leader said: 'They are like the parents but without the problems.'

The main points

- Parents value recognition of the circumstances that inhibit parental responsibility.

- Respect for different styles of parenting is important.

- Parents have needs as adults that require recognition and appropriate responses.

- The power differential between parents and workers should be openly acknowledged.

- Parents respond well to being treated with dignity.

- Parents require access to high-quality legal representation.

- The stigma of having children in the public care system remains, and requires recognition and a sensitive response.

Strategies for enhancing parental participation

So far, key factors that inhibit working with parents have been identified. These include the imbalance of power between parents and professionals and the stigma attached to having children accommodated. The 1995 Social Services Inspectorate guidance on partnership in child protection offers some useful suggestions on how parental participation may be improved.[81] At the basic level, keeping parents informed is fundamental, but giving parents information upon which they can make informed judgements is likely to enhance their participation. The Children Act studies show that the participation of parents could be improved if parents are helped in the following areas:

- clarity about expectations and parents' rights; and

- an informed understanding about the services that might be available to them.

Clarity about expectations and parents' rights

A common complaint among parents in the studies was that they were ill-informed about 'their rights' and what was expected of them. The two issues seemed to go hand in hand. This was by no means confined to studies concerned with the standard of their parenting, although rights assumed even more importance for parents who saw themselves in danger of losing their children. Parents in the planning to care study, for example, felt they had been consulted about their children's accommodation but had not been informed about why decisions had been made, whether they would be expected to pay for services and, most importantly, about complaints procedures.[10]

Once again, accommodation surfaced as an area where expectations were unclear. Some parents felt that they had been 'deceived, coerced, ill-informed and manipulated'.[9] Where the purpose and duration of accommodation was clear, parents were reassured that their parental responsibility was not at risk.[7, 15]

Parents found it confusing when they were being judged but were not sure of the rules. This appeared especially true in cases where parents were bewildered about what they had to do to regain the care of their children:

> The thing is you don't know what they want from you, what they are looking for, what they expect. Nobody tells you anything; they just carry on.[9]

An informed understanding of the services that might be available

Another contentious issue was the lack of information about services that parents might use. The Children Act 1989 requires Social Services to 'publish information about services provided by them' under sections 17, 18, 20 and 24' (Schedule 2(a)(i)).

Both in the family support studies and the studies on children looked after, there was little evidence that parents had been informed about what might be on offer.[2, 7, 8, 15, 22, 23] Social Services were failing to ensure that social workers 'took such steps as are reasonably practicable to ensure those who might benefit from the services receive information relevant to them'.[22] The implications of this for service provision are discussed in Chapter 7. The view of parents was that the absence of information left them confused, bewildered and resentfully dependent on social workers to open the door to services.[23]

Even when information about services was available, some parents also seemed genuinely confused about the outcomes that might result from different interventions. The best situations, in the family support studies and where children were looked after, were where parents felt they had gained services for themselves and their children which they understood and thought were useful.[7, 8, 23] Sometimes, services beyond the parents' knowledge had been suggested by social workers. In other cases, the parents were building on the experience of help they had received in the past. Practical services were understood best, but there were a surprising number of parents who valued what might be best described as a casework service, where social workers both co-ordinated other services and offered social work support within the context of a focused and purposeful professional relationship.

> What was helpful was with the feelings – you can get everything out of your
> system talking to a social worker. You can have a good cry and go back from
> day one and get it out and it's good to talk about it.[4]

In addition, if parents felt they had made a informed choice about a service
they understood and valued, they were more likely to participate in effecting a
successful outcome.[2, 22, 23]

Improving parents' participation in decision-making

Having struggled to fight their way through the gateway, blocked by high
thresholds and obscured services, parents had some strong messages about how
their participation in the processes of decision-making might have been
improved. These fall under two headings:

- the nature and content of consultation, planning and decision-making;
and

- improving parental participation in court.

The nature and content of consultation, planning and decision-making

Volume 2 of the *Guidance and Regulations* recognises the value of planning
activity as a vehicle for 'partnership' with parents:

> Partnership with parents and consultation with children on the basis of careful
> joint planning and agreement is the guiding principle for the provision of
> services within the family home and where children are provided with
> accommodation under voluntary arrangements. Such arrangements are
> intended to assist the parent and enhance, not undermine, the parent's
> authority and control.[47, para. 2.1]

Part of this process is engaging in consultation with parents about their
wishes and feelings. The parents' views in the Children Act studies have
much in common with those of their children, whose views are described in
Chapter 5.

Aspects of consultation that were valued by parents in several studies included:

- time to think;

- time for questions; and

- reassurance about anxieties.

It was significant that parents were happiest about consultation when they felt
they had been given space to air their agenda, even if this was not necessarily
on the social worker's list.[23]

The next challenge for parents was the nature and process of the decision-making itself. Often this took place in planning meetings, where parents were expected to be able to handle complex and sophisticated exchanges of information. One of the parents' complaints was the size of the meetings.[7, 10, 15] Another was the presentation of their lives and problems to complete strangers. This was particularly evident in child protection conferences.[4, 22] A third was the use of jargon and complex technical language,[9] and a fourth echoed the criticisms of consultation – there was not enough time to digest and respond to questions.[4, 9]

The purpose of the meeting also influenced parental attitudes. Parents experienced in these matters compared informal planning meetings relating to accommodation to previous negative experiences of conferences on child protection matters. The latter were often intimidating.[2]

Clearly, the uninitiated found these events daunting, but those with experience began to understand how they might shape the agenda and the outcome.[2, 15, 22] The issue of the quality of parental participation is important here. The Social Services Inspectorate makes a distinction between involvement and participation:

> Although involvement and participation in decision-making are closely related activities, a distinction is made between the two. Involvement may be predominately passive and amount to little more than receiving information, having a non-contributory presence at meetings, endorsing other people's decisions. However, when involvement becomes more active and when family members are asked to contribute to discussions and decision-making on key issues, they can be said to be an active participant.[81, p. 11]

However, nothing can be taken for granted, and at least one study demonstrated that parents who did not say much at meetings were in fact empowered simply because they had been invited.[2] Parents in this and other studies remarked on how they needed support to participate. Rehearsing the arguments before a meeting helped, as did a positive and informal style.[2, 4, 7, 9]

The main points

- There needs to be clarity about parents' rights in relation to services and what contribution may be expected from parents.

- Parents need to be able to make informed choices about services.

- Parents welcome consultation.

- The process of consultation should give parents time to think, time for questions and reassurance about anxieties.

Improving parental participation in court

If Social Services' meetings are intimidating, courts are daunting places for anyone not familiar with the legal processes. The court studies have much to say of value in this area. Parents found themselves ill-prepared for the experience of court. Some received poor quality legal representation.[5] The parental perspectives study found that some had problems getting to court by public transport and appreciated lifts from social workers or solicitors.[9] Some recognised that the stress of the situation had prevented them from participating as they would have wished. Parents had some useful ideas on how their participation could be improved. A common theme was the plea for 'more and better targeted information':

> I needed more help and explanation with what was going on and
> understanding things.[9]

> More advice about the court proceedings, more explanations and help from
> the social workers, in fact information on who to approach.[9]

Parents suggested that there were several ways in which they might be better prepared for court. Examples included a booklet, written in uncomplicated language, which provided specific and basic information about how hearings were conducted and on parents' rights. Visiting the courtroom and meeting the judge were also suggested, along with the opportunity to view some kind of training video and, most appropriately, the chance to practise speaking in public.[9]

Given the daunting nature of the ordeal, one important recommendation is that parents have an independent supporter to accompany them to court. Suggestions include personnel from the voluntary child care sector:

> You need someone for yourself, an adult worker. I never understood you could
> fight it. They were only doing their job but it was not done properly because
> they didn't tell me my entitlements and my rights.[9]

The forum and processes of the court could be improved to be less formal:

> It's called a Family Court but they don't involve the family.[9]

Parents had much to say about the legal profession. Barristers were generally given a very good press, especially for their confident performance in court combined with personal characteristics of warmth, humour and understanding. In spite of guardians' reservations in the expert evidence study about the quality of legal representation on offer,[5] parents themselves generally valued solicitors.[9] The study on parental participation in care proceedings reported on what, in the parents' eyes, made a good solicitor:

> Undoubtedly winning a case helps – or at least being partisan and committed
> enough to put up a good fight on their behalf and show a personal interest in
> them and their children. Being caring and understanding and developing a
> rapport with the client was particularly valued.[9]

Guardians were invariably seen as being on the side of Social Services, but frequent contact with parents mellowed the parents' perceptions.

Parents valued having the same judge throughout the proceedings and, generally, judges and magistrates were rated as fair. Highest levels of satisfaction were where judges took time and gave attention to parents:

> I wish there were more judges like her. She was like a mother with understanding and sensitivity.[9]

The parents mentioned many other issues that would have helped their participation. Giving evidence was difficult, for example. Parents would have liked more time to have their say and were confused by the language in which questions were asked. Clarity of communication was also essential, as was the avoidance of technical jargon.[9] In complex cases involving experts, parents often did not address the court from the perspective of a level playing field.[5]

Finally, it is perhaps worth noting that parents were willing to accept the decisions, provided they felt the processes had been fair and had given them the opportunity to express their point of view. On balance, one of the court studies noted that the parents' acceptance of decisions:

> gives some grounds for confidence that the judicial system retains a measure of credibility for such disadvantaged parents even if the process remains in so many respects alien and alienating.[9]

The main points

- Courts are intimidating for parents.

- Parents value an approach that treats them with dignity.

- Parents need help to prepare themselves to give evidence; they need specialist legal representation and equal access to experts.

- The presence of a supporter is helpful.

- Parents will accept the outcome of court proceedings provided they feel the process has been fair.

Evaluating Social Services

A valuable evaluation of Social Services was provided by the parents of the children in need. Their feedback, in their role as service users, on the agency that made a major contribution to service provision and delivery for them and their children should be taken seriously.

By and large, the families' verdict on Social Services was influenced by their reception by Social Services. This was not related to the type of service but rather to the attitude of the staff. Some families had previous positive experiences and turned to Social Services again when they needed help. It was an important finding that, in the services for children in need study, Social Services was seen as the agency of *first choice* in over half the cases.[23]

Satisfaction related to obtaining the services requested and to the attitudes of social workers. This was summarised by one mother:

> I stated what I wanted, and they were very accommodating indeed. I was surprised it was so easy . . . I don't know why everyone criticises social workers so much. I'd advise any one to go to Social Services.[15]

Dissatisfied parents were those who had not obtained the services they thought they needed or who had been subject to rather heavy-handed child rescue processes:

> Y'know you can't impress me with Social Services in any way 'cos I've had bad experiences with them, so, I mean, nothing what anybody says will change my mind about how I feel.[15]

A key aspect for many parents was that they were able to establish a relationship with their social worker and saw the same person each time:

> I didn't like the change of social workers. There was enough upheaval in the house without having to have that as well.[21]

The effectiveness of services will be discussed in Chapter 7, but it is worth reviewing here the key factors that delineated a good service from the parents' perspectives. The parents were very clear on what they valued:

- services that were targeted at the whole family, not just the child;
- interagency services that were well co-ordinated by Social Services:
- services that offered a combination of practical and emotional help;
- services that were offered in a welcoming, non-stigmatising manner;
- family centres that combined referred and non-referred cases and offered open access to a range of services or activities;
- transparency about the purpose and expected outcomes of services; and
- seeing the same social worker over time.

Finally, this chapter cannot conclude without giving the parents' views of what makes for good social workers. Remarkably similar views were expressed through a range of studies: family support in different circumstances, where children were looked after and in care proceedings. Social workers demonstrated attributes and actions that were highly valued. Among the most important were approachability, honesty, time to listen, understanding, reliability and helpfulness.

Approachability

This referred to parents being able to confide in workers and feel that their version of the problem would be taken at face value:

> I don't like talking to strangers but I could talk to her. She made it OK.[9]

Honesty

Parents valued directness in workers, even if this meant they did not always get what they wanted:

> They said we can't give you everything you want; we haven't got enough carers but we can offer help for three months. At least I knew where I stood.[2]

> You don't feel intimidated that you can turn round and say 'I want this and that'. But then again [social worker] is quite happy to turn round and say 'No, we can't do that.'[15]

Having time to listen

This was perhaps the most important evidence by which workers could demonstrate their interest in what parents had to say:

> When the social worker comes round and sits down, I tell him what I like and basically what I want help with.[15]

The care to accommodation study noted that sitting down was an important indicator of time to listen and of acceptance of the parents in their own domain.[15]

Understanding

This was undoubtedly related to sophisticated social work that helped parents to see the reality of their problems without blaming them. It resulted from a starting point of acceptance of the parents' perspectives:

> She helped me to see why things happened without blaming me.[2]

Reliability

This quality speaks for itself and was most evident in the family support studies. It was extremely important to parents that the rules did not change and that what had been agreed would be delivered:

> She came when she said.[2]

Helpfulness

This related to satisfaction and a positive outcome in services. Parents were satisfied with their workers when they felt they had been helpful.[2, 7] Parents were most dissatisfied when they had received an off-hand assessment. What was important was the process rather than the outcome. For example, being listened to was equated with helpfulness, even if no other service was offered.[23]

In cases where accommodation was offered as a positive service in response to parents' requests, this was seen as helpful:

> When I got in touch with [Social Services] I was in desperation . . . Talk about landing it on her lap! 'I don't want daughter moved from school. My marriage has just broken up, blah blah' – this, that and the other. And she goes 'Oh dear'. But she went straight into battle and secured [a respite carer] . . . It gave me a breathing space.[15]

The main points

Parents value:

- services that are targeted at the whole family, not just the child;

- interagency services that are well co-ordinated;

- services that offer a combination of practical and emotional help;

- services that are offered in a welcoming, non-stigmatising manner;

- family centres that combine referred and non-referred cases and offer open access to a range of services or activities;

- transparency about the purpose and expected outcomes of services; and

- social workers who are approachable, honest, understanding, reliable, helpful and have time to listen.

5 *Listening to children*

The formal involvement of children in decision-making within the Children Act 1989

Chapter 2 of this overview drew together the views of the children in need in the studies, on their circumstances and their attitudes towards families, health, school and being looked after. This chapter concentrates mainly on the opinions of the children who had something to say about their involvement in formal decision-making and planning within the context of the Children Act 1989.

The relevance of listening to children now

The Children Act 1989 anticipated and endorsed the UN Convention on the Rights of the Child[100] by establishing the right of children to participate in the decision-making that affects their lives. The UN Convention has been formally accepted by the UK government since 1991. The Convention is totally congruent with the Children Act 1989. For example:

> The parties shall assure to the child who is capable of forming his or her own views the right to express those views freely in all matters affecting the child, the views of the child being given due weight in accordance with the age and maturity of the child.
>
> For this purpose the child in particular shall be provided the opportunity to be heard in any judicial and Administrative proceedings affecting the child, either directly, or through a representative or an appropriate body, in a manner consistent with the procedural rules of national law.[100, Article 12.1]

It is increasingly recognised that, in addition to the formal arenas of court hearings, children have a perspective to contribute in many areas that are important to them, such as schools and the environment in which they live. Children and young people are being consulted about the services they use. Listening to the views of children and young people is one of the current priorities underpinning the Department of Health's *Quality Protects* and the National Assembly for Wales' *Children First* programmes.[69, 106] In Wales, taking children's views seriously is reflected in the establishment of a Children's Commissioner.

The overview and the children's participation in decision-making

Although it is implicit in the Children Act 1989 that children should be consulted about all matters that affect them, there are two domains where it is formally expected that children will be consulted: in court proceedings and when children are looked after by the local authority. The introduction of formal consultation processes in these areas is the subject of several studies because of the significant nature of the change brought about by the Children Act 1989.[2, 7, 10, 15, 17, 21] It is mainly from those studies that the children's views in this chapter are drawn.

The Children Act 1989 gives considerable weight to children's views in court proceedings:

> The checklist of particular matters to which the court is to have regard in reaching decisions about the child is headed by the child's wishes and feelings and highlights the great importance attached to them.[45, para. 1.24]

In relation to looked after children, of particular relevance is the duty placed on local authorities, before providing accommodation for children, to:

(a) ascertain the child's wishes regarding the provision of accommodation; and

(b) give due consideration (having regard to his age and understanding) to such wishes of the child as they have been able to ascertain. (Children Act 1989, section 20(6))

These sections of the Children Act are underpinned by a general operational principle, which also recognises the changing nature of children's abilities to comprehend and comment on their situation as they mature through different stages of development:

> *Young people's wishes must be elicited and taken seriously.* Even quite young children should be enabled to contribute to decisions about their lives in an age appropriate way. Learning to make a well informed choice is an important aspect of growing up and must involve more than just sitting in on reviews and conferences at which adults have power to make all the decisions. Young people should be given the chance to exercise choice and if they are unhappy about decisions or placements they should have an opportunity to be heard and taken seriously.[46, p. 12]

Ascertaining children's wishes

Two important consequences of these statements, if children's wishes are to be taken seriously, are spelt out in Volume 3 of the *Guidance and Regulations*. First, there may be inherent tensions between the views of adults and children. The child's perspectives and priorities may be very different from those of the adults, and this has to be recognised and taken seriously:

> The social worker should be aware and acknowledge that there may be good reasons why the child's views are different from those of his parents or the responsible authority.[48, para. 2.47]

Second, children cannot express their wishes and feelings unless they are well informed about the issues under discussion:

> All children need to be given information and appropriate explanations so that they are in a position to develop views and make choices.[48, para. 2.47]

Giving due consideration to children's views

The consequence of listening to children is that due consideration must be given to their views. In reality, this means that plans may need to be changed to accommodate children's wishes. The study on making Care Orders work found that plans could be sabotaged by youngsters if their views had not been heard.[11] In some practical areas, the accommodation of children's wishes may be perfectly possible without disrupting the integrity of the planned services from the adult perspective. A good example comes from the short-term fostering study, where a child was unhappy about the timing of arrangements.[2] By listening to the child's views and acting upon them, his full co-operation with the plans was assured, with consequent positive outcomes for the whole family:

> I wanted to go on Saturday not Friday night because I go to basket ball with my friends. My mum was surprised I came on so strong but she said she didn't mind.[2]

This example was straightforward but others were less so. There are inherent tensions and dilemmas in giving due consideration to children's views and acting upon them when, in the judgement of the adults, the children's wishes and feelings may not be compatible with their welfare. The matter of listening to children's views and taking them seriously has to be set within the context of safeguarding them. Children will not necessarily have the last say in what happens to them if adults believe their views will place them at risk of suffering impairment or significant harm. There is a fine balance between consultation and final responsibility for decision-making, as was shown, for example, in the short-term fostering study.[2] Here, the decision to accommodate children was sometimes made, initially, against their wishes in order to help prevent family breakdown. In spite of this, children were given a great deal of information and honest explanations about why accommodation was necessary. They also visited the foster carers in advance of their stay.

A professional decision driven by the aim of safeguarding and promoting welfare will probably win the day if there is disagreement between children and adults. However, within the context of these adult responsibilities, children deserve as much room for negotiation as possible. The age and stage of development of children will inevitably tip the balance one way or the other, as Volume 3 of the *Guidance and Regulations* asserts:

> Children should feel they have been properly consulted, that their wishes have been properly considered and that they have participated as partners in the decision-making process. However, they should not be made to feel that the burden of decision-making has fallen totally upon them, nor should they be forced to attend meetings if they choose not to do so.[48, para. 2.48]

For parents and social workers to achieve the balance between asking children about their thoughts and feelings and retaining their interests and responsibilities as adults is a very complex matter. As two studies suggest, one issue for some children in need is that their parents may be emotionally fragile. By attending to children's wishes, vulnerable parents may be threatened and undermined.[2,15] On the other hand, the impact on the self-esteem of older children when their wishes are overridden must also not to be discounted.[7, 15] Balancing all these issues calls for time, diplomacy, communication skills and informed professional judgement.

In the 1994 volume of the official chronicle of the implementation of the Children Act to parliament, *Children Act Report 1993*, it was suggested that consulting children was rather patchy in the first years of implementation:

> It was not the general practice of staff to ask children how they felt about decisions affecting their daily life or their future, and their views were not routinely recorded on case files. There was also a wide disparity in the levels of skills and experience of staff working with disabled children.[43, para. 2.30]

Twelve of the Children Act studies obtained the views of children about their involvement in decision-making and the services they were offered. Between them they span the eight years after the implementation of the Act and represent the views of a range of children in different circumstances. From the studies, three key issues emerge about listening to children:

- the nature of consultation;

- the children's participation in planning meetings and reviews; and

- the children's views on the qualities in adults that facilitate consultation.

The nature of consultation

Under the Children Act 1989, formal consultation can take place in many arenas: before family support plans are made, before children are accommodated and preceding a statutory review. It should also form part of the court processes. Alongside these formal set pieces, there is an expectation that looked after children will be consulted about any matters that are concerned with decisions related to their future, such as changing schools, placements and leaving care.

One of the problems raised by the studies is that there seems to be a lack of clarity in practice about the meaning of consultation. This could be resolved, as the short-term fostering study suggests, by breaking down the different parts of consultation into:

- information giving;

- talking over anxieties and preparing children for change; and

- giving children the opportunity to influence plans.[2]

Information giving

There are many aspects to the giving of information to children in such a way that they can make informed choices. As several studies revealed, children welcomed knowing the ground rules upon which they were being consulted. For instance, some issues may be negotiable and others may not. All of the children in the disability study had discussed placements with their parents. Whether this was consultation was a moot point:

> I say I don't want to go. Then Mum says 'You have to go'.[18]

In the study on children in need in Wales, children were most irate when asked open-endedly what they wanted. They interpreted this as material gifts, and then found the goods were not delivered. In these circumstances, children felt cheated and angry.[8] These were younger children, who were more likely to think in concrete terms, but older looked after children were also angry when promises did not materialise:

> They said I could have my own bedroom . . . you know, for at least a year, but now they say 'No'. And they didn't even write a letter or apology or anything and my foster parent said it was in my best interest to have my own bedroom because I've never had one, never had my own space. Then . . . it all folded up and that's that.[10]

Older children also felt angry and were likely to rebel against decisions they found unacceptable, sometimes with repercussions on their welfare:

> The only thing I remember about the CO (Care Order) is me going absolutely ballistic . . . 'You think by throwing a CO over my head that you are going to keep me under control, you have got no more control over me than you have now.'[11]

The studies suggest that age is a factor influencing the quality of social work consultation with children. The fostering family contact study, for example, found that social workers were more successful in eliciting the wishes and feelings of older children.[7] Similar delegation of explanations had occurred with more success in the short-term fostering study, especially where children knew many of the carers in advance of the placement and felt safe about the transition.[2]

Where arrangements are less transparent, the delegation of information-giving is open to distortion of the truth by parents, who may not be able to face telling their anxious children about how long they will be away from home, or may have their own agendas of abuse or rejection of the children. The fostering family contact study, for example, found considerable discrepancies between the views of adults and children on their anticipated length of stay.

Only one-third of the children knew both the duration and reason for fostering and had discussed the plan with a social worker.[7] Similarly, several children in the care to accommodation study found themselves removed to accommodation, occasionally from school, without any discussion. These were not emergency placements to protect children. There was no statutory reason why placements could not have been delayed, even by half a day, to allow for some preparation.[15]

In both short- and longer-term arrangements, clearly the most reassuring practice was where the social worker confirmed the parents' version of events:

> She [the social worker] came and talked to me . . . just went over what was being talked about, and asked me what I thought about it. My mum had told me, like, but I was glad that she [social worker] did too.[2]

The care to accommodation study summarises the evidence on the value of children having information to help them understand what is happening to them and recommends more explicit explanations about the process of admission to accommodation:

> The evidence suggests that young people require more explicit procedures or documentation about what is involved in admission to accommodation. Once they became familiar with social services processes, they became clearer about what might happen to them, and felt able to express themselves. However, the first hours and days were very confusing.[15]

Talking over anxieties

A second important part of consultation is to give children the opportunity to air anxieties about impending separations and to reassure children they are not abandoned once they are in accommodation. The children in at least two studies reported how difficult it was to talk over their anxieties, even with trusted adults.[2, 7] Less than half of the children in the short-term fostering study felt they could turn to their parents for solace; a minority had no one to talk to:

> I was scared but no one asked me. My mum said I had to go for her sake or else she would be ill. I didn't like it but I couldn't say.[2]

One aspect of good practice that may help to allay children's fears is visiting the placement in advance. The value of visits is summarised by the fostering family contact study:

> A meeting with prospective foster carers at the foster home could serve a number of important functions for children. For example, meetings could act as an important source of information; they would allow children to become aware of the layout of the house and find out where they were to sleep. Meetings also provided children with a sense of continuity; links between home and foster home could be made through seeing parents and foster carers collaborating. Alternatively, meetings can reassure children and dispel irrational fears. All the children who met their carers prior to placement were glad they had done so.[7]

Practice varied in relation to admissions to accommodation. The most disadvantaged children were youngsters who entered accommodation bewildered and unprepared.[7] Such events were very stressful, even if accommodation had been requested by the young people.[15] By contrast, the majority of children who met their carers benefited from these meetings. One 10-year-old boy is representative:

> I came for me tea and then the next day I came to stay . . . Me social worker brought me and then she went . . . When I went home I told me mum it was good.[7]

Giving children the opportunity to influence plans

Meeting carers may have been reassuring, but it raises the issues of the choices it is realistic for children to make. Should children, for example, be involved in choosing between different carers? Often such a choice is constrained by resources, and no child in any of the studies was offered a choice between homes. Consultation in this sense was simply softening the reality in advance of the actual event taking place. Whether this is what the Children Act intended is unclear. What is clear is that the absence of transparency in policies and practice in this respect makes children feel they have little control over their lives at the point of admission to accommodation. By contrast, in spite of anxieties about separating from parents, where children could influence the length and timing of their placements, this helped them feel in control of events.

The main points

- The meaning of consultation with children needs clarification.

- Children need as much information as possible to help them understand the realistic choices before them and their parents.

- Children benefit from being able to talk over their fears and being prepared for change.

- Children need to feel in control of events relating to separation.

The children's participation in planning meetings and reviews

Planning meetings

After the process of consultation, the preparation of children for being accommodated involves them in planning meetings designed to lead to the production of a care plan. Similar meetings were also a feature of family support plans where children were not accommodated.[23] Practice here was variable, with age again being a factor influencing the children's involvement. This is entirely consistent with Volume 3 of the *Guidance and Regulations*, which leaves a degree of flexibility about children's presence at such meetings.[48] It could be argued that some children are better served by consultation in private and would be daunted by attendance at a formal meeting. Interestingly, the children tended to see meetings as 'official' only if they took place outside their home. Otherwise, meetings to facilitate participation in the families' own homes were seen as informal 'chats' with social workers.[2]

The studies report that the value of involving children in child protection conferences and social services meetings may be accepted in principle, but there remains the task of ensuring 'that such meetings are child-friendly'.[7] Indeed, the studies suggest that not all of the children wish to attend, even the older children sometimes seeing it as the responsibility of their parents to represent their views.[3] But when meetings are 'child-friendly', many children value the opportunity of having their views heard.[10] The messages are clear that the mode of participation should be assessed individually in each case.

Once children are accommodated or in care, Volume 3 of the *Guidance and Regulations* demands that the children's wishes and feelings are ascertained.[48] There was evidence from the planning to care study that two-thirds of the children had indeed been consulted at some stage in the process, though not necessarily before the review meeting, with age once again influencing the frequency of consultation.[10] Young people over 11 were very frequently consulted, but the rate of consultation for 5 to 10-year-olds fell to almost a half and then dropped to a tenth for the under-fives.[2, 10]

Consultation forms that asked specific questions could be useful in helping the young people express their thoughts. This worked best when it was done alongside oral discussions with key workers:

> I asked my key worker to write it for me. [She] and I talked. [She] wrote it down. It was easy for me to talk but hard to write.[10]

Without this professional help to encourage children to identify and talk over their anxieties, consultation becomes a superficial or turgid exercise. Filling in details on the Looking After Children assessment and action records[67] without any help or support was a good example. Far from being important planning tools to influence the course of their lives, the Looking After Children forms were seen as boring homework assignments that had little relevance for young people's concerns.[10, 11] The length of the forms was particularly tedious:

> You get bored, just see the first question and tick 'Yes' throughout the form. Just to get to the next page.[10]

For others, filling in a consultation form, however tedious, was preferable to talking at a meeting:

> I just write it and give it to her. I ain't gonna say nothing. I just sit down there [at the meeting].[10]

Reviews and decision-making

Reviews are a fundamental part of the system designed to safeguard and promote the welfare of looked after children. The planning to care study indicated that the regulatory framework introduced by the Children Act 1989 had significantly increased children's participation in reviews, thus achieving the aims of the Act. In the planning to care study, the majority of 11 to 15-year-olds and nearly all of the 16 to 18-year-olds attended review meetings.[10]

This part of the overview is concerned with how that participation was perceived by those at the centre of it: the children themselves. The planning to care study provided detailed material on children's perceptions, which can be used to identify what is important to children.[10]

As the planning to care study suggested, in many ways the review process highlights the abnormality of the corporate parenting system.[10] Although meetings at school and discussion of health issues may demand from children their participation in a group with which they are not familiar, it is outside the experience of most children to be placed under regular scrutiny within a formal group of adults. Bearing in mind the daunting nature of this type of encounter for many adults, the nature of the review meeting itself places upon the adults concerned an almost impossible burden of combining a formal agenda with consultation and decision-making and trying to make the processes child-friendly. How far this succeeded is revealed by the children in the planning to care study.[10]

Not surprisingly, no child interviewed about reviews enjoyed them. The majority portrayed the experience as frustrating and uncomfortable. Clearly, in these circumstances children are not going to give of their best. Much can be learned from the children's views on how the process of review meetings can be improved.

Issues that were important to children:

- preparation for the review meeting;

- the size and composition of the meetings;

- the focus of the discussions; and

- being appraised of their rights.

Preparation for the meeting

Children who knew what was to be discussed and had rehearsed this with their carers or social workers managed meetings best:

> No worries. It was a straightforward meeting.[10]

Conversely, children were disadvantaged when they did not know the agenda in advance. Young people agreed:

> You get nervous when a meeting is talking about your future. I didn't know what people would say.[10]

> When meetings are about to start they give you this paper . . . you're not ready for it. They give you a paper, talk about school, education and stuff like that right there. You don't have time to think about what you are going to do in there. They say 'Is it OK? Is it OK?' and I go, 'Yeah, that's fine'.[10]

Apart from agreeing with any proposition simply to get through the meeting, nervousness was covered up by jokes or, in some cases, displays of anger, such as the tearing up of care plans. Where the stress of the review was recognised and sensitive responses were made, this helped calm young people.

The size and composition of meetings

As parents were daunted and intimidated by the size of meetings, so were their children. Large meetings with strangers were seen as intimidating and intrusive.[10, 11] As the youngsters in the planning to care study put it:

> You don't really want to sit and talk to a whole room full of people about your problems, though, do you?

> There's like people you don't know who are going 'How are you coping with your past experiences?' 'Well, it's none of your business.'

> The more people, you get scared. You get shy and try not to make a mistake in what you are saying.[10]

A good example of the impact of size was one young person who could not 'remember' why she had asked for a change of social worker when asked in front of six adults.[10]

Some of the children would have found it helpful to have been accompanied by an independent supporter who could have acted as an advocate on their behalf. However, this would have called for careful stage managing so that a 'them and us' adversarial model did not develop.[10, 15]

The focus of the discussions

Most of the children who had attended reviews felt they had been consulted in the review, and more than half felt their contribution had made a difference. This was encouraging. Although the children did not like having to discuss personal issues in front of strangers, as with their parents, they found it most helpful when discussions focused on issues important to them and they had been given opportunities to have their say in their own words:

> Everyone's asking me if I had problems with carers or anything. That's [what it should be] them asking me.[10]

Adolescents in the planning to care study had complaints about the lack of recognition of their growing maturity and their 'wish to increase the practical scope of their responsibilities'.[10] Progress to independence was, in their view, too narrowly conceived in terms of 'domestic skills':

> Sometimes they treat you like a baby.

> What they're saying about independence is all about things in the house . . . They don't give us the independence outside the house, like the times you have to be in.

> They give you independent stuff inside your house but you're not very independent outside.[10]

Some reviews attempted to conduct proceedings informally. This had its drawbacks. A free-standing informal discussion left children feeling exposed and confused. They particularly resented adults butting in:

> I didn't get a chance [to say everything] because everyone was talking.[10]

What children objected to most were ritualistic questions that went over old ground and did not leave time and opportunity for the pressing issues concerning their future. Many questions appeared mechanistic and irrelevant: 'It's like they're going through a checklist on your CV.' [10] Children rightly criticised this approach, believing it to be unnecessary and hypocritical:

> When was the last time you went for a medical? They know when we last went for a medical, but they still ask you.[10]

Being appraised of their rights

One source of concern was that less than half of the children had been told of their rights to seek court orders. Additionally, few had been told of their right to redress if they disagreed with care plans. Many had not had the opportunity to sign formal plans so were not sure exactly what was asked of them.[10]

Planning and reviews: meetings or processes

The children's views suggest that, while considerable progress has been made to involve children in reviews, more active steps should now be taken to see reviews as part of a structured and co-ordinated planning process, as envisaged in Volume 3 of the *Guidance and Regulations*.[48] With less emphasis on the meeting and more emphasis on working directly with children and parents, an incremental process of assessment and participatory decision-making should become the norm. The review meeting will then be able to concentrate on the wishes and feelings of the young people and their parents.

The main points

- The Children Act has made a difference to the participation of children in decisions.

- Review meetings should be only part of an ongoing programme of skilled direct work with children.

- Children participate best in meetings when: they are prepared, meetings are small, there is a structured, child-friendly agenda.

- Meetings should be used as vehicles for participatory decision-making and should concentrate on young people's wishes and feelings.

The children's views on the qualities in adults that facilitate children's participation

This brief review of the children's perceptions of their involvement in consultation and decision-making raises many issues about how best to make sure children's voices are heard and taken seriously. As children themselves have suggested to the researchers, ascertaining their wishes and feelings is a complex matter. Children need appropriate responses from adults if they are to feel confident enough to put forward their views.

The children in the Children Act studies had very clear ideas about the qualities in social workers and other professionals that enable them to discuss their feelings and take an active part in effective decision-making. It was clear from the research studies that children are well able to turn appropriately to individuals from a variety of agencies – teachers, doctors, youth workers, the police – as well as to social workers and residential and foster carers. There were five qualities in professionals that were important to children:

Qualities in professionals that are important to children

- reliability – keeping promises;

- practical help;

- the ability to give support;

- time to listen and respond; and

- seeing children's lives in the round, not just the problems.

Examples of these qualities, and the negative impact on children of their absence, permeate the twelve studies in which children were interviewed. Children did not like social workers who let them down, made promises they did not keep and, especially, did not keep appointments.[8] This gave children clear signals that social workers did not value them. Conversely, where adults offered practical services, counselling skills and time to listen, this was helpful. Individuals who had contributed to their well-being were remembered by children. There was the GP, who raised a teenager's self-esteem by helping her stop wetting the bed.[4] There were carers, residential workers, teachers and social workers who had more than an abundance of empathy, warmth and genuineness and had time to listen.[2, 3, 4, 7, 15] There were social workers who made children feel they were more than just cases by talking about things that mattered to children outside the problems of their family life. Such an approach seemed to help children put their problems in perspective:

> He wouldn't just talk about my dad he'd talk about other things as well like a football match.[15]

The moving on study[3] showed that care leavers appreciated being treated as independent adults and had very positive views on the combination of practical support and informal approaches of key workers in leaving care schemes. The continuing anchor function of these workers mattered. This was contrasted with the more 'parental' approach of social workers:

> What's best is the advice and help they give you.

> They don't treat you like a kid no more.

> They are friendly and you know they're there if you need help.[3]

Finally, there were carers in the short-term fostering study who understood the impact of separation upon children's behaviour and put no pressure on children when they were grieving for home.[2] They made children feel special, and understood that children need both physical and emotional nurture:

> She knows when I need to be alone – says, 'Why don't you go and give that Care Bear a hug and I'll bring you a drink and a chocolate biscuit?'

> She was kind . . . treated me special . . . gave me sandwiches and Coca-Cola.[2]

Towards a child-centred service

These views of a range of children in need give clear messages that children want the planning and reviews to be child-centred. Given the right support, many children are capable of participating fully in decision-making. To enable them to take part, they need skilled, direct work and adults who are reliable and will champion their needs. Children with severe impairments that inhibit their communication skills will need additional, specialist help.

The researchers in the Children Act studies have made their own contribution to listening to children by developing sensitive methods of talking to children and eliciting significant information from them. Such techniques can inform practice and exemplify the connections between research and practice. There are messages from the children that social workers and other professionals need to adopt similar approaches that are sensitive to children's priorities and perspectives.

Children are honest and often have very sensible views on what they see as helpful, both to themselves and to their families. If children were allowed to design the nature of meetings, communication with them might improve considerably. If children had a hand in designing the forms that record their lives as looked after children, we might see some changes in how best to safeguard them and promote their welfare.

In the end, what children want is straightforward: enough food, warmth, adults who love and nurture them, consistency, achievements and to be treated with dignity as befits their status as child citizens. The Children Act 1989 provides the framework for those aims to be achieved. The empowerment of children in need will only be achieved properly if the adults listen to what the children have to say and act upon their views.

The main points

- Children value five main qualities in professionals: reliability, practical help, support, time to listen and respond, seeing children's lives in the round.

- The techniques of research can be helpfully used to improve direct work with children.

- A child-centred service demands that adults listen to how children would like services organised and act upon the children's views.

6 *Working together to plan and provide services for children in need*

As the last three chapters have sought to show, children in need experience a diversity of problems that demand an equally broad response. Services for children in need cannot be met by one agency, but demand the pooling of resources and skills from many arenas.

This chapter draws together some key findings from the studies that inform the issues relating to joint working at different levels and between different participants.

The Children Act and interagency working

The idea that different agencies might work together to promote the welfare of children is not a new concept. Divided responsibilities between Education and Public Assistance Committees were blamed for the death of the foster child Denis O'Neill in 1944[91] and have been a subject of concern in many child abuse enquiries over the last 50 years. What is different about the Children Act 1989, as the children in need in Wales study suggests, is that 'agencies are no longer merely exhorted to co-operate but are legally required to do so'.[8] Volume 2 of the *Guidance and Regulations* confirms this view:

> Sections 17(5), 27, 28 and 30 provide duties and powers in relation to co-operation between and consultation with different authorities including social services, education departments and housing authorities, health authorities and independent organisations.[49, para. 1.13]

There are many potential players in the Children Act strategy of interagency working. Not surprisingly, health, education and social services are most prominent among the statutory services but others, such as the housing departments and youth and leisure services, alongside the Benefits Agency, the police and the probation service, are all part of local resources that have the potential to be used to promote and safeguard the welfare of children in need. The voluntary and independent sectors also have a role to play and are encouraged to do so within the remit of the Children Act 1989. Finally, the family justice system requires clear and efficient working between social workers, the judiciary, the legal teams and guardians ad litem.

The relevance of interagency work now

Under the Children Act 1989, social services departments have a key co-ordinating role to help translate the principles of joint working into action. The amendment to Schedule 2 in 1996 strengthened the mandate for interagency planning through the introduction of Children's Services Planning.[78] This has now been taken further in consultative guidance on planning children's services, issued in April 2000, which promotes planning services for vulnerable children with the full participation of NHS bodies. At the time of this report going to press the final guidance had not been issued. The potential for pooling budgets and other mechanisms under the Partnership in Action initiative, introduced in 1999, was also a major breakthrough.[71] These changes have facilitated the philosophy of the primary legislation by providing the mandate to achieve an integrated strategy for children's services. Nowhere has this been more prominent than in working together to safeguard children, as suggested in Chapter 3. Guidance on safeguarding children issued jointly by the Department of Health, the Home Office, the Department for Education and Employment and the National Assembly for Wales in 1999 emphasises the need for an integrated approach to children's services.[80]

Policy initiatives with a broader remit also have a part to play, as suggested by *Modernising Social Services*[74] and *Building for the Future*:[109]

> The Government is committed to taking action through a broad range of initiatives to strengthen family life, to reduce social exclusion and anti-social behaviour among children, and to give every child the opportunity of a healthy, happy, successful life. Examples of Government action on the wider front include the 'Sure Start' programme, the Crime Reduction Programme, Early Years Development and Childcare Partnerships.
>
> Children's social services must be seen within this wider context. However, this must not mean social services lose their focus on the most vulnerable children.[74, paras 3.4 and 3.5]

The government's insistence that public services must be performance measured has required a shift in the way planning and service provision for children is conceived. Services must be planned so as to deliver clearly articulated and measurable objectives. This idea pervades government initiatives such as Best Value and the Performance Assessment Framework as well as the *Quality Protects* and *Children First* programmes.[69, 106] The objectives have, wherever possible, been formulated in terms of the developmental well-being of children, for example in seeking stable care and improved educational attainment. Such objectives cannot be achieved unless the health, education and social care services are more integrated. This integration also needs to extend to the commissioning of services from the independent sector.

The relevance of the 24 studies to the wider agenda

These initiatives have begun since the studies were written, but the challenge of using the mechanisms for effective joint working remain. The Children Act began the process of making working together a requirement. The challenge now is for agencies to make effective use of the new mechanisms for working together. The successes of joint planning and practice in the early stages of implementation and the barriers to achieving success provide some useful insights into how objectives of the new interagency approach to children's services may best be achieved. Some authorities have taken their interagency working forward in a climate of organisational continuity and stability. Such an approach is in contrast to the damaging effects on the quality of services resulting from the turmoil of constant reorganisation reported in 1991 in one of the earlier overviews, *Patterns and Outcomes in Child Placements*.[51]

Some key terms contributed by the studies

If agencies and individuals are to work together and engage in joint thinking, planning and delivery of services for the benefit of children in need, it is helpful to define what this means in different circumstances and at different levels of decision-making. Within the Children Act studies, different aspects of working together seem to be encapsulated in three words:

- co-ordination;

- co-operation; and

- collaboration.

Although there are some differences in definition between the studies, which in themselves reflect the difficulties of the task in hand, there is enough common ground from which to offer an explanation of key terms of reference derived from a synthesis of the definitions used in the different studies.[1, 6, 8]

Co-ordination involves setting formal rules and joint goals and activities between separate organisations. Used in this sense, local authority departments such as social services and education, and health authorities and National Health Service trusts, all of which operate in a fairly autonomous way, can be considered as separate organisations in terms of working relationships. These different departments come together under the umbrella of the local authority to develop a corporate strategy along commonly agreed goals.

Co-operation involves individual organisations' goals and objectives coming together in dialogue to formulate agreed protocols for service provision and delivery while retaining their independence. It can also refer to informal contact and working together by professionals at the grassroots.

Collaboration refers to working relationships between different teams or units within single departments and to professionals from different disciplines or agencies working together with a common focus. It also refers to the participation of users in planning and managing specific services.

Some of the studies offered refinements of the terms. In relation to co-ordination, one of the day care studies suggests that:

> co-ordinating a service . . . involves more than setting up structures and communicating information: policy is subject to mediation by implementing actors, with their individual value bases.[6]

The study on children in need in Wales suggests that interagency co-operation is a four-stage process:

> intention to co-operate, formally translated into policies; dialogue between agencies for the purpose of implementing the policies; agreements or protocols resulting from the dialogue; and joint provision of services.[8]

The main points

- The Children Act contains a clear direction for interagency working.

- The original legislation has been strengthened by amendments to develop Children's Services Planning.

- Other legislation now permits the pooling of budgets, removing an important impediment to the provision of joint services as identified in the studies.

- Working together includes three key elements: co-ordination, co-operation and collaboration.

Implementing working together between agencies

Four areas of working together between agencies were explored by the studies:

- strategic planning by Social Services and other departments for implementing the Children Act 1989;

- joint planning between statutory agencies for specific groups of children in need;

- joint working between statutory agencies in relation to individual children; and

- joint working with the voluntary sector.

The early stages: strategic planning for implementing the Children Act 1989

In the early stages of implementing the Act, the means by which progress could be made towards co-ordination of services was through the setting up of implementation groups whose membership was drawn from different agencies. Both in England and in Wales, these were led, and it might be said, dominated, by Social Services. There was considerable variance nationally on how Social Services perceived the Act, with two main approaches predominating:

a)   seeing the Act as an opportunity to develop child care policy within the new broader philosophy of the Act;

b)   seeing the Act primarily as a reformulation of existing duties with the additional implementation of some new duties.[1]

These approaches inevitably influenced the processes of interagency working between Social Services and others.

Two major points emerge from the studies on early implementation:

● local authorities were starting from very different points in relation to shaping their corporate policies; and

● the extent of progress in the first three years related to the systems of communication between departments that had been operating in local authorities before implementation.[1, 6]

Co-ordination and co-operation were compounded by the fact that each agency often had a different child 'in mind'. Education, for example, saw the child who needed to be educated; leisure departments saw a child who needed play facilities, economic development units saw a child who needed to be cared for while parents were working. Social Services most often saw the child who needed to be protected from abuse or the child with behavioural problems who needed to be looked after. This in itself could cause major problems in reaching a shared understanding of children in need in an area, irrespective of any confusion around the interpretation of section 17 within individual local authorities.

As the day care and out-of-school studies reported, the finding of a common language to describe children in need was one of the major barriers to working together in many areas. It was especially needed to bridge the care–education–play divide.[6, 16, 20]

Another major hurdle in working together reported by the studies was the absence of adequate computer systems within social services departments to identify and track children in need.[1, 8, 21] Out of seven local authorities in one study, only two had any reasonable method of identifying and counting children in need in their area.[23] Without a baseline of social services data, trying to reach agreement with other departments on a common understanding of need was an insurmountable task.[1] The position in England is likely to have changed since local authorities conducted the Children in Need Data Collection for the Department of Health in 2000. However, it will take some time for most authorities to analyse and use the information they have collected about the demand for services from children in need.

In spite of the problems, in the early days of implementation the research in both England and Wales reported the generally positive attitude of Social Services in response to the call to set up consultative mechanisms for Children Act implementation strategies both within and between departments. Consultation frequently took place with education, health and housing authorities, mainly built on existing good relationships. Few links existed with transport and leisure services. Studies in England and Wales reported generally poor links at a policy level with probation services, with the police and, surprisingly in view of the extent of services offered in co-operation with social services, with the voluntary sector. However, as one study pointed out, 'little reference to co-operation in documents does not mean there is little co-operation in practice'[8] and indeed, in Wales, the evidence pointed to considerable co-operation at the grassroots in relation to service delivery in partnership between agencies, although corporate strategies for family support were not as well developed.

What the studies show is how far, in many cases, Social Services and other agencies had to go to achieve joint strategies and joint working and what could be achieved in a very short time. The fact that there were examples, even in the early studies, of achievements in co-ordination of specific services, such as those for disabled children or day care, inspires confidence in taking forward the process that has now been developed by Children's Services Planning since 1996[78], by legislation providing for the pooling of budgets[71] and by initiatives such as Sure Start[65, 107] and Children and Youth Partnerships.[108] The impact on the children and families in some of the Children Act studies of the frustrations of not having the availability of joint services is clear.[22, 23] There was also evidence, in the same studies, of the benefits for the children in need and their families who were able to access interagency services. These findings support the view that joint service planning and delivery is valuable in promoting good outcomes for children in need.

Joint planning between statutory agencies for specific groups of children in need

Setting up jointly co-ordinated services for children in need was not easy. Some social services were hampered by history and, before pooled budgets were a reality, suspicious of other agencies appropriating precious resources:

> We've always had problems with Health and Education. There is good will on our side but everyone is scared that co-operation will have financial implications.[1]

In spite of some negative attitudes, there are equally heartening examples from the studies of how the Children Act represented a legitimisation of informal strategies of co-ordination between agencies in relation to specific groups of children in need. A good example was one authority's corporate strategy for improving services for disabled children:

> When we did our sums with health and education, we realised how behind we were with children with disabilities. Given the Act says they are children in need by definition and that we had so many, we had to put a lot of money into services.[1]

There was, however, a wealth of difference between sharing joint strategies and translating these into effective systems, as shown by the two examples of setting up the register for disabled children and the mechanisms for the review of day care services under section 19 of the Act.[1, 18]

In connection with registration, Volume 2 of the *Guidance and Regulations* emphasises that local authorities, in co-operation with health authorities, local education authorities, and voluntary agencies, need to publicise widely the existence and purpose of registers to:

> facilitate collaboration in identification and a co-ordinated provision of services under the Act.[47, para. 2.19]

Over two-thirds of social services departments in England had reached agreement with others on the criteria for registration by 1992. This was a considerable achievement for many authorities where, at that time, the boundaries for health and social services were not aligned. Further, some of these authorities had set up a joint data base formulated on agreed criteria.[1] However, as the Social Services Inspectorate reported in 1994,[25] others were slow to take action. By 1998, the Social Services Inspectorate was able to report that all but one authority in England had a register of disabled children.[33] Although these had not yet become the planning tools they were intended to be, many did have an important function in the dissemination of information.

In spite of some progress, obstacles to good interagency collaboration for disabled children remain. These were summed up by the Social Services Inspectorate in 1998:

- lack of co-terminosity between health, education and social services;

- lack of agreement on priorities, and few mechanisms through which to reach it;

- inadequate management systems;

- no clear agreements on who should do what by when;

- lack of clarity about the location of responsibility for disabled children in health authorities; and

- the omission of health authorities and Trusts from planning groups.[33]

Parents told the inspection team that obtaining a service could be extremely difficult.

Another example of joint planning for specific groups of children came from the setting up of co-ordinating structures for early years services, in line with the recommendation in Volume 2 of the *Guidance and Regulations*.[47] As the day care in England study showed, the essential issue here was for 'early years professionals to move beyond their traditional boundaries to an appreciation of the complementary roles each plays in a child's development, and the difficulties this presents'.[6]

The extent of barriers to be overcome initially was shown by the fact that in some local authorities the relevant personnel had never worked together before:

> We were all strangers – never met even socially. We started a long way back, getting together to share ideas before we could do the [section 19] Review . . . to do that we had to find a common language.[6]

In spite of the barriers, the day care in England study was able to find some authorities that had an integrated approach to early years provision. One is included here as a good example of joint working at different levels.[6]

An example of an enabler authority

A metropolitan authority with above-average levels of nursery education and playgroups, and medium levels of child-minders and day nurseries (both local authority and registered), has integrated its policy and provision for early years under one department. In addition, the building that houses regulation officers also offers office space to the key voluntary sector organisations in the city, thus enabling direct liaison. The authority has constructed 'ward profiles' of early years provision throughout the city. There is, therefore, a thorough knowledge of where the provision is situated, and this helps the authority to decide where future provision should be located. There are a number of development initiatives throughout the city, such as training packages for all child care workers; a pilot scheme for a child-minders' business initiative; and a sponsored child-minder scheme for supporting child-minders looking after children 'in need'.

Joint working in relation to individual children between statutory agencies

Joint working is not confined to planning and, indeed, reports from several studies suggest that it is more often at the service delivery level that co-operation can be most effective.

Developing joint-owned referral systems

In the short-term fostering study, there was a well-developed model of referral of families to the service (Figure 2), which demonstrated co-operation between Social Services and the primary health care team. The key to success was a jointly worked out needs-led criteria for services and a high-trust professional relationship between the parties involved.[2]

Referral from local area team or health visitor for short-term accommodation

Essential features of the system included:

● a simplified system of access with well-established and broad criteria for admission to the short-term accommodation scheme;

● health visitors had direct access to the project co-ordinator, who was in charge of the whole process, both supporting families and carers; and

● the project co-ordinator shared an office with the local area team that also facilitated communication.

The referral process

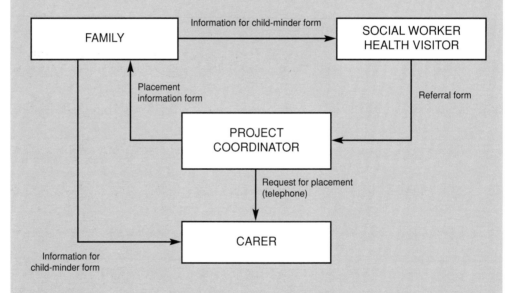

Figure 2 *An example of joint planning and provision: short-term accommodation*

This exemplar of a model of co-operation was based on a shared definition of need and excellent and frequent communication between the personnel from the two agencies. An important spin-off of this particular working together was the way in which health visitors acted as ambassadors on behalf of Social Services, emphasising the Children Act principle of promoting the upbringing of children by their families wherever possible and counteracting the image of Social Services as an agency devoted exclusively to child rescue.

Striving to improve communication within the court system

An example of how changes, however modest, can be brought about by good communication comes from the court studies. In the best-laid plans study, both guardians and lawyers were frustrated by two factors: the lack of information about the outcome of individual cases and delay in implementing care plans that involved the finding of long-term placements:

> I only find out by chance if care plans are implemented.

> There's too much emphasis on child protection, far too little on the long term. Everyone is rushing round to rescue the child from a risky situation, then quite suddenly it becomes unimportant.[13]

Although problems within the court system still obtained in some quarters,[5, 11, 13] by the time of the study on making Care Orders work,[11] there had been at least some progress in communication between the local authority and the court system, with evidence of good links between some local authority solicitors, social workers and guardians. This had occurred at a local level because of the good working relationships established between professionals. There was evidence in these court systems of productive negotiation through planning and legal meetings. Any changes in directions of the care plan at an advanced stage were due to the collapse of reunification plans rather than because of disagreement between professionals.[11] Such examples show that systems can be improved.

Areas of working together that need improving

There are several areas where the studies highlight the need for improvements in practice in working together. Three examples from different arenas illustrate the problems:

Resolving funding issues

This is a major area of tension between agencies and is reported in several studies. Educational resources for children with special needs were a particular problem.[13] The issues were summed up by one health care respondent in the children in need in Wales study:

> Working relationships and commitment to good working relationships are excellent at the grassroots and middle management levels. Case management difficulties present themselves when funding issues are being negotiated.[8]

The way forward is now being helped by the pooling of budgets that is beginning to take place under the Health Act 1999.

Clearer criteria for joint working in family support between health, education and social services

Similarly, the services for children in need study showed that, in spite of the fact that school was often the place where children's problems first came to light, the education authority only referred children to Social Services when there was a child protection concern. Whether this was because of a social services gatekeeping policy or whether it was because the education authority preferred to deal with cases through its own welfare system was difficult to ascertain. What was clear was that families who had multiple problems were sometimes shunted between different agencies. Where the problem was grasped, it was left to Social Services to take the lead in resolving it. As one parent reported:

> We would get on to Health we would get on to Education, nothing happened. In the end the social worker took a grasp of things.[23]

Reversing the impoverishment of mental health services for children and parents

A serious impediment to joint working for children with mental health problems was the absence of therapeutic or mental health services for children and young people. This was a matter of concern in several studies, both of children at home and those looked after by local authorities.[13, 22, 23] Child psychiatrists in the expert evidence study reported that they were unable to provide much follow-up work after court proceedings.[5] The Children Act studies reveal the widespread impoverishment of child and adolescent mental health services in different areas and an urgent need to review the state of these services.[4, 5, 13, 22, 23] Of particular concern was the absence of the early intervention of mental health services for children in their middle years who were displaying a range of behaviours associated with clinical depression and other identifiable disorders.[23] Similar concerns were expressed in several studies about the availability of mental health services for parents.[2, 4, 15, 22, 23] In the care to accommodation study,[15] the authors suggested that the unmet mental health needs of parents contributed to the accommodation of their children in over a quarter of cases, a finding supported by the fact that one-third of the families in the services for children in need study were said to have mental health problems.[23]

Joint working with the voluntary sector

Although an important part of the Children Act was to improve interagency working between statutory agencies within and outside the local authority, as Volume 2 of the *Guidance and Regulations* suggests, an equally important aim was to ensure that children had access to a wide range of services:

> In putting together packages of services, local authorities should take account of the services provided by the voluntary sector and other agencies.[47, para. 2.16]

The research on early implementation of family support under the Children Act suggested that voluntary agencies were not automatically seen as an essential part of the planning process. In both England and Wales, voluntary agencies were not always included in developing strategies for ascertaining need. The day care in Wales study showed that the large voluntary sector in day care provision could have been more actively consulted in section 19 reviews.[20] In England, the picture is more complex, with consultation hinging on whether voluntary agencies were used on an *ad hoc* basis or were in service agreements with Social Services.[1]

The involvement of the voluntary sector in the provision of services was also varied and could operate at a number of levels. Family centres were a good example: the pattern of social services involvement varied from sole funding to co-funding with a voluntary agency, to voluntary agencies providing centres themselves or, more rarely, providing them in collaboration with the education or health services.[1, 20]

Other types of provision show equally varied patterns. Respite care for disabled children was often provided through joint funding between Social Services and voluntary agencies.[1] Sponsored day care for children in need could be purchased through one-off arrangements, through specialist schemes involving approved providers, or through ongoing funding to keep places open for children in need.[21]

However voluntary agencies were funded, their value in augmenting family support services permeated the family support studies – providing that these agencies were not used in an *ad hoc* way that rendered them liable to collapse because of unreliable funding.[1, 21, 23] The study on family centres gives some good examples of genuine 'corporate' responsibility for children in need through the working together of health, housing and education services.[19]

A useful framework for planning interagency services

Several studies mention the planning framework developed by Hardiker[87] as a useful tool to plan and target discrete and interagency services at different levels.[2, 22, 23]

The Hardiker framework: policy contexts of prevention in child welfare

Base level: This level identifies overall populations for whom universal services are mobilised.

First level: Services at this level target vulnerable groups and communities and aim at preventing problems from arising.

Second level: This level targets early stresses, such as those experienced by families in temporary crisis or early difficulties; it covers all 'children in need', including disabled children.

Third level: This level targets serious stresses, including the risk of significant harm, family breakdown or compulsory entry into the care system.

Fourth level: This level addresses a diverse range of issues and problems from social breakdown and placements outside the home to children abused within the care system.

The Hardiker framework is useful for interagency planning on where to target services to avoid duplication. It helps to show where different agencies are positioned in relation to different levels of services. It emphasises how important it is to connect service intervention within the Children Act 1989 to more general initiatives to promote children's welfare at both universal and primary preventive levels across a range of agencies, including health and education.

The main points

- A common language is the key factor in joint strategic planning and in working together.

- There is some evidence of the capabilities of agencies to engage in joint planning.

- Obstacles to the provision of joint services for disabled children remain.

- There is evidence of good working together within the courts.

- Links between Social Services and education authorities need to be further improved.

- Working together between Social Services and child and adult mental health services is hampered by a dearth of services.

- The dearth of mental health services for children is affecting the process of care proceedings.

- There are examples of good partnerships between Social Services and the voluntary sector, especially in the provision of family centres.

- The Hardiker framework provides a useful tool for interagency planning.

Social Services – a unified department?

A major aim of the setting up of social services departments following the 1968 Seebohm Report[96] was that there would be integration within the personal social services so that duplication of services to adults and children within the same family could be avoided. It was also the intention that families could be moved appropriately and easily between adults' and children's services. Whether such integration still exists is worthy of debate. In practice, as several of the 24 studies show, the impact of the National Health Service and Community Care Act 1990 on children's services has been to separate adults' and children's services within the same department in many authorities. The introduction of quasi-markets through the purchaser/provider ethos has created, in some social services, serious structural hurdles for social workers and other professionals working with both children and parents.[2, 22, 23] The negative effects of this separation for parents with learning disabilities has also been highlighted by the Social Services Inspectorate.[35]

Three issues that come out of the Children Act studies:

- the management of joint working between adults' and children's social services;

- the need for integration of different social services for children; and

- working with service users in planning services.

The management of joint working within Social Services

Although it might be expected that the process of developing a *modus vivendi* for working together between agencies would bring tensions, it might also be expected that collaboration within Social Services would be rather easier. However, the Children Act studies reveal that this has been as much of a challenge as joint working between agencies. A major omission from the studies is the relationship between social services departments and elected members. There are, however, several areas that reveal useful findings.

One major area of frustration for parents and social workers in children and families' teams was the difficulty of providing an integrated approach to services for children and parents, especially in cases where a parent might have a mental or physical disability or a chronic illness.[4, 11, 22, 23]

In two of the family support studies, there were several examples of the frustrations caused to parents by not being able to have their problems seen in the context of the support they needed for their children.[22, 23] Workers from children and families' teams spent much time negotiating with their colleagues in adult teams to recognise this need and supply help to their clients so they might fulfil their parental responsibilities and not impair their children's welfare. A particular problem was the very high threshold set by mental health teams.[4, 20] This meant that some parents who had serious mental health problems that were having an impact on their children's well-being were unable to gain an assessment of their needs or the provision of appropriate services under the National Health Service and Community Care Act 1990.

The picture was not all negative. There are also examples of good collaboration between adults' and children's teams. In one of the family support studies, one social services department had drawn up excellent collaborative procedures between adults' and children's teams and was planning to pilot a new system of assessment that would ensure a joint response to meet both adult and child need.[22]

The need for integration of social services for children

Social workers do not have to be separated by adults' and children's teams to encounter problems of collaboration. Just as many problems can result where there are no joint goals and no mechanisms for collaborative direct work between different branches of children's social services. Two of the court studies[12, 13] recount that one of the major reasons for delay in implementing care plans for children resulted from the structural separation of short- and long-term teams. For example:

> There is a real problem between long- and short-term teams. It's like different worlds, there is that split. If you could sort that out.[12]

> The Children Looked After sections have less work than we do but they're precious about taking cases on.[12]

Clearly, such feuds and impediments to smooth joint working call for the development of collaborative and effective systems at all levels of management and practice within Social Services. Where good systems existed in the studies, they reinforced trust between workers and inspired the families to have confidence in Social Services.[23]

Finally, it is relevant to rehearse here the points made in Chapter 3 about the best way to integrate the safeguarding and promoting of children's welfare. Several studies made the point that separate systems for assessing the needs of children at risk of suffering significant harm and those in need of services because of significant impairment were counterproductive to meeting children's needs.[4, 22, 23] The studies provide clear evidence of the overlap between these two categories. One system of referral and assessment – so that needs relating to the safeguarding and promotion of welfare can be addressed simultaneously – is likely to provide the most timely and cost-effective service for the children and their families. This point is taken further in Chapter 8.

There is also a need for flexibility in the timing of the transfer of children and families from assessment to long-term teams. Such transfers are best done in consultation with the children and families themselves.[4, 20]

Involving service users in planning services

In England and Wales, consultation with service users is increasingly being seen as an important prerequisite for any plans to improve the quality of services. However, this rarely happened at the time the studies were undertaken. *Modernising Social Services*[74] and *Building for the Future*[109] reinforced this point:

> Service users and carers often play little or no part in shaping services. Attempts at consultation can often turn out to be public relations exercises, rather than genuine attempts to listen to what people want and their view of services. Genuine consultation cannot only make services more responsive but also increase public confidence and trust in the services.[74, para. 2.43, p. 29]

The studies on early implementation showed clearly that users were rarely seen as part of the consultative process: 'Working with user groups seemed more like an aspiration at the back of planners' minds rather than an ongoing reality'.[1] There was no evidence of individuals being involved in strategic or service delivery planning in any of the studies on the provision of social services.

The situation was different in the independent sector. The family centres study provided illuminating information on different models of service delivery in those family centres in which joint planning and participation in the running of the centres by users and staff featured to a lesser or greater degree, according to the scope and purpose of the centres. The study suggested three levels of user participation in planning and delivering services:

- participation in the form of local control of management;

- participation of individuals in helping with groups; and

- participation in planning activities and accessibility or user-friendliness.[19]

The study raised the dilemmas of participation for clients of Social Services 'where children's safety and the principles of good child care cut across self-determination'.[19]

The family centres study is highly relevant to a discussion of the concept of collaboration between parents and professionals. It recommends greater precision in terms of reference as a first step to disaggregating what is meant by participation:

> We should ask whether there is local control of management; whether project staff, or parents, take decisions about the organisation of activities, in contrast to parents helping at sessions: how the views of referred parents are taken into account; whether users recognise a user friendly project style; how and what information is made available.[19]

The main points

- The management of joint working within Social Services has been hindered by the separation of social services for adults and children and the internal markets set up between these two sides of Social Services.

- Within children's social services, separation of child protection enquiries and family support has hindered a needs-led assessment of children in need.

- The integration of children's and families' views into the planning of services is in its infancy.

7 *Effective services, good outcomes*

Chapter 6 explored the role of an interagency approach to services for children and families. This chapter looks at some of the roles and tasks that are the remit of Social Services, and particularly social workers, under the Children Act 1989.

Part III of the Children Act 1989 is very much concerned with the provision of services, either co-ordinated or provided by social services departments for all children in need and their families irrespective of whether the children are with their families or elsewhere. For the first time in child welfare legislation in England and Wales, specific services to support children and families are named. These services include: advice, guidance and counselling; activities; home helps; day care and family centres; and financial assistance in certain circumstances.

There are also services for looked after children, including accommodation, the facilitation of contact between children accommodated and their families and services for young people leaving care.

Disabled children, as a special category of children in need in their own right, have a right to services to minimise the effect of their disabilities and to give them the chance to lead lives that are as normal as possible (Schedule 2(6)).

The Children Act 1989 expects that services will produce good outcomes for children, both safeguarding them and promoting their welfare needs. To emphasise this point, the relevant volumes of *Guidance and Regulations* provide those delivering the services with information on the purpose of the services and the manner in which they should be delivered.

The relevance of the Children Act to services now

In specifying services to safeguard and promote the welfare of children in need, the Children Act 1989 seeks to provide the primary legislative foundation for good practice. More recent initiatives such as *Quality Protects* [69], *Children First* [106] and the objectives for children's services spelt out, in England, in *The Government's Objectives for Children's Social Services* [73] and, in Wales, in

Building for the Future[109] have built on the Act by drawing attention to the vulnerabilities of particular children and the improvements that are needed in services. More rigorous measures of accountability and standards for services are proposed, with the introduction of external regulation and inspection of a broad spectrum of residential and day care services for children, including the inspection of private fostering agencies, administered through national inspectorates. Most of the studies in the overview pre-date these initiatives. Nevertheless, they are valuable in providing exemplars of good practice and identifying the challenges that still have to be met.

In looking at the studies in the overview, it is of course fair to repeat the question asked in Chapter 1. How far can legislation lead to changes in practice? Asking such a question will inevitably raise questions not only about the provision of services but also about the standard to which they are provided. The measurement of standards and outcomes was not a major focus of the studies in this overview, but is rightly included in the discussion of service provision, with some examples of service outcomes where these exist.

Exploring key areas of practice

This chapter selectively explores some of the key areas of practice that are within the domain of Social Services, either working alone or in partnership with other agency providers.

The messages from the studies can be divided into five main groups. Messages about:

- access to services;

- assessment for individual children and families;

- planning for looked after children;

- good practice in particular services; and

- the role of managers and social workers.

Access to services

One of the aims of the Children Act 1989 was to make access to services easier for families. Under Schedule 2, Social Services have a duty to publish services available to families with children in need. Volume 2 of the *Guidance and Regulations* states: 'authorities should take such steps as are reasonably practicable to ensure that those who might benefit from services receive the information'.[47, para. 2.35] Special attention should be given to making publicity take account of cultural and language needs of minority ethnic families and being sensitive to those with sensory disabilities: 'as far as possible, the relevant publicity should encourage parents to seek help if it is needed'.[47, para. 2.36]

It was clear, from several studies, that such aspirations had not been met and that thresholds for access to services often continued to be linked to service criteria and concerns about significant harm. The danger is that need becomes defined in terms of whether services to meet the need are available; if the services are not available, then the need goes unrecognised.

There were two main reasons for limited access:

- fear of overstretching limited resources; and

- a policy of gatekeeping that sets high thresholds for receipt of services related to interpretations of suffering significant harm.

Fear of overstretching resources

Families who were seeking help from Social Services for the first time found it hard to find out which office to go to. Initial phone calls could be frostily received, and there was an aura of what one study called 'deterrent prevention', which faced those referring themselves for help.[22] There was little available publicity about family support services, although the importance of publicity and helping families learn about specific social services was recognised by some workers.

One justification for such a controlled approach was that publicising services would open the floodgates to families turning to Social Services for help.[1] Such an approach, it was argued, would strain to the limit the already stretched resources. There was little evidence that such fears were justified. Families in the short-term fostering study fully appreciated the need for rationing services.[2] Where authorities had adopted an open access policy and had encouraged families to seek help through children's resource centres or family centres, this seemed to work well. A good example came from the short-term fostering study.[2]

A collaborative model of working between a family resource centre and a family placement team

A protocol for assessing the needs of children needing short-term accommodation had been developed jointly between a family resource centre that acts as an access point for families and the family placement team.

This model provided the opportunity for the assessment of children in need and their families to be carried out by one of several personnel, using the same criteria and template for gathering information. Sometimes a joint assessment was undertaken by the centre worker and the member of the family placement team; sometimes the family placement worker did the whole assessment. But more often the family placement worker, clear about eligibility criteria for a placement, simply followed the direction and work of the resource centre worker. Good communications, aided by both workers occupying the same building, ensured that the children's needs were met as promptly as resources allowed. Furthermore, while children were accommodated, parents could continue to receive direct social work services within the context of a centre that was familiar to them, a factor not unimportant in facilitating a good outcome for parents and children. Above all, evaluation was built into the system.

The conclusion from this example, which was reinforced by recommendations from three other studies,[4, 22, 23] was that 'a one-stop shop' approach enhanced accessibility and was cost-effective in terms of swift and appropriate responses to families, including referral to specialist sources of help or agreement that a service was inappropriate. It was also advocated as a way of providing cost-effective support and non-stigmatised services to those needing them for longer periods, thus avoiding the 'revolving door' type of processing whereby cases were closed as rapidly as possible only to be opened again soon after.[22]

Equally important in accessing social services was to bring to the attention of other professionals who regularly came in contact with families – such as primary health care teams and teachers – what Social Services could and could not offer. Setting the boundaries was an important part of interagency collaboration. As one social worker said:

> What is important is to get the information to the people that families will
> see regularly and who understand what they need . . . and what we can
> and cannot do . . . it's vital.[2]

Without clarity in policies and practice, a lottery of access to social services will persist. However, in spite of this, two-thirds of the families in the study on services for children in need and the majority of families in the short-term fostering study saw Social Services as the agency of first choice.[2, 23]

Gatekeeping and high thresholds for Part III services

In spite of the families' perception of Social Services as a helping agency of first choice, the existence of a broad range of services for children in need remains patchy and does not have the universal endorsement of every social services department.[23] A report by the Social Services Inspectorate (1999) on the delivery of family support services suggested that the success achieved by social workers in helping families to respond to the needs of their children and to take control of their lives was often achieved without sufficient support from managers. The report recommends that the issues managers should pay attention to include:

- the formulation and implementation of their own strategic priorities for family support services;

- the implementation of planned changes in a way that addresses practice culture, real change and review processes;

- the equipping of their information systems to monitor the distribution of resources on the basis of need;

- the development of performance monitoring to link service objectives to performance indicators and individual case outcomes.[35]

Even if services were available, the studies suggested that a significant inhibitor to receiving them was the setting of eligibility criteria for access to children's services. In practice, these meant that services were offered to children in need only where issues of child maltreatment were evident. The findings from the studies on this issue are strongly reinforced by several SSI reports on family support,[27, 30, 31, 35] disabled children[25, 33] and looked after children.[29, 32]

The evidence from the two studies on safeguarding children where there are concerns about maltreatment showed that there was no consistency of approach to children in need between authorities.[4, 22] Similar children were being treated very differently in different authorities. Whether they accessed services through the gateways of section 17 or section 47 was rather haphazard.

Decisions about who might access services were not transparent and were likely to vary from agency to agency, according to the individual judgements of workers processing requests for services, the services available on the day and the departmental guidelines that listed priorities for the receipt of services. Parents who were disabled or whose children had impairments were especially disadvantaged and resented the fact that only families who mal-treated their children seemed to get help.[1, 22] The combination of poverty and high costs of caring for disabled children caused much distress and placed children in need of services:

> My husband lost his job. I asked if they could help with a playgroup as we are
> struggling with money. I didn't think I was asking for much. I would have paid
> for one day if they would pay for the other. How do you find out what you are
> entitled to? You shouldn't have to lie or beg or grovel.[22]

Consequently, families were confused about what services they might ask for, and it was equally unclear why some were offered services and others in similar situations were refused services. Families had more chance of gaining a single practical service, such as day care, but even here the grounds on which such a service might be offered were rarely revealed to families in any written family support plan. It is of interest that the researchers in the family support and child maltreatment study took leaflets with them to explain Part III services. This information was warmly received.[22]

Many families, across several studies, believed the gateway to services lay in a constructed biography of their troubles that hinted at potential maltreatment to a child rather than the impact of that maltreatment on a child's welfare. A fine line was drawn between presenting a convincing case of stress that might place children at risk of impairment and one that was not sufficient to trigger an enquiry under section 47.[2, 4, 8, 22, 23]

The main points

- Fears of overstretching resources by providing more open access to social services were unfounded.

- A one-stop shop approach to accessing services was very helpful to families and workers.

- Social Services was seen as an agency of first choice for many families under stress.

- Access to services often related solely to concerns about child abuse or neglect and should be widened to other children in need.

- Access to social services was like a lottery. There was little consistency about who might get services both within and across departments.

- A more discerning approach to accessing services is needed.

Assessment for individual children and families

Given the confusion around accessing social services, it is not surprising to find that the Children Act studies have some rather robust messages about the inadequacies of assessment, inadequacies that have also been identified by the Social Services Inspectorate:[31, 82]

> We found it was unusual for families to be assessed systematically taking account of their strengths and weaknesses. Departments more often simply responded to the problem that was presented. As a result some families who needed support were inappropriately caught up in the child protection system, whilst in other situations obvious risks to children were overlooked.[82]

The criteria that determined why some children were sent down a 'child protection route' and others were assessed as being in need of Part III services were not necessarily based on children's needs. Some social workers deliberately manipulated the system to ensure that the children they judged to be in need gained access to services:

> We haven't very clear statements of policy anywhere. Sometimes it (the child protection route) is the only way to get a detailed assessment. It is not using the system appropriately, but out of sheer desperation with children who have huge needs but are not necessarily at risk . . . If you are a good salesman you can sell anything as a CP issue or as a child in need. It's a case of how you present it.[22]

Little matching of needs to services

With one major exception,[2] there was little evidence in the studies that particular services were matched to need because they were likely to be the most effective. At least three studies drew attention to the fact that families were sometimes offered services inappropriately, drawing from a pool of existing services that did not meet families needs rather than providing services based on assessment of need.[15, 21, 23]

Unusually, the short-term fostering study was an exception, demonstrating the link between a focused assessment of families' abilities to use the service and successful outcomes for children and families. Here, gatekeeping did take place but was based on assessments of families' capacities to use the service. These careful assessments led to successful outcomes in terms of relieving stress, improving children's quality of life and behaviour and helping parents feel more in control of their lives.[2]

The more normal pattern was what might be called a 'sticking plaster' approach to assessment, based on what services might be in the medicine box. Families with complex problems were not assessed fully but were offered single services, which happened to be available, too late, at a time when problems had become entrenched and required a more sophisticated response. Not surprisingly, brief interventions were not effective at this stage. The research evidence suggests that the needs of these families cannot be ameliorated by short-term intervention or a single service.[4, 21, 23] Longer-term packages of intervention, in excess of twelve months, co-ordinated by social workers and delivered by skilled professionals from a range of agencies, are more likely to be effective.[2, 23]

Even here, complex needs will demand complex assessments that will identify what can and cannot be changed. The family support and maltreatment study suggests that it is much harder to help children when they have been harmed over a long period.[4] The need for long-term services should be recognised, but complex interdisciplinary packages are expensive and therefore it is important that they are only given to those who really need them.

Conversely, families responded well if they were offered practical services such as day care, attendance at family centres or brief social casework at an early stage. The conclusion from the studies is that 'prevention' is likely to be easier and more cost-effective than 'cure', though both are needed.[4, 21, 23] Clearly careful assessment is needed to identify which children might benefit from early intervention.

The recommendation from the research is that a joint strategy of assessment is needed:

- On the one hand, it is important to assess and prioritise the children most at risk of impairment or significant harm for complex services that may need to be long-term, i.e. in excess of twelve months.

- On the other hand, it is important to place alongside this another priority: one that can identify children and families who can respond positively to well-targeted, supportive services at an earlier stage.

The studies suggest that more work is needed in identifying the services that are likely to be most effective and helpful for black and minority ethnic families. It was encouraging that, on the whole, the studies found examples of services that were responsive to the needs of black and minority ethnic families even though they were not necessarily targeted at them.[22, 23]

The purpose and processes of assessment

The variability in gaining access to appropriate services raises many questions about the purpose and processes of the assessment of children and the accurate identification of children who are 'in need' of services. The 'quick-fix sticking plaster' approach to assessments and services was inefficient because little attention was given to the wider profile of the families' needs. Some families approached Social Services asking for single services with which they were familiar, but they might also have benefited from other services they did not know about.[22, 23]

Conversely, where there is no evidence to suggest parents are placing their children at risk of suffering significant harm, the wheeling out of the full panoply of enquiries under section 47, including conferencing and registration, in order to gain access to Part III services, is a misuse of the system designed to protect children seriously at risk of maltreatment.

The evidence also suggests that such an approach is not cost-effective. In the safeguarding children study, in similar cases, there were no obvious differences in outcomes after one year in cases where court action was used to safeguard children and in those where it was not.[4] Had this more discerning approach been adopted, there would have been a reduction in workload costs and stress to all concerned. This 'would have been achieved at no cost to the welfare and protection of the children'.[4]

Not surprisingly there is a consensus from several studies that:

> Neither the reason for referral, including whether the case is referred because of concerns about maltreatment or for a special service, nor the type of service requested in response to the need identified by the referrer are adequate bases for a quick decision about the sort of service to be provided.[22]

The need for one system of assessment for all children in need

The evidence from the studies points clearly to the need for one differentiated system of assessment, where judgements about the need for the safeguarding and promotion of welfare are part of the same system. This applies across the board, whether plans are for children to be helped in the community or for children to be looked after. In other words, the 'child protection system' and the family placement systems are part of an assessment process where decisions are made using Children Act definitions of 'in need'. Indeed, as the best-laid plans study concluded, services should be structured to provide 'effective liaison and mutual understanding between different teams within the local authority'.[13] Such a system should differentiate between children at different levels of impairment and those at risk of suffering significant harm, grounding professional judgements in the knowledge of individual children's developmental needs and the capacities of parents to respond to those needs. The issues identified by the studies have now been taken forward in the *Framework for the Assessment of Children in Need and Their Families* of the Department of Health et al. and the National Assembly for Wales.[79, 92]

The evidence from the family support studies supports the assessment framework by pointing to the use of assessments that place children in need and their families in the wider context of their histories, their living circumstances (including income levels), their strengths, their relationships as a family, their social supports and their communities.[22, 23] Such assessments should also contain information on previous intervention and why this was found to be effective or ineffective. The perspectives of the children and their families on what they found helpful should be included.

The issues and way forward are succinctly summarised by the family support and maltreatment study:

> In the light of the very large numbers of families seeking assistance with apparently similar environmental and practical difficulties, ways have to be found to sift referrals so that the most effective service is provided to those who can make use of it at an earlier stage to avoid further impairment of children's health and development; and to provide cost-effective longer-term help for those whose children are already suffering significant harm and are likely to continue to do so without sustained support. The notion of triage, more often used when considering the health services, provides a way forward. Central to this sifting process is the continuum of types of assessment . . . The sifting process starts when families themselves or other professionals or neighbourhood support workers decide whether or not to make a referral.[22]

Finally, the views of both families and social workers across several studies remind professionals that the process of assessment itself is often seen by families as a helpful intervention in its own right. In the course of the study on services for children in need, simply talking over problems in a brief casework relationship with a social worker was sometimes enough to enable families to gather their often considerable strengths and find their own solutions to the problems they had presented to Social Services.[23]

The main points

- The process of assessment described in the studies was not always based on need but rather on presenting problems that would access the system.

- There was little matching of needs with appropriate services but rather a sticking plaster, service-led approach.

- There is evidence of positive outcomes of early intervention in some cases, but assessment should distinguish between complex cases and others.

- Complex cases require a longer-term and more discriminating response.

- Culturally sensitive services can be effective for children from black and minority ethnic families.

- The studies point to an integrated needs-led approach to the assessment of children in need.

Planning for looked after children

Assessments go hand in hand with planning, and planning is important for all children. The Children Act 1989 sought to introduce a systematic and effective system of planning for looked after children. It paid particular attention to the care of children looked after by the local authority – in response to earlier research that had reported the negative consequences of drift for children in the care system in the 1980s.[50, 51] It is important to distinguish between the decision-making that obtains for all looked after children and the presentation of that decision-making to the courts in the process of seeking a Care Order. Both are called *care plans* in Volume 3 of the *Guidance and Regulations*.[48] Ideally, the Children Act intended that planning for all looked after children should be executed using the same principles and with the same aim of safeguarding and promoting children's welfare. What happens to each and every looked after child will be the subject of an individual care plan.

Four studies deal specifically with planning for the care of looked after children[10, 11, 13, 24] and others contain sections on the process of planning for looked after children.[2, 4, 15] Most of the studies were undertaken within the first five years of implementation of the Act. One investigates practice in the late 1990s in cases of compulsory care.[11] Thus, the studies not only provide information on key aspects of planning to care for looked after children as envisaged in the legislation and guidance, but also throw some light on the process of implementation and the continuing challenges.

The evidence from all the studies is that effective care planning remains one of the most significant challenges facing Social Services, although the evidence is by no means all negative. Such are the vulnerabilities of some children who are the subject of Care Orders that to expect to achieve optimal outcomes quickly in all cases may be unrealistic. On the other hand, as the studies suggest, it is precisely because of the needs of the most vulnerable that planning and the direct work that flows from it must be sound, flexible and effective to ensure that the best possible outcomes can be attained for this special group of children in need.

To take a snapshot of some of the results from the best-laid plans study:

- two in three of children's eventual destinations were in accordance with the original firm care plan;

- 57% of all new placements were made within six months of the final court hearing; and

- 22% took more than nineteen months.[13]

How are these results to be judged? Do they represent success or failure? These may not be the most appropriate questions to ask. The best way forward may be to strive towards bringing the actual close to the ideal, rather than analysing the pros and cons of the targets already reached.[13] So what needs to be done at different levels to improve the planning to care for looked after children? The studies suggest some refocusing of the fundamentals.

Refocusing the fundamentals
The planning to care study suggests that clarification is needed on:

- the care plan;

- the planning process;

- the review;

- the concepts of participation;

- the scope and timing of statutory reviews; and

- the linking of planning to outcomes.[10]

The study suggests that the *Guidance and Regulations* should be amended as follows to reflect the good practice that has emerged over the last eight years as a consequence of the introduction of the Looking After Children assessment and action records:

> The complete care plan should consist of objectives (the overall plan) and steps that should be taken to achieve them (the executive arrangements).[10]

Recognising planning is a process

The point is well made by the planning to care study that planning is a process and consists of the four components laid down in Volume 3 of the *Guidance and Regulations*:

- enquiry;
- consultation;
- assessment; and
- decision-making.[48, para. 2.43]

The research found that reviews were led by rigid time-scales rather than by responding to children's changing needs, circumstances and fresh experiences. The planning to care study concluded that reviewing is 'planning informed by monitoring, not a separate activity in its own right but a periodic continuation of planning assisted by the wisdom of hindsight'.[10]

Improving participation

As described in earlier chapters (4 and 5), children and adults in the review process have views on their participation. Ensuring the increased participation of young people in the planning process is an important aspect of good practice, as is working in partnership with the families and carers of all looked after children.

Developing more effective management and accountability

Although there are no studies dedicated to management practices, the role of management in influencing the provision of services is present in most of the studies. The planning to care study suggested that there was need for a designated manager to spearhead development of effective care planning and assure quality control for individual children.[10] In addition, the day care studies and those on looked after children all stressed the value of external accountability in helping to raise the standard of services.[6, 10, 18, 20, 21]

Linking planning to outcomes

Putting together the findings from several of the studies on looked after children, there remains a fundamental challenge: to achieve positive outcomes for looked after children. In the moving on study, the distress and loneliness of young people who had left the care system is powerful evidence of the need for improvements in the system to give these looked after children the best possible life chances.[3] The evidence of poor educational outcomes, poor health and social skills remain to be addressed, as the SSI inspections on looked after children confirm.[29]

There is evidence from the studies that the Children Act 1989 provides the framework in which planning can improve. The planning to care study showed that the process of planning was taken seriously, with 70% of local authorities having demonstrated satisfactorily that they had absorbed the key messages of *Guidance and Regulations*. By comparison with the 1980s, there were signs of a more systematic approach to promoting participation. The use of standardised records – asking for accountability from professionals on actions agreed at a review – appeared to enhance the process of planning.[10]

Care plans and their implementation have also shown a steady improvement over the last eight years. The evidence from the study on making Care Orders work suggests that such improvements are important because fulfilling the plan is associated with good progress in children's welfare.[11] This study reported progress, but perhaps not as much as might have been expected. With just over six out of ten children at the end-point of the study living in the placement type specified in the court plan, it seems that Social Services are taking the implementation of care plans very seriously but have not yet achieved the desired outcome for all looked after children.[11] Best practice has not been reached across the board. At the conclusion of the study on making Care Orders work, almost two-fifths of the children still fell short of reaching their optimal potential in family and social relationships, in emotional and behavioural development and in educational attainment.[11] The studies suggest that, without effective and skilled supportive and therapeutic services, plans will not be translated into good outcomes.[3, 7, 24] The studies showed that, where good casework services were offered to ensure plans are carried to fruition, outcomes for children in need and their parents were much more satisfactory.[2, 7]

A common language and shared goals between agencies

Finally, a common language and a clear framework for interagency working is needed in relation to looked after children. One way forward, which has provided a framework for addressing the issues of planning and outcomes, is the introduction of the Looking After Children assessment and action records.[67] These records were originally developed in response to concerns about poor outcomes for looked after children. A working party under the chairmanship of Professor Roy Parker was set up to discuss and analyse the concept of outcome and how it might be assessed. The activities of this working party culminated in the development of outcome measures for looked after children that were piloted and introduced by some social services departments in 1992. The Department of Health supported national implementation from 1995. The implementation of these Looking After Children assessment and action records, as they became known, is the basis of one of the studies in this overview.[24]

Two other studies on children looked after by the local authority draw attention to the use of the Looking After Children assessment and action records to inform and improve planning.[2, 10] The records have now been adopted, at least in principle, by the majority of social services departments in England and Wales and are being increasingly used by countries elsewhere across several continents. These records serve as a study of a systematic approach to planning for looked after children.

The Looking After Children assessment and action records – a framework for improving practice and management

The aim of the Looking After Children records was to provide a method of assessment that covered all those milestones in growing up that are informally monitored and promoted by 'reasonable' parents. The working party identified seven developmental dimensions along which children need to progress if they are to achieve satisfactory outcomes, defined as 'long-term well-being in adulthood'. These were health, education, identity, family and social relationships, social presentation, emotional and behavioural development and self-care skills. Assessment materials were fashioned which not only showed how much progress children were making but also showed how the care experience contributed to the realisation of their full potential.[24]

The looking after children study was innovatory in that it linked the concept of outcome to the processes needed to bring about those outcomes.[24] Research knowledge was employed to assess children's needs and chart their progress. The use of the records is ongoing and more research is expected which will show if the records can help professionals to improve outcomes for looked after children.

The looking after children study was completed in 1995. The study confirmed that the dimensions were valid and, further, could be applied to all children. It also showed that the Looking After Children records were beginning to introduce a common language about the needs of children and had the potential for gathering aggregated data on looked after children to aid strategic planning. With regard to individual children, the records reinforced the value of the participation of children and families in decision-making. The system also assumed that accurate information was the key to effective policy development.

The looking after children study revealed potential omissions in the records, such as the emphasis on individual children deflecting attention from siblings and detracting from wider structural factors that can inhibit children's life chances. There were also questions from this study and the study on making Care Orders work about the detail and the amount of time required to complete the forms.[11, 24]

The findings on the Looking After Children records need to be seen in tandem with the national audit of their application undertaken in 1999, in

England[72] and in eleven authorities in Wales.[93] These audits questioned the time taken to complete the records and showed that they were not being used as effectively as they might be, with only one-third of authorities in both England and Wales using the records properly. Clearly, as with any developmental programme, further refinements will need to be made, but the coherence of the records in providing a framework for safeguarding and promoting the welfare of children in need remains. This coherence was noted in two other studies on looked after children.[10, 15]

The main points

- Guidance on planning for looked after children needs refining to reflect the good practice that has developed.

- It should be recognised that planning is a process not an event.

- The role of management and inspection are important in ensuring the quality of planning.

- Plans for children in need should be linked to welfare outcomes.

- There is a need for a common language of planning between agencies.

- The Looking After Children assessment and action records are proving a valuable framework to link planning to outcomes by accounting for changes in children's progress over time.

- Planning is ineffective without knowledgeable professionals to implement plans through skilled service delivery.

Good practice in particular services

The need for a broad range of services

There can be no escape from one factor that permeates all the Children Act studies: the question of resources. The studies of children in many different circumstances show clearly the struggle that faces social services managers and practitioners in responding appropriately to children and families when they have a serious shortfall of trained personnel and have to contend with the ever-shifting sand of annual budgets subject to fluctuations in amount of funding. This question has to be faced even if it is to recognise that the perfect solution may be elusive, no matter what changes take place in policy and practice at both governmental and local levels. Nevertheless, the studies reveal there is a will to improve the provision and delivery of all services for children, including social services. The strategies are many and varied: the pooling of interagency budgets, better information systems about which children are in need and those who should be prioritised, partnerships between Social Services and the independent sector, and better training for the workforce. All these will, it is hoped, have an impact on improving the effectiveness of services for children in need and their families.

The Children Act studies contribute to this debate by acknowledging the challenges facing Social Services, by cataloguing the kinds of services families find helpful, by indicating pointers to good practice and by exploring whether there are connections between good practice and good outcomes.

The studies conclude that a broad range of services is needed to respond to the needs of those for whom Social Services already have responsibility, such as children identified at risk of suffering significant harm and children looked after both in accommodation and in care. Equally, the studies make the case for judicious use of family support services in the community, including day care, playschemes, family centres, practical and financial help and the mobilising of community and multi-agency resources, especially health and education, although leisure and recreation and advocacy and advice services also have a part to play.

The development of services for looked after children remains a major focus of policy and practice. The Children Act studies show the impact that coherent planning systems, such as the Looking After Children records, can have on practice and reaffirm the importance of planning and reviews combined with high quality relationship-based casework.[10, 24]

Issues relating to looked after children include more choice of foster and adoptive families. The fostering system rarely offers choice to its users, a factor that the court studies suggest inhibits effective care planning and the outcomes of Care Orders.[12, 13]

Although services to help young people leave care have made considerable progress over the last decade, meeting the needs of this vulnerable group still remains a priority and, as the views of the young people revealed (Chapter 5) there are still challenges to be met, under section 24 of the Children Act, to assist the transition of these vulnerable youngsters to independence. These challenges are being addressed by strengthening the legislation through the Children (Leaving Care) Act 2000.

Finally, there is the role of social work itself, which is of some significance across all the studies in contributing to the provison, delivery and outcomes of services.

Within the scope of this chapter it is impossible to review all the services described within the studies. These remain the subject of an in-depth reading of the books that accompany this volume. However, it is possible to offer a brief review of selected examples of practice that illustrate the challenges and outcomes of implementing some of the fundamental principles of the Children Act 1989. These have been chosen for two reasons: they represent new or changed areas of practice under the Children Act 1989 and they are particularly relevant to current policy initiatives.[69, 106] Some of the examples emphasise the enhancing of parenting skills and the mobilising of community resources. They also represent different parts of the continuum of Part III services and illustrate the translation into practice of four fundamental Children Act principles:

- the duty to safeguard and promote the welfare of children in need who are looked after by their families or by the local authority;

- the value of a continuum of services;

- the importance of supporting families in relation to the promotion of children's welfare; and

- the importance and potential impact of well-regulated systems of planning, monitoring and practice on safeguarding and promoting children's welfare.

Day care, including playschemes

Most of the day care studies were conducted in the early 1990s.[6, 16, 20] They show the struggle day care underwent to upgrade itself to meet the new regulations and in this respect are a testament to the structure of the legislation that underpinned the principles with a clear regulatory strategy.[26] The study on services to disabled children showed evidence of improved standards in day care, with children being offered a wide range of stimulating and educational experiences as a direct result of the Children Act.[18] On the other hand, the first study of out-of-school services for disabled children presented a mixed picture, and in some cases gave cause for concern about children's well-being and safety.[16] The later out-of-school study suggested that services had improved.[17]

Practice and provision have developed considerably since the time of the early day care studies, but both they and the later day care studies have messages relevant to the current initiatives on child care. The importance of training and support for day care staff are highlighted as factors influencing provision. This is especially important in the light of the diversity of provision revealed by the studies, and the fact that many independent services are providing an important form of family support for children in need.[21]

Funding is an important issue and relates to issues of cost-effectiveness. In Wales, for example, a good model was provided by the special needs referral schemes, which offered supported places to children with learning difficulties or other disabilities in their local playgroups.[20]

Out-of-school schemes also offer a range of options and may be separate or integrated into longer day care arrangements. Strong messages also come from the first play and out-of-school study about the value of regulation and training and the linking of schemes to a national childcare strategy to avoid *ad hoc* schemes of a low standard.[16]

Family centres

Family centres are specifically listed in Schedule 2 of the Children Act as a service that local authorities are required to provide 'as they consider appropriate in relation to children in their area'. Family centres may be run by the local authority or others, singly or in partnerships. Volume 2 of the *Guidance and Regulations* outlines the possible uses of family centres, emphasising that they may provide therapeutic services to families experiencing severe difficulties, provide neighbourhood-based activities and meeting places for parents and children and be a source of informal support to families.[47]

The question has to be asked: is there evidence from the Children Act studies that family centres have justified the place given to them in legislation? What have the users of centres made of them and are there lessons to be learned about how they may best be organised?

The summary of the study on family centres in Section II gives the study's findings in more detail.[19] Here, specific points relating to the key issues are presented. The six centres run by the Children's Society offered three or four different models of support.

It was clear that the centres were well valued by those who used them, but little information is available in the study about those who chose not to use the centres. It may be, as in the study on services for children in need and the short-term fostering study, that parents' views were influenced by their gratitude for having been offered a service.[23, 2] Nevertheless, this does not detract from the fact that over 80% of the parents said the family centres had made a difference to them and their children. These high rates of satisfaction are similar to those in the study on services for children in need[23] and the short-term fostering study.[2]

The centres were all located in highly disadvantaged social areas. They recruited via local networks or referral from professionals and most were heavily used. Centres met young children's developmental need for a safe play space and for social experiences, while at the same time supporting and educating the parents. Centres were non-stigmatising meeting places for parents to share problems and make social contacts, 'helping the most vulnerable to gain confidence and learn to cope with their children'. There was also an adult education function in helping parents learn new skills and develop self-confidence. Centres were also a valuable resource in the community, helping to sustain a sense of community and providing resources in neighbourhoods with few facilities.

There remain questions about the use and targeting of family centres. Should they be part of an open-door strategy for the under-fives or should they target families who might be likely to place their children at risk of suffering impairment or significant harm? The study on family centres,[19] supported by the family support and maltreatment study,[22] comes down on the side of the former, arguing that this model is more cost-effective in reaching and impacting on a wide range of individuals, especially within socially disadvantaged neighbourhoods. In summary, if the families in this study are representative of others, family centres as envisaged under the Children Act have an important part to play in any strategy to promote the welfare of young children.[19] Their effectiveness in the long term must be the subject of further evaluation.

Short-term accommodation

This service was introduced as a family support measure and was intended to break down the barriers between children in and out of care, but also to offer a standardised regulation of placements and carers for children with disabilities and for children in families under other types of stress.

The short-term fostering study charts the processes and outcomes of the service for 60 children in four local authorities.[2] All of the children who used the services had been assessed as priorities for services under section 17 of the Children Act 1989.

As in the study on family centres,[19] from the point of view of the parents and carers who were offered the service, the aim of helping to prevent family breakdown was achieved with 56 families intact at the end of the study.[2]

Parents used the service to address a range of problems. Though some children had natural fears of separating from their parents, these were handled well by social workers, parents and carers, with the result that the service enhanced the children's quality of life and in some cases addressed behavioural issues.

The success of the service depended on multi-agency access, clear assessment processes, including parental capacity to use the service appropriately, focused social casework and the careful selection, training and support of carers. Carers and parents shared neighbourhood locations, and placements were easily accessed by public transport.

Good user and service outcomes were achieved because the targets set for children and families were realistic, intervention was carefully planned, time-limited and subject to sensible implementation of regulations. Additionally, as with the family centres, parents were grateful that they had received some help when they needed it.[2]

The short-term fostering study and the safeguarding children study both dispel myths about any form of accommodation being a 'last resort'.[2, 4] Families and professionals from these two studies were clear that short-term accommodation was a service of first choice, whilst the care to accommodation study distinguished between the reluctant use of full-time accommodation and the first choice of short-term accommodation.[15] The studies show how planned and careful use of short-term accommodation can support a range of children in need and their families in the community. The role of well-supported extended families as short-term carers is highlighted.[4] There is potential to extend the service to some children who are at risk of significant harm providing the purpose and boundaries of the intervention are clear.[4]

Supporting families living apart

Organising contact between children and families is a major activity when families are separated from their children. As suggested in Chapter 3, in the light of the research of the 1980s about the association between reunification and contact,[50] the Children Act imposed a new duty to promote contact between a child being looked after and those with whom he or she has a significant relationship. Contact must also be offered in accordance with children's developmental needs and take account of their wishes and feelings. There are consequently some important practice messages from the research on:

- the circumstances that facilitate contact;

- the circumstances when contact is not in the children's best interests; and

- factors that facilitate reunification.

The aims for contact should be clearly identified and integrated into the care plan. Contact aims should have clearly stated and measurable objectives that identify:

- the identity of visitors and the timing, frequency and venue for contact;

- the arrangements for indirect contact;

- the carer's role in contact;

- the social worker's role – in supporting parents, carers and the child; and

- the services required to support the contact plan.[7]

The venue of the contact is important. The research shows that contact in the parental home is most effective in offering continuity with immediate and wider family and friends, and in assisting the child's sense of identity. Visits to the foster family are also welcomed by children, but reveal tensions between parents and carers. Given that almost two-fifths of the children saw their families at a social services venue, the research concludes that Social Services play a major part in facilitating contact that safeguards children's welfare while allowing them to maintain links with their families. This is especially relevant where there is potential for erratic or violent parental behaviour. However, some families found the venue of social services uncomfortable. Thought needs to be given to the further development of specialist contact centres that have facilities to help parents and children feel as easy as they can in what is clearly a rather unnatural situation.[4, 7]

Indirect contact through thinking and talking about families, through phone calls and less commonly through letters was instrumental in keeping links alive. The value of treasured toys and objects as symbolic links was also noted.

There seem to be few cases where some links are not desirable. It is suggested that caution should be exercised in cases of sexual abuse and violence, although for some children supervised contact was successfully used in these instances.

Direct social work with children and with parents is extremely important in keeping contact going and attending to any changes in attitudes and behaviour that need to take place before a child returns home. It is suggested that meetings between social workers and parents should take place at least monthly. Ongoing social work meetings also ensure that the worker will know if contact arrangements are not going well. Additionally, a harmonious and supportive relationship between social workers and carers will help facilitate the carers' relationship with the parents.

Contact between children and parents, supported by social workers and carers, remains the key to reunification. A successful return was associated with the following factors:

- a good attachment relationship between parent and child;

- a well-motivated parent who is willing to change and seek help;

- purposeful contact aimed at improving the parent–child relationship;

- contact that is adequately resourced and supported;

- contact that is a positive experience, with the child responding well to increased contact;

- the return process being taken at a steady pace and being regularly reassessed;

- the involvement of parent and child in the planning and process of return; and

- where appropriate, support services being used to assist the family after reunification.[7]

Young people leaving the care system

Section 24 of the Children Act 1989 placed new duties on local authorities to prepare young people for leaving care and to advise and befriend young people who left care after their sixteenth birthday up to the age of 21. Two studies and one inspection report are concerned with care leavers.[3, 14, 28] These young people were also the subject of the 1996 overview *Focus on Teenagers: Research into Practice*.[53] Both of the studies in this overview and the inspection report commented on the vulnerability of young people and the young age at which they leave the care system. The moving on study reviewed four schemes and found there was no blueprint for the ideal leaving care scheme. It was more important that a scheme had a sense of direction, good management and adequate resources.[3]

The moving on study concluded that leaving care schemes provide a valuable service: helping young people to plan their futures, providing follow-up support and meeting accommodation needs. Even for young people experiencing the greatest instability, the schemes' continuity of support often either prevented a descent into homelessness or provided a rapid escape from it.[3]

The moving on study[3] and the leaving care in partnership study[14] both addressed the issue of family links, which the young people themselves have recounted in Chapter 5. The issues for service delivery are the important role social workers and scheme leaders have in facilitating the retention of family networks and using their knowledge to help young people develop alternative supportive networks. This help was highly valued by the young people.

The main points

- There is a need for a broad range of focused services.

- Day care improved in quality and scope under the Children Act.

- Family centres provide a valuable service for parents and children.

- Short-term accommodation can be an effective family support service provided it is aimed at children and families who can benefit from it.

- Contact between looked after children and their families remains the key to reunification.

- Leaving care schemes are valuable in supporting vulnerable young people.

- Linking young people leaving care to their families is an important service.

The role of managers and social workers in delivering effective services

Managers
The Children Act studies were not primarily commissioned to study the impact of management on the organisation and delivery of services. However, throughout many of the studies there is a permeating and consistent message that the role of management at every level is influential on service delivery. Good managers are germane to good outcomes for children and families. There are several examples where management influenced service provision.

Who was able to access family support services was very much determined by management processes. Authorities with far-sighted and competent managers made a significant difference to the initial implementation of services for children in need, as these examples show:

> The Children Act has given me clout to push support services. Before it was all child abuse investigation. Now we get fieldworkers coming to my team asking us to take on a family where there is some risk. If we get in early, sometimes we can prevent a crisis.[1]

> One of the central messages of the Act we identified at the planning stage was the importance of leaving care issues, and we followed this through at the stage of prioritisation.[1]

There was also evidence, from the same study, of senior managers using evidence from research to plan their services:

> We felt that we had to know some of the basic grids [by Hardiker] which had appeared in the literature we knew, and using a three level model was common as well as giving us an obvious way to define priorities. We could always refine it later on.[1]

Managers also struggled with unsatisfactory information systems and inappropriate computer systems, which made it harder for agencies to work together to identify children in need.[1] However, this may well have improved since the studies in this overview were undertaken, as additional resources have been made available under the *Quality Protects* programme to improve management information systems.

As the Social Services Inspectorate has suggested, a poor understanding of section 17 in relation to the assessment of children in need living with their families or being looked after by the local authority leaves a continuing challenge for managers, as does the management of effective services within budget constraints.[31, 32]

In spite of the difficulties, the Children Act studies provide evidence of the influence of managers on changing systems to improve services. As discussed earlier in this chapter, management was instrumental in implementing the regulatory framework for looked after children. The looking after children study suggests that managers have a key role in using aggregated data to target services effectively.[24] Responses to the refocusing debate reported in at least two studies had been driven by both senior and middle management.[22, 23] In short, the key message is that managers can effect positive change, but they need to develop effective systems to support their aims and objectives.

Social workers
The looking after children study serves to emphasise what permeates many of the other studies: the key role social workers play in effecting outcomes that

safeguard and promote the welfare of children in need.[24] The studies provide a wealth of evidence on the roles and tasks social workers can and should undertake in this process.

The social work role as described in the studies is multi-faceted. It is very clear that what happens to children in need, both in the community and when they are looked after by the local authority, will be heavily influenced by professional judgements. Several of the studies draw attention to the knowledge and skills needed by social workers and the gaps that exist in some areas.

Social workers need to be able to undertake skilled assessments, make plans informed by evidence from theory and research and both co-ordinate and provide services for children in need in different circumstances. Assessments, planning and helping are not separate activities. They rely on professional judgements informed by a theory and knowledge of child development, the factors that have shaped parental capacity, the impact on families of poverty, disruptions and social disadvantage, and the contribution of extended family and community to families' advantages or disadvantages.[2, 4, 22, 23] Above all, they should be shaped by evidence about the effectiveness of different modes of service delivery.[2, 3, 4, 15, 21, 22, 23]

Care planning and reviews demand forward-looking plans and a dynamic approach. Workers should be able to present themselves well in court and be their own expert witnesses, but they may need support from colleagues in dealing with the stress of court proceedings, and also access to sound legal advice.[11] All work needs an interagency context where knowledge of networks and clear lines of communication and accountability are supported by management.[4, 5, 12, 13, 24]

The management and organisation of individual cases is only part of the social work role, albeit an important one. What is equally important are interpersonal relationships with children and families – in short the processes of psycho-social casework.

As suggested in Chapters 4 and 5, there is a need for social workers to be skilled in direct work with parents and children and to be able to work closely with foster carers. Research on looked after children, the courts and children in the community all give the same messages. Skilled social work combines evidence-based decision-making with sophisticated direct work and the effective use of other services. The vulnerabilities of both children and adults – and especially of children who have been subject to prolonged significant harm or impairment or who are being separated from significant attachment figures – demand special attention.

Social workers need an understanding of the meaning of life events for children of different ages. They must be able to translate this knowledge into practice through appropriate interventions aimed at counteracting negative events and promoting children's welfare.

Chapters 4 and 5 provided examples of the difference social workers made to the process of admission to accommodation, contact with parents and leaving care. Many troubled parents found their interactions with social workers facilitating and empowering. Even in court cases, the process of altering the balance of parental responsibility could be achieved reasonably and without harm to the children if social workers were working in partnership with parents.[10]

Unfortunately, good practice is not universal and there were instances when parents and children felt belittled and unheard, when children were moved between placements without plans and adequate preparation, and when young people left the care system without appropriate skills and supports. There were also some inappropriate judgements about the frequency of contact arrangements between children and parents and ineffective and indiscriminate uses of practical Part III services to appease requests for services that were not available. There was also, on occasion, an inappropriate use of accommodation which failed to safeguard children. Conversely, there was inappropriate use of formal child protection procedures when negotiation would have worked as well, if not better.

Several of the studies drew attention to the need for more specialist training for children and families' social workers. The absence of knowledge of child development was noticeable, as was the scarcity of expertise in direct work with children and methods of working in partnership with families in child maltreatment cases.

These caveats apart, across the full range of studies, there is consistent and cumulative evidence that social work activity in the form of psycho-social casework is the foundation stone of any services that are likely to make a positive difference to the lives of children in need and their families. The response of parents and children to such good social work practice has been described in Chapters 4 and 5. There are many examples across the studies which warrant further reading. The one described here shows good, evidence-based social work practice:

Rachel – a case study of reunification

The fostering family contact study describes the process of reunification for one child.[7] This case illustrates how interdisciplinary work, careful planning, adequate resources, professional judgement and skilled direct work combined to both safeguard and promote the welfare of the child:

The placement

Rachel (5 years) and her two younger half-sisters had been fostered with their grandparents. The mother, who was the primary carer, experienced considerable shock and grief when the children were accommodated.

Rachel regarded her mother as her key parenting figure. Feelings towards her stepfather were more ambivalent (assessed using the Family Relations Test).

At the time of the admission Rachel's mother and stepfather separated. Rachel's mother left the area. The social worker's efforts to encourage her to keep in touch with the children failed, and the mother wittingly lost contact with her ex-spouse, the children and Social Services.

Contact

Supervised visits for the stepfather took place on a twice-weekly basis at the nursery. The aim of contact was to improve the relationship between the father and his children. The contact was well resourced. The social worker regularly transported Rachel from school to join her sisters at the nursery for the contact. Rachel's stepfather travelled by a social services department's pre-paid taxi. Social workers, nursery staff and the foster carer worked together to support the relationship between father and children. In addition, Social Services arranged for a psychologist to work with the stepfather.

The foster carers believed the contact sessions improved the relationship between the stepfather and his children.

Return

After six months the three girls returned to live with their stepfather. His verdict was:

> It took a couple of months for me to think right [after the children were fostered] but I thought I've got to get them back, got to get myself sorted out.

Outlook

The results of the Family Relations Test suggested that the direct work with Rachel and her stepfather had proved successful. At the follow-up interview the main attachment relationship was between Rachel and her stepfather. Rachel also expressed considerable pleasure over her move home:

> I'm happy now . . . happy all the time.

Social workers believed that the long-term reunification between the children and their stepfather to become a one-parent family was a real and desirable possibility.

The importance of social work and good services

Putting together the findings from the 24 studies, there is clear evidence of improvements in the organisation and delivery of services for children in need and their families in spite of major financial constraints. There are more examples of well-planned, imaginative, inter-disciplinary programmes of help and support than appeared in previous overviews, including good work in the field of safeguarding children within their families. Family support services are highly valued and can be effective if there are careful social work assessments and a network of relevant services.

Social workers are not yet so good at helping looked after children effectively. In part, this is because the absence of family support services at an earlier stage means that so much harm has occurred before the child is looked after that it is difficult to effect optimal outcomes for the children concerned. This said, there were, in the studies, some excellent examples of tenacious efforts to improve children's lives and many instances of good practice in listening to children and making careful plans that identified their needs and strove hard to meet them.

The children and families in the studies were clear about what they valued in social workers – the psycho-social caseworker who provided emotional support and a range of services. There was evidence of highly skilled, sensitive responses to troubled parents and children, and casework was used to deliver effective services that both safeguarded and promoted the welfare of children in need.

The main points

- Managers have a significant influence on the scope and character of services and how they are delivered.

- There is a central place for social workers and psycho-social casework in the provision of effective services for children in need and their families.

8 The Children Act now – messages for policy and practice

When the Children Act was introduced, the Department of Health emphasised the opportunity for change it presented for practice in children's services:

> The Act gives the opportunity to rethink practices and unless this is done
> there will be lost a rare and vital opportunity to improve the lot of children.
> [45, para. 1.2]

Almost a decade after implementation, this overview has explored whether that opportunity has been grasped. To what extent has there been a rethinking of practices and, if so, what impact has any rethinking had on children in need and their families? The studies in this overview provide evidence about various aspects of the implementation of the public law parts of the Children Act. The evidence from the 24 studies shows how the philosophy of the Act has been interpreted and points to the areas of practice in which the Act has met its aims and to those where there have been difficulties.

Because some of the studies have taken place over time, there has been opportunity to show the dynamic nature of implementation. There is no doubt that government initiatives, such as the refocusing initiative begun in 1996 and the implementation of the Looking After Children records from 1995 onwards, have had an impact and this is reflected in the studies.

What is the overall verdict on the Children Act 1989? Basically, the Children Act as the overarching primary legislation is sound and has provided a working framework for the provision and delivery of services to children in need and their families. The principles of the Act – such as safeguarding and promoting children's welfare in all circumstances; promoting the upbringing of children by their families wherever possible; working with parents to enhance parental responsibility; and providing a wide range of services for children in need and their families – have underpinned practice. Although there have been some flaws in practice, the principles of achieving a balance between voluntary and compulsory measures have also had an impact. The participation of children and families in the processes of service delivery has begun to improve but more needs to be done. Some parts of the Act have proved problematic, either because the Act's intentions were unclear or have been misinterpreted or because of sluggishness in changing old habits. There have also been considerable difficulties in meeting the requirements of the Act in a climate of intense competition for resources for public welfare services.

The implementation process

The Children Act 1989 was launched with an intensive training programme. In spite of this, the research studies show that change in some areas was slow. It took a long time to grasp the principles behind defining children in need. This was for several reasons. The concept of linking need to children's development was not fully understood. There was reluctance to change from the certainty of narrow eligibility for services based on risk of harm to a concept of service provision based on the needs of children and with the aim of optimising health and development. Social Services and other agencies found it difficult to reach a common definition of children in need in their area. Information technology systems were not developed sufficiently in the early stages to be able to catalogue who were children in need. Although considerable progress was made with the introduction of Children's Services Planning in 1996,[78] the search for a common understanding of the definition of need remains. The parallel introduction of the National Health Service and Community Care Act 1990 brought with it a philosophy at odds with concepts of continuity and stability for children in need, and this hindered an integrated approach to the planning and delivering of services for children in need and their families in some areas.

The later studies do show that changes are beginning to take place and that the broad definition of 'in need' linked to children's developmental needs is entering the language and actions of social services departments. The Looking After Children assessment and action records introduced a common language of child development for assessing and taking action on the needs of children looked after.

Putting children centre stage

There is clear evidence that there has been a substantial cultural shift to include children in planning and decision-making that affects their lives. The voices of children are now heard in the planning process in a substantial number of cases. In this respect, the Children Act 1989 has been consistent with UK ratification of the UN Convention on the Rights of the Child in 1991.[100] The Children Act studies support the view that, given the chance, children across a variety of ages are able to participate in decision-making. However, the development of more sophisticated, skilled direct work with children and child-friendly meetings is required in child welfare agencies to enable children to make their views heard effectively and appropriately. Professional practice is not yet consistent in this respect.

The process of children's participation is sometimes not as child-centred as it should be. What the studies reveal is that the skills of facilitating children to express their wishes and feelings are variable. Professionals are better at communicating with older children. There is evidence of excellent work with children – giving them full information on which they can make informed choices, preparing them for admission to accommodation – and also evidence of a sensitive response to children's perspectives. Children's views are taken seriously on many occasions. There is also evidence that social workers are not as sophisticated in communicating with children as the participatory framework of the Act demands. Sometimes the professional task of reconciling tensions between children's wishes and their needs is not fully addressed. Such findings have implications for the training of skilled social workers who understand child development and their role in arriving at a decision about the child's welfare.

Working with parents

Working in partnership with parents has been a major challenge for social workers, a challenge to which, on the whole, they have responded. However, the evidence from the studies is that practice is variable. Sometimes partnership has been seen as an end in itself rather than as a process to facilitate the attainment of good outcomes for children. This approach has confused parents in cases where safeguarding issues remain. In these situations parents have felt coerced or betrayed when the goalposts change. There were examples of excellent practice where parents were treated with dignity, were able to gain the services they felt would be helpful and fully participated in decision-making. This was particularly evident in cases of children at risk of significant harm, family support services for children at risk of emotional maltreatment and neglect and in a range of family support services. Family centres can make an important contribution to participatory practice for families.

There were also examples of parents who felt marginalised and degraded, especially those who were involved in care proceedings and those whose children were looked after. A major issue was the handling of the balance between voluntariness and compulsory measures, such as in the provision of accommodation. It was clear that some social workers did not have the ability to exercise a positive use of authority when working with parents who were not seen to be the subject of intensive child protection intervention. There is a need to revisit the well-developed skills of working openly and honestly in negotiated partnerships with parents whose children are at risk of suffering significant harm and to apply them in the arena of family support. The positive use of authority, combined with clear aims and objectives of intervention, could improve practice in the areas where there is a need to safeguard and promote children's welfare simultaneously in order to prevent risk of impairment, without the use of court action.

The balance between compulsion and voluntariness in the courts

Slow progress has been made in achieving the balance intended in the Act between voluntariness and compulsion. Simultaneously safeguarding and promoting children's welfare has been difficult to achieve. It is clear that, on the one hand, some children have not been made the subject of care proceedings soon enough. In other cases, the operation of a high threshold for family support has led to insufficient emphasis on intervention at an early stage.

One major problem has been the absence of a common framework for assessing the needs of children and the capacities of parents to respond to those needs. Another has been an approach to the 'no order' principle that aims to keep children out of the courts at all costs. This is a misinterpretation of the Act and needs to be remedied. Each case should be decided within a framework of meeting children's developmental needs, as the Children Act 1989 intended. There is evidence from Children Act statistics that the balance is changing. It is important that this reflects need rather than fashion and that the trend is not allowed to bring about a return to the position prior to the Act when compulsion was used indiscriminately.

Safeguarding children with the courts

The court system has been changed for the better by the Children Act 1989. Even the early studies were reporting considerable improvements in the flexibility provided by the overlapping jurisdictions. In the court setting, there has been an appropriate balance between the 'no order' principle and the paramountcy principle. By the time of the later studies, there was clear evidence that cases were being brought to care proceedings with carefully prepared evidence. The range of orders has not been used as might have been expected. Supervision orders have been little used for reasons that are not entirely clear. Lawyers, guardians and social workers are working together well within the court system. Early fears about Social Services not being able to make and implement good care plans are not borne out by the research findings, and some progress has been made.

The Children Act 1989 has generally had a positive impact on court practices in the public welfare system with one major exception. The aim of the Children Act to reduce delay in court proceedings in order to take account of children's time-scales has not succeeded. Delays still occur in getting cases to court, in the process of the hearing and in the implementation of care plans. There is some evidence from the later court studies that the time-scales originally set by the Children Act were unrealistic, however laudable. There are many reasons for the delay, reinforcing the urgent need for further scrutiny of the way the court system is working and for remedies to be developed.

An interagency approach to children's services

It was not the intention of the Act that Social Services alone should be responsible for services for children in need, although they were given the lead in co-ordinating such services. The multi-faceted nature of children's development demands a multi-agency response. The Children Act 1989 laid the foundations for interagency collaboration, but this was not an area of dedicated attention in *Guidance and Regulations*, except in the case of children in need of protection from suffering significant harm.[49] Nor was it a well-developed way of working, either in England or in Wales. Considering the low baseline for collaboration that existed in many areas before the Act, considerable progress has been made in creating mechanisms for planning and working together to provide children's services.

There is still a long way to go. The studies show that progress within Social Services has been hampered to some extent by the separation of adults' and children's services. The studies show that collaboration with health services has been developing well in many places and will now be further aided by legislation to allow the pooling of funding. Early into implementation, the fragmentation of the education services and the establishment of self-governance of schools initially impeded progress in collaboration between education and social services but the later studies suggest that good collaboration is beginning to happen.[11, 24]

Family support services

The impact of the Children Act 1989 on the provision and delivery of family support services for children in need and their families is the subject of several studies. There is some good news. Social Services are viewed as an agency of first choice by many families who need family support services, but gaining access to services is often difficult. The studies point clearly towards the integration of different routes to accessing Part III services. The current system of separating child protection enquiries and family support assessment is ineffective and counter-productive to meeting the needs of children and families. The studies suggest that, by separating the two systems, some children have missed the value of early intervention to prevent more intrusive and intensive activity at a later stage. Conversely, some children who need safeguarding because of neglect are slipping through the net of family support services because these services fail to address the importance of safeguarding children's welfare.

Progress has been made on the scope and level of family support services available, but there still exists considerable discrepancy in the provision of services and access to those services. The designation of disabled children as children in need has not improved the access of these children to services as much as had been expected.

The use of accommodation as a family support service remains contentious. There is evidence of the burgeoning use of short-term accommodation as an effective service for a range of children, including its selective use for children at risk of significant harm. There is evidence that many children and families have also been helped by using full-time accommodation appropriately. However, too often accommodation is still seen as a last resort rather than as part of the services to help prevent family breakdown. Courts, social workers and families also remain unhappy with its use as a gateway to the courts. There needs to be a more discerning use of accommodation as a family support service and clearer aims and objectives against which the progress of families can measured.

Improvements in standards of practice

Finally, there is evidence that the Children Act 1989 has provided a framework for more focused and effective practice. In spite of problems, there are examples of good interagency practice between health and social services. There are many examples of excellent social work practice in the different domains of family support and looked after children. Leaving care schemes introduced within the scope of the Act have been much valued by young people making the transition from care to independence. Although the practice to promote contact between children and their families has been variable, the Children Act aim of maintaining connections between separated children and their families has been relatively successful. There is supporting evidence of more robust maintenance of links with families after young people have left the care system than existed prior to the Act. The studies give cause for optimism that services are improving, but standards are not yet consistent nationally in both England and Wales.

The Children Act studies show that the regulatory strategy and guidance given on service delivery has had an impact on standards, but not consistently in all authorities. Although this overview is not primarily concerned with the outcomes and best value of services, there is evidence that many children in need and their families have been supported appropriately. The Children Act 1989 has provided an appropriate framework for the delivery of services. Much of the *Guidance and Regulations* is still relevant and necessary. Where changes have occurred, these have been in the form of additions to respond to issues requiring a stronger approach to safeguarding, such as for children looked after in residential care or leaving care, or changes that aim to support good practice. The overarching message is that the provision and delivery of services for children and families has made considerable progress under the Children Act, but there remains a need to refine systems, management and practice to use the Act even more effectively to safeguard and promote the welfare of children in need.

The messages and current policy

There are many messages from the Children Act research studies that are relevant to contemporary policy objectives for children's services. These objectives have, in turn, translated some of the key messages into actions to improve services for children in need and their families.

Combating poverty and social exclusion

There is no doubt that living in enduring poverty remains a major problem for many of the families of children in need and places them at risk of being socially excluded. The studies have poignantly chronicled the circumstances of children and their families, including care leavers. Social isolation, poor health and poor self-esteem are common problems. The government's commitment to combat child poverty and social exclusion in the objectives for children's services[73] are supported by the evidence from the Children Act studies.

Early intervention strategies

There is also evidence from the studies that many children in need live in families who are beset by conflict and turmoil. Relationships between partners and the management of the behaviour of their children are major sources of stress for many parents. The studies suggest that many children and their families would have benefited from easily accessed services at an earlier stage. The early intervention strategies such as Sure Start[65, 107] and the Childcare Strategy are helpful in providing a focus for better help and information on parenting.[64, 105] Many of the parents in the Children Act studies would have welcomed the availability of such help.

An interagency agenda for children's services

The studies present evidence of the multi-faceted needs of children and support robust measures to take forward interagency co-ordination and collaboration, both in planning children's services and in the provision of services that can be easily accessed between agencies. Children's Services Planning has built upon the intentions of section 27 of the Act and has helped take forward implementation in this area. It has also challenged local authorities to improve their information systems and arrive at a common understanding of the definition of 'in need'. There are now in place significant government initiatives that should help the Children Act ideal of interagency collaboration to come to fruition.

The assessment frameworks in England and in Wales highlight the importance of an interagency assessment of children's needs and the value of agencies working together to strengthen parents' capacities.[79, 92] Guidance on the education of looked after children emphasises the need for better collaboration between education and social services and suggests how this might be brought about.[78] An increasing number of services are provided on a interagency basis, whereby teams operate with a pooled budget and shared responsibility, such as Sure Start and Youth Offending Teams.[73]

The importance of planning has been emphasised throughout the overview. The draft consultative guidance on Children's Services Planning[77] is intended to strengthen the expectation that all bodies providing services for children participate throughout the planning process and throughout the provision of integrated services. Similarly, guidance on safeguarding children has been issued jointly by several government departments and emphasises that working together is fundamental to safeguarding children's welfare.[80] To make an integrated approach work, the Health Act 1999 has enabled budgets to be pooled between health and social services so that opportunities may be created for maximising resources and targeting them effectively.

The framework for assessing children in need and their families

The Children Act studies show cumulative evidence about the inconsistencies of assessment. Several studies recommend that a common framework for assessment should be developed. What has been absent is a consistent approach that looks both at children's needs and at parents' responses to those needs, i.e. the inhibitors to parents fulfilling their parental responsibilities. The effective provision of family support services is dependent on just such an accurate assessment.

The assessment frameworks in England and in Wales[79, 92] move the agenda for assessment from one that assesses only risk of significant harm to a child-centred approach that identifies impairment or significant harm in the context of children's development, as the Children Act 1989 intended. The frameworks are accompanied by practice guidance that explains and expands on many of the key principles upon which the assessment frameworks are founded.[76] The Children Act studies make clear recommendations that the safeguarding and promoting of welfare are intertwined aims of intervention. A system that allows families to access services via a common route and assesses children's developmental needs differentially, at different levels of intervention, is to be welcomed. The assessment frameworks also build on the Children Act principle that parents have needs of their own that must be addressed in order to help them respond appropriately to the needs of their children. The messages from the studies also support an approach that takes into account the impact of environment on parental capacity and on the children themselves.

Improving outcomes for children in need –
Quality Protects and *Children First*

Legislation rarely sets specific objectives but rather reflects broad policy object-ives. So it is with the operational principles of the Children Act 1989.[46] They offer an explanation of what is considered to be the underlying philosophy of the Act. The collected volumes of *Guidance and Regulations*[49] describe why and how the principles are there, but do not set objectives by which the imple-mentation of the principles can be measured. Nor can legislation be concerned with the measurement of outcomes and performance indicators. That is left to those who translate the law into service provision.

The *Quality Protects* programme was set up in England in the autumn of 1998 and the *Children First* programme in Wales in spring 1999.[69, 106] Both provide comprehensive and outcome-focused objectives for children's services. These have been taken further in *The Government's Objectives for Children's Social Services*, which sets eleven objectives aimed at improving management and practices in children's services.[73] Several of the objectives build on the research findings of the Children Act studies in relation to family support, looked after children and children leaving the care system. They take forward the research messages in relation to the organisation, management, provision and delivery of services. The messages from the research in this overview have a key part to play in supporting these new policy initiatives. They provide evidence about the services that children in need and their families value and give practical ideas on how services might best be delivered.

Children's participation

Listening to the views of children and young people is one of the current priorities underpinning the *Quality Protects* and *Children First* programmes. It will become more important as the UN Convention on the Rights of the Child is integrated into all children's services and the Children's Commissioner begins work in Wales. The messages from the Children Act studies give insights into children's perspectives and ideas on how services may be devel-oped to become child-centred.

Developing more effective regulation and inspection

The importance of accountability and a good standard of service provision is highlighted in several of the studies on day care and looked after children. At the time of the studies, any accountability was generally in the hands of Social Services themselves. This internal scrutiny will soon be overtaken by more rigorous independent inspection and regulation. This is being taken forward by the establishment of the new national inspectorates.[74, 109] The system whereby the local authority is both the purchaser and inspector will be abolished and be replaced by independent inspectors and regulators. There will be new national standards for inspection and regulation within a broad spec-trum of health and social care facilities in the statutory, voluntary and private sectors. Inspectors and regulators will have training based on a national curriculum. These changes, along with the Care Standards Act 2000, will help develop further the infrastructure to safeguard and promote the welfare of a wide range of children in health settings, day care and residential care.

The training agenda for post-qualifying social workers

In January 2000 the Post-Qualifying Award in Child Care was launched by the Department of Health, the National Assembly for Wales and the Central Council for Education and Training in Social Work (CCETSW) to help train a more competent workforce to respond more effectively to children in need and their families.[57] The objectives and curriculum of this award address many of the issues raised by the studies. These include the importance of understanding children's development and creating opportunities for children to maximise their life chances in adulthood; being able to safeguard and promote children's welfare simultaneously; understanding and implementing the law; the value of children being securely attached to their families; the importance of skilled direct work with children and families; the ability to present evidence in court; the value of taking a broader approach to assessment; helping families access a broad range of services; and demonstrating the value of working with other agencies. Above all, the award demands that workers understand the importance of taking responsibility for their own professional development so that they may be able to offer children in need the services from which they would benefit.

Such advances in the training agenda are extremely important. There is much that post-qualifying social workers can learn from research about how to deliver effective services for children in need. It is clear that the Children Act 1989 has provided a foundation for change but, in the end, it is the quality of the workforce that will improve the standard of services for children in need and their families.

Endnote

The Children Act 1989 is alive and generally well but needs some remedial attention in specific areas. Overall, we have come a long way in a short time. Much has been accomplished and much has been learned from successes and mistakes. There has been a rethinking of practices that has made a difference to the lives of many children in need and their families. Now the task is to ensure that, across England and Wales, all children in need receive consistently good and effective services to safeguard them and promote their welfare.

The final verdict, however, rests with the children and families whose quality of life the Children Act set out to improve. In spite of the difficulties in achieving uniformly good services, there have been some significant changes in practice, which, in their turn, have produced positive outcomes for children in need and their families. It is fitting, therefore, that this overview should end with comments from two parents and four children whose lives were improved by services under the Children Act 1989.

Working with parents

A parent: You can actually talk to them now. When [social worker] comes round and sits down, I tell him what I like and basically what I want help with, this sort of thing. Whereas in the past if you said, 'I'm having trouble coping,' I mean, their answer was to send someone round, and 'cos the housework was done, that meant I was coping. Whereas now they'll actually listen, y'know: why you aren't coping, this sort of thing.

A parent: When I met [social worker], my whole outlook on Social Services changed. They were there for me. They have been there every time for me. I had a real barrier about them . . . they've always done good for me every time. I've never had to moan or anything. When I moved I sent her a thank you letter, just for all her help and backup and just for being there really. Today, she's not even my social worker, I phoned her up and she was there to listen . . . she's an absolute diamond.

Contact

Helen, aged 7: I draw pictures for me mum though and they're lovely. I did a love letter for me dad and mum.

Children's participation in decision-making

Tom, aged 13: She [the social worker] came and talked to me . . . just went over what was being talked about and asked me what I thought of it. My mum had told me, like, but I was glad that she [the social worker] did too.

Short-term accommodation

Neil, aged 9: I don't know really. I think I feel happier, sort of less worried. I don't get so tired now. My dad says I'm easier to deal with.

Dave, aged 10: It did seem to help my mum . . . I suppose she could relax a bit. Things got much more sorted out . . . she just got a lot more relaxed.

Section II

A. Study summaries

In the first part of Section II we present summaries of the 24 studies included in the overview chapters. These have been prepared in consultation with the researchers. They highlight a selection of key findings but cannot substitute for a careful reading of the full reports. Each summary begins with the title and the authors of the main publication arising from the study. This is followed by a brief description of how the study was carried out, an overview of the main findings and an indication of their relevance for current policy and practice.

The 24 research studies

1

Making Sense of Section 17: Implementing Services for Children in Need within the 1989 Children Act

Jane Aldgate and Jane Tunstill

Published by HMSO (1995)

> This study addressed a key aspect of the Children Act 1989, the replacement of the relatively narrow concept of preventing children from being received into local authority care, with a broader duty under section 17 to support families through the provision of services for children in need.

Study design

This was one of the earliest studies commissioned by the Department of Health into the implementation of the Children Act. It was a short project designed to obtain a national picture of the range of approaches that authorities were adopting to implement section 17. The findings were based on the results of a postal survey sent in autumn 1992 to all 108 social services departments in England, of whom 82 replied, and on in-depth interviews with senior and middle management in ten local authorities. The researchers looked at four main topics: how local authorities had tried to assess the extent of need; which children and families were given priority for receiving services; what kind of services were offered; and how far social services departments had collaborated with other agencies in defining and meeting need.

Key findings

- Most local authorities were finding it very difficult to estimate the number of children in need, and information systems were poor.

- Resources were focused on 'high-risk' families at the expense of promoting the welfare of a broader group of children through the provision of family support services.

- Few authorities defined children as 'in need' if they were living in substandard housing, were truanting or excluded from school, or lived in low-income families.

- There was some evidence of a national shift towards a mixed economy of provision within children's services.

- There was substantial variation between authorities in the amount of interagency working, and this needed to be developed.

Estimating the extent of need

Most local authorities had found the task of estimating how many children should be regarded as 'in need' a difficult one, although it is an essential first step in order to plan how services should be provided. Few authorities could draw on an effective system for collecting and analysing statistics, especially when these were obtained by districts in different ways and not pulled together by a central team for planning purposes. Although computer databases were increasingly being introduced, their effectiveness was often limited by technical problems and insufficient staff time to analyse and make use of the information. The challenge was not only a technical one; some authorities clearly found the forward-looking notion of ascertaining need alien to their usual practice of monitoring need based on the level of existing services and numbers of referrals; and there were concerns about identifying levels of need that could then not be met. Assessments were very social services based, with few authorities seeming to use information on educational matters to help them judge the extent of need, such as school exclusions and truanting.

Establishing priorities

The second task for authorities was to establish priorities for service provision. The intention of the Children Act was to encourage local authorities to offer support to a wide range of children and families, but this study found (like others since), that most authorities were continuing to put most of their efforts and resources into identifying and providing services for 'high-risk' families, at the expense of promoting the welfare of a broader group of children through the provision of family support. The majority of authorities had not included as 'children in need' those who research has suggested are at risk within the community, such as child truants, children living in substandard conditions and those from low-income families. Whilst three-quarters of the authorities gave high priority to children at risk of harm, at risk of neglect or who were being looked after, only one in eight gave high priority to children living in homes where the gas, water or electricity was disconnected or where the child was excluded from school. In fact, there was a common misperception that the statutory duty to provide for children in need referred only to cases for which the local authority already had some responsibility, in particular child protection, and that family support and preventive services were some kind of optional extra, to be offered if resources allowed, rather than part of the same continuum of services for children in need.

Providing services

The third area that the researchers considered was how local authorities were carrying out their new duty to provide a broad range of services to support families, either directly or by facilitating the provision of services by voluntary organisations and others. They concluded that there was a broad range of services on offer, although it was difficult to say much about the quantity or quality of this on the basis of the postal survey, and that there was some evidence of a national shift towards a mixed economy of service provision.

Social Services departments seemed to be retaining control of services such as the provision of accommodation and investigative work, but were starting to develop partnerships with other agencies in order to offer services such as after-school provision and community-based youth activities (in partnership with education and leisure services) and family centres (with voluntary organisations). However, although there was a fairly wide range of services on offer, they were generally targeted on those children assessed as being at risk of significant harm, with only a minority of authorities managing to open up services to a wider group.

A corporate approach

Finally, the study looked at the extent to which local authorities had succeeded in developing a corporate strategy for delivering services to children. The amount of joint working between departments varied substantially, and depended largely on the strength of links before the Act. Where good relationships already existed between different agencies, these had provided a sound basis from which to move to a more corporate approach. Where links were poor, old barriers had proved more difficult to break down. However, most social services departments had embraced the spirit of the Act by consulting with other organisations, such as health and education, and were beginning to involve voluntary agencies too. The researchers concluded that there was 'much to be applauded' in the way authorities had responded to the need for closer interagency working, but that this needed to be built on and developed. In particular, it was much more common for authorities to consult over specific issues (such as the register for disabled children) than to develop wider partnerships involving joint planning of services to support children and their families. Also more needed to be done to involve the users of services, which in general remained 'an aspiration in the back of planners' minds rather than an ongoing reality'.

Some local authorities had clearly seen the Act as an opportunity to rethink their service provision and develop a new child care policy within the philosophy of the Act, but others – the majority – were responding in a more limited way, by reformulating their existing duties and adding in some new ones. The central shift in the balance of service provision between child protection and family support had yet to be achieved.

Relevance now

This study showed the difficulties that local authorities experienced in the early days of implementing the Act, especially with adopting a broader, more corporate approach to planning and delivering children's services. There have been many government initiatives since to encourage interagency working, such as mandatory Children's Services Plans, Sure Start and (in Wales) Children and Youth Partnerships, and some authorities are exploring the use of sophisticated IT approaches to mapping need. However, there are still problems with agreeing on common definitions of children in need, and with re-focusing children's services towards family support.

2

Supporting Families through Short-term Fostering

Jane Aldgate and Marie Bradley

Published by The Stationery Office (1999)

> This study is about a particular kind of family support that local authorities can offer under section 20 of the Children Act 1989. It provides for children to have short-term breaks away from home, defined as no more than four weeks at a time or 90 days over a year with the same carer. Such short-term placements have traditionally been offered to families of disabled children, but this study investigated their use for other children in need.

Study design

This intensive study of 60 children explored the expectations and outcomes of this particular form of family support from the perspectives of the different parties involved: parents, children, carers, social workers and other professionals. Using a 'before and after' design the researchers traced the progress of 60 children and their families, who were recruited sequentially to the study in four different parts of the country. Parents, children and social workers were interviewed when the service was about to be taken up and then again six to nine months later, or when the arrangement ended if that was sooner. Standardised psychometric tests were administered to parents and children at the start and end of the period to serve as outcome measures, and carers were also interviewed at the second point.

Key findings

- Families using the service were all living in circumstances of considerable stress.

- Parents were very positive about the service and felt it had helped them gain more control over their lives.

- Children had some reservations, but by the end most were reasonably happy with the placement.

- The community basis and voluntary nature of the service helped to make it acceptable to parents.

- More attention needed to be paid to arrangements for ending the service.

- Social workers played a key role in holding the arrangements together.

- For parents with chronic needs, the key to success was the combination of breaks plus other social work support.

The families

The families using the service were all living in circumstances of considerable stress. Most were on very low incomes, with few sources of emotional and practical support and a high incidence of health problems. They were definitely 'in need', but could be divided into those who were facing particular crises but normally coped (acute cases) and those with more ongoing, chronic difficulties who were often already known to the social services departments. For the former, short-term accommodation on its own was generally enough to prevent early stresses becoming more serious, but for parents with more chronic needs the key to success was the combination of breaks plus other services, including social work support for themselves and sometimes direct work with the children.

Both groups of parents judged the short-term accommodation service to be a resounding success. They thought it had helped them to address health problems, relationships with partners if they had them, and problems of social isolation. They felt that breaks had given them a chance to build informal support networks, both through re-establishing links with extended family and friends and through developing links in the community via the carers, who mostly lived in their own neighbourhood. Parents described feeling more in control of their lives, and said the breaks had helped them to get things more in perspective. On a more objective level the placements were also shown to work, since only 2 of the 60 failed to prevent family breakdown. Social workers were slightly more cautious in their evaluation than families, but even so they believed their original aims for the placement had been met in practically two-thirds of the cases.

The children

The children were more ambivalent in their views. The older ones could appreciate the value of the breaks for their family but were less sure for themselves. Many children worried about what would happen without them at home, about being rejected and not wanted back, and about practical issues like not being able to watch favourite TV programmes or having to eat food they didn't like. Children over 5 often felt homesick, and coped with this by wanting to be alone – not as a rejection of their carer family, but as a way of coming to terms with their feelings. By the end of the placement, however, most children were more positive about the experience, and with one or two exceptions their needs did not appear to have been subordinated to the needs of their parents.

The social workers

The study also looked at the social work processes that form an essential link between the principles and regulations of the Children Act and successful outcomes for children and families, such as how parents access the service, how social workers consult and work with parents and children, and how the planning and reviewing process is carried out. The findings were broadly positive. Although parents had often found it hard to get information about family support services, two-thirds had no difficulty in accepting short-term accommodation for their children once it was offered, partly because many had positive experiences with social services in the past (such as being offered child-minding or day care) and so did not perceive social workers in a 'child rescue' role. It was harder for new families without such previous links or for those subject in the past to child protection enquiries, but a model of referral that worked particularly well was when health visitors based within the community and trusted by families were able to refer them directly.

Once families had accepted the service, family support social workers played an important role in holding the arrangements together and managing the placement. The consultation process specified in the *Guidance and Regulations* seemed to be working well. Almost all parents felt they had participated fully in the planning meeting and had helped to shape the child care plan. Social workers often underestimated the extent to which parents had felt consulted, and the researchers suggest that the concept of partnership needs to be sensitive to different ways of involving parents. Some may be content to be quietly present and consulted; others may need help to rehearse their views prior to the meeting so that they feel confident to express themselves in public.

The one aspect of short-term accommodation arrangements that was unsatisfactory was the way in which they were ended. Too often the carer was left with responsibility for managing the ending of the placement without social work support. When a family had been offered six weekend breaks but was still desperate for support, it was very difficult for carers to say good-bye, and parents had no chance to reflect on what had been achieved. Parents, children and carers all found this a difficult time, and there was a clear need for a more formal and symbolic ending.

What worked

A number of factors helped to make the short-term accommodation services in the study a success. First, this was a positive service being offered to families on a voluntary basis, which was greatly appreciated. Second, it was a community-based service, which meant that parents and carers lived in the same area, used the same shops and schools, and parents could identify with the carers and see them as role models. They saw the carers as 'like us, but without the problems'. Third, the carers were carefully recruited, often from child-minders who were used to offering a service on a business basis to families, and they were reasonably well supported by social workers. Social workers also tended to choose families whom they felt would be able to make good use of short-term breaks, and they were unlikely to offer this particular form of family support to very chaotic or disorganised families who would find it difficult to sustain the arrangement, to families where children were at risk of serious harm, to children with severe behavioural problems, or as a crisis resource. Most importantly, the input of social workers was crucial in effecting a positive outcome for parents and children. Successful short-term accommodation offered not just relief from stress for harassed parents, but also a social work service that attempted to strengthen families. Social workers worked in partnership with parents, undertook direct work with children and casework with parents, organised and supported the placement, and worked collaboratively with other professionals on behalf of the family.

Relevance now

This study exemplifies the value of an approach to children's services that focuses on promoting and safeguarding children's welfare. It uses measurable outcomes to show that this kind of short-term fostering, when well targeted, can bring about changes in levels of family problems and help prevent family breakdown. The *Quality Protects* programme encourages local authorities to develop such provision.[69] The study also underlined the importance of traditional casework and demonstrates how social work is a family support service in its own right, which is valued by parents and children.

3

Moving On:
Young People and Leaving Care Schemes

Nina Biehal, Jasmine Clayden, Mike Stein and Jim Wade
Published by HMSO (1995)

Section 24 of the Children Act 1989 placed new duties upon local authorities to prepare young people for leaving care, and to advise and befriend young people who left care after their sixteenth birthday up to the age of 21. It also provided discretionary powers to offer financial assistance to young people in relation to housing, education, employment or training. Specialist leaving care schemes had been developed in some authorities since the mid-1980s, and this study set out to describe what such schemes offer, which type is most effective in helping young people to move on, and whether the experiences and outcomes for young people using the schemes are better than for those who have not had access to them.

Study design

The study had two stages. The first was a survey of patterns of leaving care in three different English local authorities, based on questionnaires completed by social workers concerning 183 young people aged 16–19 who had left care during a six-month period in 1991 (this represented 91% of all those leaving care during this period). The second was a longitudinal and in-depth qualitative study of the process of leaving care and the support offered to care leavers by four different leaving care schemes. There were 74 young people in this qualitative sample, 45 girls and 29 boys, divided between a 'participating' group (receiving support from a scheme) and a 'comparison' group of non-scheme care leavers. Their experiences during their transition from care to living in the community were charted through interviews with the young people, their social workers and (where applicable) their scheme workers, on leaving care and on two subsequent occasions over the next 18–24 months.

Key findings

● Young people often leave care at the age of 16 or 17, but they are still very vulnerable and need support during their transition to living in the community.

● Seventy-five per cent of young people who had access to a leaving care scheme had positive outcomes after two years in terms of good accommodation, a regular source of income and a sense of purpose.

● Educational and employment outcomes were poor for all care leavers compared to the general population.

● There was no significant difference in outcomes between those who had attended a leaving care scheme and those who had not, but the schemes were working with the more disadvantaged young people who had least support from their families.

● There was no best blueprint for an ideal leaving care scheme. It was more important that a scheme had a clear sense of direction, good management and adequate resources than whether it was located in the statutory or voluntary sector.

Moving on

The study found that young people continue to leave care at a much earlier age than other young people leave home, a quarter of them at just 16. Sometimes this was because their foster or residential placement had broken down, but often it was just assumed that they should move on when they reached 16 or 17. Changes in housing benefit since the research was carried out have created an additional financial incentive for local authorities to discharge a much larger proportion of young people from care at the age of 16, since the Benefit Agency then has to pay their housing costs. Yet they are often a particularly vulnerable group. Many in this study had experienced a high degree of movement and disruption during the time they were 'looked after', and over two-thirds had spent four or more years in substitute care. They were thus dependent on social services to equip, prepare and support them in their key transition to adulthood.

The schemes

The four leaving care schemes all played a major part in this 'moving on' process, helping young people to plan their futures, providing follow-up support and meeting accommodation needs. Between them, the schemes offered directly managed accommodation in trainer flats or specialist hostels, 'floating support schemes', arranged access to supported lodgings or hostels provided by other agencies and arranged and supported young people in independent tenancies. Even for those young people experiencing the greatest instability, continuity of support by schemes often prevented a descent into homelessness or provided a rapid escape from it. The analysis of accommodation outcomes showed not only that leaving care schemes were working with those who had the most unstable early housing careers, but also that they were able to help the vast majority find good accommodation within two years.

Education and work

Schemes were less successful in counteracting the poor educational histories of many of the young people. Half of the young people in the study were unemployed within a few months of leaving care and nearly two-thirds failed to establish a stable career pattern, facing periods of short-term casual work interspersed with episodes of training and unemployment. As a result, most were living on or near benefit levels. The developmental role of the schemes in promoting education, training and employment was less developed than other areas of their work, and educational and employment outcomes for all care leavers were very poor compared to the general population. Poor attainment was associated with a high degree of movement while being 'looked after', and better educational attainment was achieved by those whose last placement was in foster, rather than residential, care.

Family links

Many of the young people had poor relationships with their families, which ruled out a return home. However, family links were very important to most of them, including links with brothers and sisters, grandparents and other members of their extended family. The leaving care schemes were playing only a minimal role in mediating between young people and their families, tending to assume (often erroneously) that the social workers were still taking responsibility for this. However, the schemes were very active in helping young people develop friendship networks, using their specialist knowledge of local youth and leisure provision as well as running their own groups and drop-in arrangements. This help was highly valued by the young people and was an important aspect of the schemes' work, given the links that the research revealed between young peoples' social networks, relationship skills and a secure sense of identity.

There was no best blueprint for an ideal leaving care scheme, and the four schemes differed in perspective, methods of working and the balance sought between 'young person demand-led' and 'planned worker-led' services. It appeared less important whether a scheme was located in the statutory or voluntary sector than it was for it to have a clear sense of direction and a sound managerial and resource framework within which to operate.

Outcomes

Among the 53 young people who remained in the study over the two years, three-quarters were judged to have achieved a broadly positive outcome (in terms of good accommodation, a regular source of income and a sense of purpose), or at least to have made noticeable improvements considering their starting point. There was no clear difference in successful outcomes between those who had attended a leaving care scheme and those who had not. However, given that the schemes were working with the more disadvantaged youngsters, who were far less likely than those in the comparison group to have positive supportive relationships with a parent or other family member, the researchers conclude that such schemes do have a valuable contribution to make in helping local authorities meet their duties and powers under the leaving care sections of the Children Act.

Relevance now

Since the research was completed, the government has enacted new legislation, the Children (Leaving Care) Act 2000, to improve the life chances of young people living in and leaving local authority care. Based on the consultation document *Me, Survive, Out There?*, the Act imposes a new duty on local authorities to assess and meet needs; a new duty to keep in touch with care leavers, young person's advisers and pathway plans; help with education and training; and new financial arrangements. In addition, increasing support for care leavers has been identified as a funding priority under the *Quality Protects* programme[69] 'to ensure that young people leaving care, as they enter adulthood, are not isolated and participate socially and economically as citizens', and within National Priorities Guidance to improve the level of education, employment and training for care leavers. Wider government initiatives to combat social exclusion – especially in respect of homelessness, underachievement in education, training and employment, and teenage parenthood – will also impact upon care leavers. The profile of young people leaving care could not be higher.

Safeguarding Children with the Children Act 1989

Marian Brandon, June Thoburn, Ann Lewis and Ann Way
Published by The Stationery Office (1999)

The term 'significant harm' was introduced in Parts IV and V of the Children Act 1989 to mark the threshold at which courts could intervene in the lives of children. Before a court order can be considered, a child must be suffering or likely to suffer significant harm. This research set out to explore whether children were being protected from maltreatment and neglect under these new provisions, and to address concerns that the emphasis in the Act on working in partnership with parents might be placing some children at increased risk of harm.

Study design

Consecutive cases of all children newly identified as suffering or likely to suffer significant harm were collected over an eight-month period (March 1993 to May 1994), from eight area social services teams in four local authorities. They included rural and urban areas, all with pockets of acute material deprivation. The inner city areas contained above average numbers of people from minority ethnic groups, including refugee families.

A sample of 105 cases of significant or likely significant harm were identified and followed through for a year. Most cases were collected following an initial or a 'repeat incident' child protection conference, but a few were included which did not reach a child protection conference because protective services were already being provided under Part III of the Children Act. Information was collected from case files and interviews with social workers at the time the child was identified for the study and again a year later. The parents of 51 children agreed to allow their child and family to be followed up in detail. These cases (the 'intensive sample') were studied in greater depth, involving additional interviews with other professionals and also with the parents and children themselves, at the start and end of the study, to allow them to tell their own story. Play techniques and observation were used with the youngest children, whilst parents and older children completed a range of standardised scales about their health and well-being.

Outcomes

Of the 105 children in the study, 87 were living at home at the start of the study, and a year later 70 were still living with at least one parent. Legal orders had been used with just over half of the children. There was significant and successful use of informal protection by means of section 20 accommodation and placement with relatives. By the twelve-month stage eighteen were already living in permanent substitute placements (twelve with relatives, four with adoptive families and two were already adopted). Eighteen (19% of those under 5, for whom delay will be the most damaging) were already placed with permanent substitute families. Long-term plans were unclear for only three under-fives and three of those over 5 (6% of the cohort).

The well-being of more than two-thirds of the children had improved by the end of the study, but 55% still had problems. The child protection system was, on the whole, more thorough and consistent at dealing with risk than with need. Although by the end of the study most children had been protected from serious episodes of re-abuse, nearly half were still suffering significant harm and many were in high or moderate need of services to avoid their health or development being 'significantly impaired'. Some children who still needed services to stem significant harm were not getting them. The welfare of all except four of the 48 children under the age of 5 at the start of the study had been safeguarded. (One of these four was in unplanned foster care; three were closely supervised at home but their care at times fell below acceptable standards.) For many of the older children the actual or likely impairment to their health or development was due to their own risk-taking behaviour. This applied to more of the young people who were 'looked after' than to those living with parents or relatives.

Abuse or harm?

The concept of 'significant harm' requires a shift in social work thinking and practice, from a consideration of the *abuse* that is inflicted on the child to one of the *harm* that this causes to the child. The study found that this shift was slow to happen. There was no clear relationship between the abusive behaviour that might have led to a child protection conference and the type of harm the child was likely to suffer. Yet child protection conferences still concentrated on measures to counteract specific acts of maltreatment or neglect and tended to produce protection plans that ignored important causes of harm to the child. For example, violent marital conflict was present in nearly half of the cases and was an important factor contributing to significant harm to the child, but this was overlooked in most child protection plans.

Children with long-standing problems tended not get a concerted service until an often comparatively minor event triggered the child protection system into action. Once significant harm was apparent, there was generally an adequate response to helping the child, but not always to helping other members of the family, especially if the child was removed from their care. Once concerted attention was given to meeting the needs of parents and children, improvements occurred in families that had been known to social services teams but had made no apparent progress for years. There was evidence from cases which were ultimately recognised as significant harm' that earlier provision of services to families of 'children in need' could have prevented situations of stress from deteriorating and resulting in significant harm to the children.

The child protection system

In 42% of the cases the formal child protection assessment and monitoring system was judged necessary, compared with the 73% of cases where it was used. In 33 of the 76 cases where the child's name was entered on the Child Protection Register, the researchers judged that protection via support plans could have been provided just as successfully without registration. They suggest that there should be a 'presumption of no registration', similar to the presumption of 'no order' in court, so that registration would occur only if it was considered to be of positive benefit to the child. In making these decisions, the willingness of parents to become involved in the protection process and the degree of danger to the child would need to be taken into account.

There was little to confirm fears that minimal use of coercion and attempts to work in partnership with parents would put children at increased risk of maltreatment. In all four authorities the welfare and protection of the child was given the highest priority. Because of this, although working in partnership was taken very seriously, only a minority of the parents interviewed in the study felt that they had been involved in the work and the decisions.

Apart from the small number of youngest children for whom permanent out-of-home placement was needed, there was no obvious difference in the interim outcomes between apparently similar cases where coercion and court action were used and where they were not. The study concludes that a more discriminating use of the formal child protection system and the courts could result in a more cost-effective service to the most vulnerable children and free up resources to provide more help to children at an earlier stage of need.

Relevance now

A major recommendation of the study – that the formal child protection procedures should only be triggered if they were necessary in order to safeguard the child's welfare – has been incorporated into the new *Working Together* guidelines.[80] The conclusions do not support the view that large numbers of children are left too long in harmful circumstances, though vigilance is required to stop this happening. Nor was delay in making care plans a feature of this group of 'run-of-the-mill' protection cases. In the spirit of the Act, relatives were playing important short- and long-term protective roles. On the other hand, there is a recent trend towards fewer children being accommodated as part of a short-term protective service and a larger proportion of children being in care on Care Orders. These changes run contrary to the findings of this study.

Expert Evidence in Child Protection Litigation: Where Do We Go From Here?

Julia Brophy with Phil Bates, Louise Brown, Suzanne Cohen, Polly Radcliffe and Christopher J. Wale

Published by The Stationery Office (1999)

The Children Act 1989 and the attendant rules of court changed many aspects of legal proceedings under Part IV – applications for the care and supervision of children. Against a background of criticism about length and drift in care proceedings, the Children Act and rules aimed to increase the control of the court over every aspect of proceedings. Directions appointments were introduced as a mechanism whereby courts were expected to exert direct control over both the content and timetabling of cases. The role of the guardian ad litem as both adviser to the court and representative of the child was also increased. This project, consisting of four separate but interrelated studies, explored the use of expert witnesses by all parties in 'care and related' proceedings following the Act. It also considered how courts exercised control over the use of experts, and the views and practices of experts themselves in providing assessments and opinions in public law proceedings.

Study design

The research was undertaken between 1992 and 1996. It adopted a three-stage multi-method approach using both qualitative and quantitative methods. Stage I of the study consisted of a national postal survey of guardians in England and Wales which focused on guardians' views about the use of experts and the level of satisfaction with the services of experts. The survey also collected extensive information on 557 cases (concerning just under 1,000 children), all of which contained expert evidence. The response rate to the national survey was 71%. Also included in Stage I was a court-based study in one local authority area. This study tracked 65 cases involving 114 children. It focused on the court processing of all 'care and related' applications in five family proceedings courts and one care centre. Stage II of the study was based on in-depth interviews with 35 guardians in three geographically diverse panels in England and included the use of a vignette to explore the guardians' views towards the use of experts. Finally, in-depth interviews were undertaken with seventeen child and adolescent psychiatrists on various aspects of their role as expert witnesses.

Key findings

● The Children Act has improved many aspects of child care proceedings and has strengthened the interdisciplinary nature of child protection litigation.

● However, improvements were undermined by lack of resources and skills, in particular the failure of courts to provide a consistent tribunal to prepare cases for trial, and the failure to reduce the delay incurred by decision to transfer.

● Many parents received poor-quality legal representation and often did not have access to the same experts as the professional parties.

● Joint letters of instruction to experts can be problematic and do not meet many of the weaknesses identified in current procedures.

● Most guardians are experienced and skilled social workers, although relatively few have additional clinical training.

● Guardians now occupy a central and multidimensional role in proceedings, but some of the tasks they have acquired are not entirely compatible.

● Key features to the guardian's successful case management were: independence and flexibility, an ability to draw on high-level practice-based experience and analytical skills and reasoning backed by academic training.

● Child and adolescent psychiatrists provided the majority of expert evidence.

● However, the service as a whole is fragmented and uncoordinated. There was also heavy reliance on consultants undertaking this work outside of NHS provision.

● This meant that work was outside of medical audit; there were no measures for accountability or feedback to clinicians. There was also little evidence of pre- or post-court involvement of clinicians in cases.

The courts

The study demonstrated that in many respects care proceedings under the Children Act 1989 have improved enormously and become a multidisciplinary exercise. Nevertheless, there is little room for complacency. The management of cases by courts suffered because of a lack of information technology and an inability to insist on consistency in the judge, magistrates and justices' clerks hearing directions appointments throughout the life of a care application. The continual attention to improving the quality of instructions to experts was offset by the inability of courts to control the delay incurred when cases were transferred. The movement from largely oral to written evidence has increased the use of child welfare knowledge and child specialists in care proceedings. This has benefited both the work of the court and the children and parents within it, but further changes are needed to capitalise on this process.

Child and family mental health services

The shift towards a multidisciplinary approach to the problem of child abuse/neglect had not been matched by serious attention to the way this type of service is provided by local child and adolescent mental health services (CAMHS). The service continues to rely on a relatively small number of consultants who, historically, have provided much of this service outside of mainstream NHS practice. This method of supplying assessments and reports for courts has serious limitations for the development of this service and for the training and accountability of those who provide it. Consultants themselves indicated a need to review this process and its narrow reliance on a 'forensic' model.

The position of parents

The study raised considerable problems about the position of parents during proceedings. Many received poor-quality legal representation. Certain child psychiatrists were unwilling to accept instructions from parents, which meant that many parents did not have access to the same pool of highly experienced expert witnesses as the professional parties in the proceedings. This was reflected in part by a lack of comprehensiveness and the poor quality of some of the second opinions filed by parents.

Joint instructions of experts

The study raised serious concerns about issues of fairness and social justice and the implications for 'due process' arising from an indiscriminate move towards joint letters of instructions in care proceedings. Rather than providing an example of a continued move towards a more 'inquisitorial' as opposed to an 'adversarial' approach, the findings of the study raised questions about the underlying reasons for this shift and suggested it was essentially driven by cost rather than welfare or justice reasons. Despite pressure from the courts, guardians ad litem and child psychiatrists questioned this shift and its fruitfulness in terms of achieving the aims and objectives of the Children Act. Experts raised serious concerns both for the courts and for their own role in proceedings, including loss of the 'critical factor', which allowed their views to be challenged. Guardians were concerned about maintaining an apparent and a real independence from local authorities when cases demanded additional evidence, and they saw this as critical to successful case management in order to keep parents involved. They were, therefore, very sensitive to the implications of jointly instructing experts with an authority at the very beginning of proceedings and saw it as the responsibility of a local authority in the first instance to acquire evidence necessary to 'prove' their application. This did not mean the guardians would not have an input at this early point. But they saw little advantage to joint instructions if the end result was that the parent effectively withdrew from the proceedings because they perceived the professionals to be united against them, or because they had not had a real opportunity to consider and question the local authority's evidence. If parents were made even more angry and disaffected by their experiences of the legal process, it would be even harder for the authority to work in partnership with them in the future.

The guardian ad litem

The study demonstrates that guardians now occupy a central and multidimensional role in child care proceedings, which arguably moves beyond the role that was envisaged by the original rules governing their appointment. They act as overseer, mediator, negotiator, broker and, in some cases, gatekeeper to the work of experts. They have become something of a 'safety net' in a system where there are some serious shortcomings in the resources and skills of others. Some of these roles are not entirely compatible. Many guardians are very experienced and highly skilled social workers, although relatively few have any additional clinical skills and training. Many cases requiring the use of experts are highly complex. For effective case management, both within and without the courtroom, guardians require a range of analytical and reasoning skills. The researchers argue that these skills must be backed by sound academic training and a high level of practice-based experience, and that independence and flexibility in decision-making hold the key to effective case management.

Because of the resource and skills limitations of some local CAMHS and the resistance of many local services to undertake assessments for court proceedings, many guardians and local authorities looked to 'national' figures to provide expert evidence. This approach creates difficulties where there is a need to instruct someone who can offer some ongoing treatment for children.

Much of the important work and decision-making about the use and choice of certain experts was undertaken outside of court hearings. Guardians, child advocates and others achieved considerable success in these negotiations, but they did not occupy a formal stage in the proceedings. This informality could be advantageous in achieving agreements, but not when decisions had to be taken at breakneck speed in order to try and comply with the needs of courts to demonstrate reductions in the delay in the processing of cases.

Relevance now

This study demonstrates a need for the increased training, availability and accountability of certain experts undertaking assessments of children and parents within public law proceedings. Strong arguments are put for this service being part of rather than peripheral to mainstream NHS practice. The tasks now required of child and adolescent psychiatrists demand an increasingly high level of skills, training and experience, and these may be best acquired within mainstream training and practice.

Considerable additional funding was made available to the under-resourced CAMHS during the early part of 1999, but the government decided not to include public law work in the range of core services CAMHS was committed to supply. However, it is likely that the incorporation of Article 6 of the European Convention on Human Rights (ECHR) into English law through the implementation of the Human Rights Act 1998, in October 2000, will necessitate a further rethink of the supply, training and independence of experts for family proceedings, and of the indiscriminate use of joint letters of instructions to experts. In these circumstances courts are likely to become even more dependent on the development of a high-quality, highly skilled and highly trained 'guardian' service, especially given the absence of any substantive moves towards developing a family justice system and the recent plans to introduce a united family court welfare service. Like the provision of a service of clinical expertise, the guardian service will require appropriate support and funding to fulfil this role.

Policy into Practice: Day Care Services for Children under Eight

Mano Candappa, Julie Bull, Claire Cameron, Peter Moss and Charlie Owen

Published by The Stationery Office (1996)

Whilst much of the Children Act 1989 concerns the service local authorities should offer to children who are in need, looked after or subject to court proceedings, the day care sections of the Act relate to services used by the majority of young children and their families. Day care services for young children (including child-minders, playgroups and private day nurseries) have been registered by local authorities since 1948. The Children Act clarified the duties of local authorities with respect to such services and introduced some new requirements, including annual inspections (Part X), a three-yearly review of day care and educational services for children under 8 (section 19) and a duty to make day care services available to children in need (sections 17 and 18). This study investigated how local authorities had responded to the day care parts of the Act.

Study design

This study had two parts: a monitoring exercise that looked at the process of implementing the day care parts of the Children Act and an evaluation of the impact of the Act in its first few years on services for young children. A stratified random sample of eighteen English local authorities took part, and a linked study was carried out in Wales (Study 20). A variety of methods were used, including document analysis, interviews with key people involved with under-eights services both within local authorities and in voluntary and private organisations (one set of interviews concentrated on the implementation of the Act, another set two years later asked about its impact) and case studies in a small number of authorities on the themes of provision, regulation and co-ordination of day care services. A survey of over 400 child-minders, playgroups and day nurseries was commissioned, which provided the first national evidence of how the Children Act had been experienced by the people who provide day care. The views of parents were not sought directly, but the researchers attempted to collate the findings from parent surveys carried out by local authorities.

Key findings

- The Children Act resulted in some worthwhile improvements to day care services for children under 8, but did not address important issues such as the separation of 'care' and 'education'.

- Communication between agencies and awareness of early years services improved, largely through the mechanism of the section 19 review.

- Playgroups, child-minders and day nurseries accepted the principle of regulation and were mostly satisfied with the standards set by local authorities.

- Workloads of regulatory staff varied widely between authorities.

- Some aspects of regulation were proving difficult, such as assessing 'fitness' to look after young children and attitudes towards equal opportunities.

- Few authorities had used their power to cancel or refuse registration.

- Independent day care providers were generally willing to accept 'children in need' who were placed and paid for by the local authority. Nearly half of the playgroups and nurseries and a quarter of child-minders had at some time done so.

- Most local authorities were unable to offer adequate support and training to day care providers.

Impact of the Children Act

The overall conclusion of this study was that the Children Act was evolutionary rather than revolutionary in relation to day care services for young children. It built on existing policy but did not address long-standing issues of concern to those working in the field, such as the division of services into those offering 'care' and 'education' or the issue of how the responsibility and costs of day care services are shared. However, the Act did result in a number of worthwhile improvements in day care services for children under 8. Overall, they gained a higher recognition and profile within local authorities. The Children Act introduced the mechanism of the section 19 review, which for the first time placed a statutory duty on social services and education departments to co-operate in reviewing and planning services for children under 8. As a result, most authorities now have more information about day care services, both what is available and what is needed. The Act also encouraged a process of better communication and closer working between local authority departments and with the voluntary and private sector, with the section 19 review again playing an important role, although most authorities felt they had failed to find adequate ways of involving minority ethnic communities.

The Children Act reinforced the importance of day care services as a form of support for children in need and encouraged local authorities to think creatively about how to provide such services, for instance through developing family centres in partnership with voluntary child care organisations or through placing and supporting children in local community services. A surprisingly high proportion of voluntary and private day care services (around half of the playgroups and day nurseries and nearly a quarter of the child-minders) had at some time taken a child referred by a social worker or health visitor. There was considerable willingness among independent providers to offer such a service to children in need, but at the same time there appeared to be insufficient local authority support to enable this potential resource to be fully used. The position of disabled children was judged by most local authority policy officers to have improved since the Children Act required them to be treated first and foremost as 'children in need'. However, the study found that there had been little change in the amount of local authority day care provision for children in need, largely because planned developments had frequently been offset by budget cuts.

Regulation of day care

The revision and broadening of the regulatory system was one of the most significant aspects of the Act for day care services and was initially a cause for concern among voluntary and private day care providers, who feared that stricter requirements might put them out of business. The study found that these fears had not been realised. The survey of day care providers showed almost unanimous support for the principle of regulation and a general acceptance that the standards required were 'about right', although day nurseries were more critical than either child-minders or playgroups.

At the local authority level, the registration and inspection of day care for young children was being taken on by inspectors in independent 'arms length' units in a number of authorities, rather than by day care officers based in child care or under-eights teams within social services departments. These arrangements reflected different views about the relationship between inspecting and supporting services. Workloads of regulatory staff varied widely between authorities. However, a recurring theme was that current staffing levels did not allow local authorities to offer adequate support and training to independent day care providers, partly as a consequence of the support function being only a power, rather than a duty, under the Children Act. On the whole, the Children Act had led to improvements in the regulatory process and probably in standards of care, but some areas remained difficult to implement. These included assessing if someone was a 'fit person' to look after young children, assessing day care providers' attitudes towards equal opportunities and offering sufficient support to help services improve.

When the Children Act was first introduced it was welcomed by many in the day care field as it provided local authorities with more 'teeth' to get rid of poor-quality services, but in practice few authorities had used their power to cancel or refuse registration. This was partly because officers preferred to work with service providers over a period of time, or to counsel them out of the registration process early on if necessary. But it was also because it was widely believed that there would be little chance of winning a case in court, especially following a 1993 government circular, which instructed authorities to be 'flexible' in the standards they applied, and the case of the 'Sutton smacker', a child-minder who successfully appealed against the council's decision to refuse registration because she was prepared to smack a child.

The study concludes that the Children Act has had a 'worthwhile but limited' impact on services for young children and raises some serious questions about the future of policy on early childhood services and the consequences of the Children Act for this field.

Relevance now

The findings of this study are highly relevant to current attempts to develop and integrate early childhood services, for instance through the National Childcare Strategy, the transfer of responsibility for regulating day care services from the Department of Health to the Department for Education and Employment, the requirement to produce Early Years Development and Childcare Plans and the Sure Start programme. Many of the issues raised by this study have become central to the policy agenda of the current government, for example the relationship between education and day care, the role of regulation and the need for stronger information on the supply and demand for services. The messages about what is needed to produce a coherent, integrated early childhood service are particularly topical in the light of the many new initiatives to support and develop services for families and children.

7

Fostering Family Contact:
A Study of Children, Parents and Foster Carers

Hedy Cleaver

Published by The Stationery Office (2000)

When children are looked after by a local authority, unless contact orders stipulate otherwise, the Children Act 1989 presumes reasonable contact between separated children and their parents. However, a legal requirement need not necessarily result in a change of practice. This study explores the impact of the Children Act 1989 on contact between foster children and their families.

Study design

The study was set in six local authorities and had two parts: a retrospective survey of 152 social work files to identify whether practice regarding contact had changed since the Children Act; and a qualitative study of 33 foster children aged 5–12 years who social workers expected to be looked after for at least four months. Interviews with children, key family members, foster carers and social workers were conducted six weeks after placement and twelve months later. Outcomes were measured using a number of dimensions, including placement stability, levels of contact and the children's behaviour and well-being.

Key findings

- The amount of contact foster children have with their parents has increased considerably since the Children Act 1989.

- Home was the most popular meeting place for children and families.

- Carers were more likely to promote contact if they were trained, understood the purpose of contact, had a good relationship with the child and felt well supported.

- Indirect contact was also important to keep emotional links alive.

- Parental contact was positively associated with the child's behaviour and well-being when fostered and with reunification.

The frequency of contact

The implementation of the Children Act 1989 has had a fundamental impact on contact between foster children and their families. Prior to the Act only some 11% of the children saw their parents on a weekly basis. Findings from the survey of social work files suggest that this has increased fourfold. None the less, the proportion of children (a third) who were not in contact with a parent has changed little, although only 17% were cut off entirely from all their family members. Contact with mothers was most common (nearly two-thirds of the children) followed by contact with separated siblings (nearly half). Visits with fathers were less common and rarely occurred when families had broken up. Although contact with wider kin was not the norm, a fifth of the children saw a grandparent, aunt or uncle. The greater emphasis since the Children Act on ensuring stability of education for looked after children also meant that most foster children were able to continue their school-based friendships with peers and teachers.

The venue for contact

The survey of social work case files showed that approximately half of the sample either saw their family at home (24%) or at the foster home (23%). Social services venues, such as nurseries or family centres, served as meeting places for the children and their families in 38% of the cases. The qualitative study found that home visits were valued by both the children and the parents because they offered continuity. Children were able to see other relatives and friends, re-acquaint themselves with their neighbourhood and engage in typical family activities, while parents were enabled to continue actively to parent their child. Contact at the foster home was met with mixed feelings: children were often positive, but parents expressed less satisfaction and often resented carers for usurping their role. Social services venues were generally used when contact required supervision. Supervised contact was often brokered with parents in order to avoid a Care Order and more formal restrictions. Social services venues were seldom popular meeting places because they offered little privacy and restricted everyday family interactions.

Partnership with parents

The majority of families in the study were experiencing considerable adversity, and social workers encountered a great deal of difficulty in translating the Children Act principle of working in partnership with parents into practice. The findings from the qualitative study suggest greater levels of involvement by parents in some aspects of the planning process than in others. Few parents felt they had any control over whether or not their child was looked after or who the child should live with. Moreover, parents were rarely actively involved in preparing their child for the placement or accompanying the child to the foster home. But working in partnership with parents proved important because involvement in early decisions about placement and contact was positively associated with parents remaining in contact with their children.

Supporting contact

Social services departments played an important role in promoting and supporting contact. Regular social work visits to parents were associated with continued parental contact with children. With regard to the contact visits themselves, social services enabled contact through supplying the venues and resourcing transport. In 60% of the cases included in the qualitative study, parents believed social workers had helped them to keep in touch with their absent child. In contrast, many of the factors associated with *lack* of parental contact were indicative of chronic parenting difficulties, such as a long history of social services concerns about the child, two or more previous care episodes, the child being subject to a Care Order, poor attachment and parental drug and alcohol misuse. In such cases, a lack of parental contact may well be appropriate.

Involving children in the decision-making process

To work in partnership with parents may prove difficult, but ascertaining the child's wishes and feelings (a local authority duty under the Children Act 1989) can be particularly problematic when children's experiences have left them with a deep distrust of adults. Effective communication is especially hard when children are young or have communication difficulties. The findings from the qualitative study of children aged 5–12 suggest that in two-thirds of the cases children were ill-informed about their forthcoming placement, and only half of the children fostered with strangers had met their prospective carers prior to placement.

Indirect contact

Contact between the children and their families was not restricted to visiting. Links were also kept alive through thoughts and feelings and through more physical methods such as telephoning and letter writing. Emotional ties were also strengthened through special activities and projects, such as treasured toys, photographs and clothing. In half of the cases telephones were regularly used to connect children and families. Calls were a source of information and reassurance. Postal contact, although not common, was highly prized. The low rate of letter writing should be set within the context of frequent visiting and high levels of parental illiteracy. Talking is a further way in which bonds of affiliation may be kept alive, and around half of the children talked to someone about home and family. The qualities that children valued in deciding who to talk to included friendliness, trust, empathy and a willingness to listen.

The role of foster carers

The principle of contact between children and their families was accepted by all foster carers. When parental contact ceased, this was usually the result of the parents' behaviour and wishes rather than because carers blocked or hindered contact. However, contact was rarely a trouble-free process. Three types of problems dominated the carers' perception of contact: parents who demanded too much of carers' time for their own needs; parents who played the child off against the carer; and erratic and unreliable visiting. The role carers played in contact arrangements varied, but a number of factors were associated with carers promoting contact: formal training, a shared understanding with social workers of the aim and duration of placement and purpose of contact, a good relationship with the child and being well supported themselves.

Outcomes

The survey of social work files showed that four years after admission 41% of the children were living at home or with relatives, a quarter were with their original carers, 5% were living independently, 12% had been adopted and 17% were living with new carers or in residential care. The factors associated with children's well-being and adjustment while fostered were strong parent/child attachment relationships and continued parental contact. These were also associated with the likelihood of reunification.

The qualitative study suggested that a return home may not always be in the child's best interests. In half of the cases the parent/child relationship remained problematic, with parents, carers and social workers holding reservations about the homecoming. Return was more successful when the following factors applied: good parent/child attachment, well-motivated parent(s), well-resourced and purposive contact, the contact was a positive experience for both parent and child and the return was part of a shared plan. In more than half of the cases included in the qualitative sample, children had experienced a change of placement. For many children a single, well-planned placement move, particularly when children went to live with relatives, had a positive impact on their well-being and benefited contact. Although a stable placement has frequently been used as an indicator of a successful placement, the findings from the qualitative study suggest this presumption is unsafe. Whilst half of the children in stable placements improved their relationship with their carers, the remaining children failed to form a secure, stable, affectionate relationship.

Relevance now

Accommodation is generally used as a service of last resort. To set accommodation within the context of family support would encourage a more imaginative attitude to contact. In cases where parents' chronic difficulties prevent them from fully parenting their child but there is evidence of good attachments, accommodation and contact should be used to promote ongoing shared-care arrangements.

Children in Need:
Family Support under the Children Act 1989

Matthew Colton, Charlotte Drury and Margaret Williams
Published by Gower (1995)

This study examined the provision of services for children in need and their families under Part III of the Children Act 1989, primarily in Wales but also in England. It was carried out before local government reorganisation in Wales in 1996 and looked at policies and plans in all eight authorities, followed by an in-depth study of services provided to children in need in two Welsh authorities.

Study design

The first part of the project was based on an analysis of local authority policy documents and interviews with leading child care managers in all eight social services departments in Wales. Information was also gathered by questionnaire from voluntary child care agencies, community and consumer groups and other statutory agencies in Wales about the extent to which they linked with social services departments over children in need. The progress of the Welsh local authorities in implementing Part III of the Act was later compared with the progress made by eight similar authorities in England. This analysis of policies and plans was followed by an in-depth study in two Welsh authorities on how need was actually assessed and responded to in practice. This involved interviews with over 100 social workers and their managers and with 122 parents and 123 children (from families on social workers' lists) to discover how far they felt their needs were being properly met and their views taken into account.

Key findings

- Guidance on interpreting definitions of need was generally unavailable, and social workers resorted to using materials designed for child protection work.

- Managers would have liked to give a higher priority to pro-active, preventive work than they felt able to do in practice.

- Some progress had been made with interagency co-operation, but problems remained.

- Almost two-thirds of the parents were satisfied with the help they received from social workers, and they especially valued emotional support. Children were also positive about their social workers.

- The concept of partnership sometimes resulted in parents being left with responsibilities that they did not feel ready to assume.

- Services focused on a particular child, often at the expense of the family unit.

- Cultural issues were not given a high priority and were often seen as irrelevant by social workers.

Local authority policies

The study found wide variation in the length, quality and content of the policy documents produced by social services departments. Local authorities had generally followed the definition of need given in the Children Act but offered very little, if any, guidance to social workers on how to interpret the concepts in practice. In the absence of such guidance social workers tended to fall back on their own individual value systems and experience, or resorted to readily available material designed for use in child protection work. This had a number of potential disadvantages: provision could become inconsistent, with some families receiving services whilst others in similar circumstances did not; and the emphasis on child protection was reinforced at the expense of broader notions of prevention and family support.

Defining need

At the time the research was carried out social services departments were clearly finding it difficult to develop a definition of need that would maintain the spirit of the Children Act while ensuring that the children in greatest need were adequately served. Managers generally wanted to give more emphasis to preventive work, but in practice they concentrated resources on children at risk of abuse and neglect, as demonstrated by their rankings of categories of children who would have priority for services under ideal circumstances and those who had priority in practice. Pro-active prevention work came much higher up their 'ideal' than their 'actual' list. The level of services available to support families was judged by both managers and social workers to be generally inadequate, especially with regard to family centres, social and recreational facilities, suitable housing and day care. They thought that those most likely to be affected by inadequate service provision were children living in poverty, children in unsatisfactory home conditions and children with disabilities, whilst children at risk of abuse or neglect were most likely to receive the services they needed.

Interagency working

Like many other studies, this research found that some progress had been made with interagency co-operation but that problems remained. In particular, conflicts had arisen over referrals, lack of understanding between agencies of each other's roles and disagreements over who should take responsibility for particular clients. Pressure on resources tended to promote conflict, as agencies were anxious to pass responsibility for clients to someone else.

Partnership with parents

In respect of local authority partnership with parents the results were also mixed. Most parents did feel that they had participated in decision-making. They had been asked how they felt about their children going into care; they had been invited to and had attended reviews; they had been encouraged to express their opinions; and people had taken notice of what they had said. However, a quarter had agreed to 'voluntary' care of their child because they thought they had no choice, and some parents (and older children) felt they were invited to reviews simply to 'rubber stamp' decisions made by the authority. This was especially the case when they were left until last before being asked for an opinion, when there were a lot of people present at the review and when a number of the people present were unfamiliar.

The value of social work

Interviews with parents provided encouraging comments on the extent to which social work input was valued. Two-thirds of the parents felt that Social Services had helped them in bringing up their children, and they particularly appreciated the provision of emotional support. Their satisfaction seemed more closely linked to how far they felt social workers were supportive and doing their best to meet the family's needs than to the actual services provided or even the amount of service they received. The majority of children were also positive about their relationships with their social workers, believing the social worker would help them with problems if possible and selecting the social worker as one of the very few people with whom they would discuss a personal problem.

Sharing responsibility

However, the concept of 'partnership' held by social services departments did not always coincide with what parents thought it should mean. Whilst social workers saw the purpose of partnership as supporting parents in the exercise of their responsibilities, some parents felt that social services were pushing back on to them responsibilities that should belong to the state, for example responsibility for truanting, pregnant, drug-addicted or delinquent youths. Parents sometimes felt that children were returned to them before they were ready to cope. They were also critical of the way the social workers' attention usually focused on a particular child and ignored the needs of the rest of the family.

When children were accommodated away from home in particular, siblings were often jealous of the treats and benefits the accommodated child enjoyed, and parents resented financial support being available to foster parents but not to themselves or relatives. Similarly, some parents with disabled children, while grateful for the help they were receiving, felt that this help should be extended to their other children whose 'normal' lives were being disrupted by their sibling's disability.

The element of partnership most lacking between agencies and families was the sharing of information. Only 29% of the children interviewed felt that their social workers had told them things that they needed to know, and only 13% of the parents felt that they knew enough about the kinds of services available to help them (from other agencies as well as from Social Services).

Responding to diversity

The study found that social services departments were attempting to comply with the requirements of the Children Act by formulating general policies to the effect that the ethnic, cultural, linguistic and religious needs of children would be taken into account when providing services. However, they had drawn up few detailed policies on how this might be put into practice; nor had they developed systems for collecting data on the background of service users. Cultural issues were rarely given a high priority and were often seen as irrelevant. Of 103 social workers who had been provided with training on ethnic and religious issues (according to their managers), only 25% seemed to be aware that they had been trained.

The researchers conclude that progress in implementing Part III of the Act has been uneven and that the basic contextual requirements for an effective system of family support are lacking. They note that action is needed at a national level to reduce social inequality and tackle primary poverty, but they also recommend steps that local authorities could take, such as decentralising family support services on a local neighbourhood basis and giving family centres a more pivotal role.

Relevance now

The study provides useful information on taking forward strategies for developing a common definition of need, which is especially relevant in the light of the new framework of assessment for children. Like other studies in the series, this study provides support for the philosophy of a broader definition of need and for agencies to work together to promote children's welfare, a philosophy that is now incorporated into the framework for post-qualifying training in child care and the framework for the assessment of children in need. In line with the *Quality Protects* and *Children First* initiatives,[69, 106] the study highlights the importance of incorporating the views of children and families into service planning and delivery.

9

Parental Perspectives on Care Proceedings

Pam Freeman and Joan Hunt

Published by The Stationery Office (1998)

A key principle underpinning the Children Act 1989 is the importance of working in partnership with parents. This includes families at the far end of the child protection spectrum, families for whom all preventive resources appear to have failed or else a dramatic incident of abuse has catapulted them into the court process. This study examined the extent to which the new emphasis on working with families was reflected in the experiences of parents who are unwilling but key players in the legal process. It forms one strand of a project evaluating the impact of the Children Act on the use of the courts in child protection (see Study 12).

Study design

This study used in-depth, semi-structured interviews to explore the perspectives of 35 parents and adult relatives in 25 families in which care proceedings were brought under the Children Act. These were drawn from the 83 families involved in Study 12. Compared to the sampling pool, this group of parents over-represented families who had been involved with social services for some considerable time over against those who arrived in court as a result of a crisis or were subject to compulsory emergency protection.

Key findings

- Parents often held very negative views of the child protection system, especially where court orders were sought on children who had already been accommodated on a voluntary basis.

- The services offered to families before they reached court were seen as inadequate and focused only on the child's needs rather than on those of the parents.

- Few parents felt they had participated in decision-making even when they had attended case conferences.

- Most parents were ill-prepared for court proceedings and felt marginalised and unsupported. Many found the court experience intimidating and confusing.

- The majority of solicitors representing parents did not have specific expertise in this area of law.

- Little support was available for parents after care proceedings had ended, whether or not they retained their child.

- Despite the generally negative views held by parents, there was potential for improving their experience of the court process.

Parents' views

Parents brought to court extremely negative views of their contact with the child protection system. They often denied the legitimacy of statutory intervention, even when acknowledging that there was some cause for concern. Parents suffering from mental illness and learning difficulties felt particularly unjustly stigmatised at being drawn into a system that labelled them as child abusers. The services offered to families before they reached court were seen as inadequate and overly focused on the child. Key issues for parents were poor housing, the impact of their own damaging childhood experiences and the effects of domestic violence; but they felt that their own needs, which in part created the parenting difficulties, were often ignored by social workers.

Few parents had any sense of having participated in decision-making or having been engaged in partnership with social services prior to court action. Although they welcomed the opportunity to attend case conferences, most had felt unable to make proper use of this and found the experience confusing, intimidating and demeaning. Estranged fathers and members of the extended family felt especially marginalised at this stage of the process. Parents were particularly negative when court orders had been sought on children who were already accommodated, usually as an alternative to earlier court action. Such parents felt they had been coerced and manipulated into accepting accommodation in the first instance and deceived about the agency's intentions.

Preparation for court

Most parents were practically, as well as psychologically, ill-prepared for proceedings and voiced a unanimous need for more information, including written information that they could take in later when they felt less stressed. They found the often lengthy period that their case was before the court highly stressful, and they felt that delays increased the problem of managing their relationships with separated children. In court, few parents gave oral evidence and those who did felt unable to do it well. What they most wanted was to be able to put their view of things directly to the judge or magistrates. They were mostly satisfied with the service provided by solicitors, despite the fact that few solicitors representing them had specific expertise in this area of law, and with the fairness of their treatment by the judiciary. Many of the children were looked after or accommodated in foster homes for at least part of the court proceedings. Although there were a number of complaints about foster placements, almost all were situational: inappropriate ethnic matching, separation of siblings, distance from home, disruption of schooling or of friendship groups. Almost all the parents spoke positively about the carers themselves. However, supervised contact was universally loathed.

After court

In the aftermath of care proceedings, whatever their outcome, parents were frequently in a state of turmoil, struggling to come to terms with what had happened and to rebuild their lives. They had frequently lost the informal support of extended family or the local community, and were ambivalent or hostile to continuing involvement with social services. Parents who needed help with their children in future said they would be unlikely to turn to social services and would prefer to turn instead to health professionals or voluntary agencies.

What worked

Despite the generally negative view of Social Services, there was evidence that where social workers were perceived by parents as honest and sensitive, able to listen and communicate in a straightforward way, they were able to turn around relationships that had initially been hostile. A key theme throughout the research was the need for practitioners to be honest and straightforward rather than to fudge issues, even though parents may be caused initial distress. Other suggestions for improving the experience of families involved in care proceedings were an information pack for parents, appropriate training for all solicitors engaging in this area of work, an independent supporter to guide and support parents through the court process and a less intimidatory and impersonal court system. One of the clear messages from the research was that small indicators of respect or concern − a foster parent asking permission to take some action in relation to a child, a social worker assisting with transport, a judge looking at the family photographs − were of great importance to the parents, probably far more than the practitioners realised.

Relevance now

Working in partnership with parents at the 'heavy end' of child protection is difficult. The insights this study provides into the experiences of parents involved in care proceedings have a continuing relevance in the promotion of good practice by all those involved in the child protection and family justice systems.

10

Planning to Care:
Regulation, Procedure and Practice under the Children Act 1989

Roger Grimshaw and Ruth Sinclair

Published by the National Children's Bureau (1997)

Care planning is central to effective social work intervention with children and young people. In recognition of this, the Children Act 1989 introduced a new requirement that every young person who is looked after by the local authority should have an individual care plan, and that this should be reviewed regularly. The *Guidance and Regulations* accompanying this part of the Children Act constitute a set of national standards that spell out in unprecedented detail how local authorities should undertake this planning and review duty. This project collected evidence about the impact of this regulatory strategy on child care planning.

Study design

The study had two main components. The first was a national survey of local authority documentation about plans and reviews. Documents received from 80 authorities in England and Wales were analysed using rating scales based on the standards and principles of the Children Act. In the second phase, three contrasting local authorities were selected for a detailed examination of the actual practice of care planning and reviewing. Over the period 1993–95 a sample of 180 cases were studied, using a range of methods: case file study; observations of review meetings; interviews with children and parents, as well as senior managers and a range of professionals; and a survey of social workers. A group of senior managers were also asked about arrangements for chairing review meetings and how well this worked.

Key findings

- The *content* of planning and review documents was usually adequate, but the *process* of producing and distributing them had rarely been undertaken in a shared, collaborative way.

- The right balance between supporting sound professional judgement and putting effective procedures into place was proving difficult to achieve.

- Better information for planning was available where authorities used good paper forms such as the Looking After Children materials.[67]

- Much of the real planning happened outside review meetings. Reviews were seen as a meeting rather than a process.

- There was a more systematic approach to promoting the participation of children and parents, but they often experienced review meetings as uncomfortable and frustrating.

- Education and health assessments had been undertaken for most children, but they were of variable quality.

- Over 60% of the decisions in care plans were implemented. Legal and placement decisions were the most likely to be successfully implemented; those concerning contact with parents the least.

- Monitoring was a weak link in the whole planning and review process.

Policy and planning

The survey of local authority documentation found little evidence of an open, shared and collaborative approach to the process of preparing and distributing the documents. There had been little consultation with health, education or other local authority departments and even less with child or parent advocacy groups or representatives of minority ethnic groups. However, when the content of the documentation was analysed, seven out of ten were rated as 'adequate' or better, suggesting that the key messages from the Children Act *Guidance and Regulations* had been absorbed. On the whole, local authorities had responded well to the administrative challenge of creating new procedures for planning and reviewing their care of children. However, there was a risk that an overemphasis on procedures (the 'administrative model') could leave little room for professionals to use their experience and judgement to find the best ways of dealing with specific cases. Whilst a proper regulatory framework was needed to replace the old *ad hoc* planning system, this needed to be flexible enough to serve the interests of individual children. The researchers suggest seven principles to guide the planning process: openness and sharing, cogency, integration, flexibility, sensitivity, responsiveness and continuity.

Having translated the Children Act *Guidance and Regulations* into local policies and procedures, the next step for local authorities was to use these procedures to effect changes in social work practice, which in turn should lead to better outcomes for children and young people. The second part of the study addressed these questions of practice, looking at the planning process in action, the extent of participation by children and parents, the involvement of other agencies such as health and education, the output of reviews and how effectively plans were put into practice. It also considered the arrangements local authorities had made for monitoring the planning and review process.

Obtaining information

The first stages of the planning process involve obtaining information. For almost all of the looked after children in the study, there was evidence that the local authority had collected together the basic information needed for planning. However, the quality of this varied, and in only a quarter of the cases was the enquiry process rated by the researchers as 'positive' or 'excellent'. Better results were achieved where the authority used good paper forms, such as the Looking After Children (LAC) materials, which were being tested out in one of the study areas. Education and health assessments had been undertaken for most of the children, but they were of variable quality, and the particular needs of some groups of children were less likely to be assessed – for instance the health needs of adolescent young women and the educational needs of young people in further education. Education and health decisions had been taken for two in three children, but when the researchers examined the outcomes of plans, these education and health decisions had been implemented less frequently than many other aspects of the plan. Of some 1,500 decisions made in care plans in this study, six out of ten were successfully implemented overall. Legal and placement decisions were the most likely to be implemented and those concerning contact with parents the least.

The review meeting

The review meeting was seen as the focus for decision-making, but in fact much of the real planning happened outside of these meetings. This was especially the case for younger children, those undergoing changes of placement and those in the first year of being looked after. The researchers note that this separation of planning from review was associated with several difficulties: children and parents attended a limited proportion of all the meetings that occurred; time-scales for implementing planned decisions were often imprecise; and monitoring of previous decisions was fairly cursory. Monitoring was a weak link in the whole planning and review process. The findings of the fieldwork study revealed significant gaps in local authorities' arrangements for monitoring. Despite the adequacy of their written procedural frameworks, they had an uneven grasp of what was happening on the ground.

Children's views

A particular focus of this study was whether the new procedures were giving children and young people and their families a clear and active voice in decisions that were made about them. Compared to practice in the 1980s, there were signs of a more systematic approach to promoting participation. Most children were consulted about their wishes and feelings and attended reviews, as did most mothers, but reviews were attended by only a small minority of the fathers. However, attendance at meetings did not guarantee participation. The evidence from interviews with young people and their parents showed that their experience of trying to participate had mostly been uncomfortable and frustrating. They rarely received information to help them understand the planning process, or support to help them through it. Young people in particular often found formal meetings a difficult place in which to express their views and often painful feelings, especially if there were large numbers of strange adults present. As one young person in care pointed out: 'None of my friends who live with families have to sit down with all these people and talk about all these things.'

The review as process

One of the key conclusions from the study is the need to give greater emphasis to the review as a continuous process of planning rather than simply as a meeting. The researchers make a number of recommendations as to how the *Guidance and Regulations* could be amended to make the functions of planning and review clearer, to encourage closer working between agencies and to facilitate the participation of children and parents. They conclude that the regulation framework introduced by the Children Act is providing practitioners with the tools to improve the planning process, but that a lot remains to be done at both national and local level to create a structured and co-ordinated planning system for the children and young people who are looked after by local authorities.

Relevance now

There is now widespread agreement about the central importance of care planning and reviewing to social work with looked after children. Local authorities strive to achieve compliance with the regulations of the Children Act. But the issues raised by this research – especially practice concerns and ensuring that the procedures for planning and reviewing do add value for children and families – are still very pertinent to local authorities as they work towards achieving the objectives of *Quality Protects*, and especially of Objective 8: 'To actively involve users and carers in planning services and in tailoring individual packages of care'.[69]

11

Making Care Orders Work:
A Study of Care Plans and their Implementation

Judith Harwin, Morag Owen, Rachel Locke and
Donald Forrester

The Stationery Office (forthcoming)

The Children Act 1989 introduced a series of measures to strengthen the planning and review processes for looked after children, including the care plan that has to be presented to the court in care proceedings. This helps the court to establish whether making a Care Order will promote the child's welfare better than no order [section 1(5)] and also provides a framework for management. This study examined the influence of the care plan on case management by social services and explored a range of outcomes nearly two years later.

Study design

The study was a 21-month follow-up of 100 children from 57 families who were made subject to Care Orders between March and September 1997. Five authorities took part. The study used a mixture of quantitative and qualitative methods and was carried out in two phases. In Phase I, information was collected from court files and followed up by semi-structured interviews with social workers, guardians ad litem and local authority solicitors. Phase II was carried out at the 21-month point. It involved further interviews with social workers as well as analysis of social services' file data. Interviews were also held at the end point with current carers, children aged 7 or over and birth parents to find out their views on care planning and their experiences since the Care Order was implemented.

Key findings

- The implementation of court care plans makes a difference to the stability and life chances of children on Care Orders. Children whose plans were implemented showed the best welfare progress over the 21-month period and displayed the fewest unmet needs at the end point. Non-implemented plans were associated with the poorest welfare progress.

- Social Services were committed to implementing the care plans that had been presented to the court and there was no evidence of capricious changes.

- Care plans contained fairly full information on the children's needs and the proposed placement type. However, 49% omitted time-scales and 27% lacked contingency plans. Contact plans were frequently short-term and service plans relied heavily on the resources of social services.

- At the end of the study 60% of the children and young people were in the placement type specified in the care plan. Placements with relatives had the highest fulfilment rate, whilst plans for children to live at home proved the most fragile. Fifty-eight per cent of adoption plans were implemented within the study period.

- Foster care was the main collecting ground when placements of young children broke down. By the end of the study almost double the planned number of children were living with foster carers. Older children whose placement had foundered tended to move towards independent living.

- Although the well-being of many of the children had improved since the time of the Care Order, at the end point 40% still had moderate or severe unmet needs in emotional and behavioural well-being or in family and social relationships and 30% in education.

The role of the court care plan in decision-making

The care plan presented to the court has established itself as an important planning framework. The majority of those interviewed felt there was a moral obligation to implement it, and serious efforts to carry out the plan were made in all cases.

Care planning has strengthened links between local authority solicitors, social workers and guardians, with differences in professional viewpoints generally being productively negotiated through planning and legal meetings. In court, the final recommendations of the care plan – and especially the proposed arrangements for placement and contact – helped to determine the parents' attitude to the order. In one-third of the cases the final hearing was contested; but in approximately half of the cases where it was not contested positive agreement had been reached on these important issues.

The implementation of the plan

By the end of the study, six in ten children were living in the placement type specified in the court plan. The rate of fulfilment was highest for kinship care (78%), which included placement with some non-resident fathers and placement with members of the extended family. It was lowest for children living at home (41%). Fifty-eight per cent of the adoption plans were implemented successfully within the follow-up period. When placements at the end of the study were evaluated to assess the degree of permanency they offered the child, 70% of the children were found to be in permanent placements, and placement fulfilment and permanency were closely linked. Altogether 82% of the children had their original contact plans fulfilled, inasmuch as contact was continued or terminated with named individuals as specified in the care plan, although only 45% experienced contact of the expected duration and frequency. Face-to-face contact was almost never recommended for children to be adopted, and children spoke of their regrets at losing contact with younger siblings. They also valued their contact with parents and significant adults and only 2 of the 26 children interviewed did not want contact maintained – even when parents had severe problems such as chronic substance misuse.

Despite the social workers' commitment to implementing the plan, the results do not allow complacency. Of the 40 children whose plans were still unfulfilled at the end point, 15 had never entered the preferred type of placement and 25 had suffered placement breakdown. The rule of optimism had clearly prevailed in respect of children living at home, since more of these placements failed than succeeded. Furthermore, at the end point 30% of the children were still not living in a permanent placement. Just over one in ten had moved three times or more, and some were still on the move.

Foster care was the main collecting ground when placements of young children broke down. Foster care had initially been recommended for 22 children, but the number living with foster carers had virtually doubled at the end to 42. Older children who failed to find a foothold in specialist fostering or residential care tended to move towards independent living, where they struggled to survive. The clear message from the small number of young people concerned was that ongoing support was needed to help manage the transition to independence.

Reasons for variation

A complex interplay of factors helped explain why some children never entered their chosen placement and why some placements broke down. These factors varied with the placement type. For adoption, non-entry was far more common than placement breakdown. A shortage of suitable adopters and certain child risk factors (membership of a large sibling group, developmental delay and being aged 3 or over at the time of the final hearing) weakened adoption chances. Age also influenced implementation rates in foster care. All the children with unfulfilled fostering plans were aged 9 or over. They were also more likely to have had emotional and behavioural problems, learning difficulties and educational needs identified at the final hearing. When children were placed at home, fewer initial difficulties were noted in the children; but young children were removed during the follow-up period because of continuing child protection concerns. The child's wishes and feelings were important, particularly in explaining non-fulfilment of foster care and residential care plans. In both types of placement, difficulties arose when the initial commitment to the care plan was less than wholehearted, and children played an active role in either ending their foster placement or running away from residential care.

The relationship between plan implementation and welfare outcome

The study found a clear relationship between plan implementation and good welfare progress over the 21-month follow-up period. Using the framework of the Looking After Children schedules to evaluate progress across seven dimensions of child well-being,[67] the researchers found that children who obtained the highest scores were more likely to be living in the placement type specified in the court care plan and vice versa. Fulfilled adoption plans accounted for the highest proportion of children with high welfare progress scores. Kinship care was in second place.

In addition to measuring welfare change, the researchers examined the children's welfare status at the end point. With 40% of the children displaying moderate or severe unmet needs either in their family and social relationships or in their emotional and behavioural development and 30% in education, the neediness of the sample emerges forcefully. But so does the link between welfare progress, final welfare status and plan implementation. Children with the best overall welfare progress scores had the fewest unmet needs at the end of the study and vice versa. The best welfare profiles at the end point were found among children living in placements set out in the court plan.

Relevance now

The study highlights the impact of care plan implementation on children's life chances. There are clear differences in welfare outcome between children whose plans had been implemented and those whose plans had not. For this reason the emphasis placed on the court care plan by the Children Act is extremely important, as is the need for careful initial assessment in order to choose the best possible placement for the child.

The study draws attention to the need for a rapid expansion of substitute carers to ensure that the full potential of section 1(5) is achieved; for better planning through the inclusion in care plans of time-scales and contingency plans; and for ensuring that contact plans address children's longer-term needs and safeguard sibling relationships in the face of placement changes. Recommendations for avoiding delay include negotiating services from community health, education and other agencies prior to the care plan and approaching permanency panels prior to proceedings in long-term fostering as well as in adoption cases. With children taking an average of 9.6 months to reach an adoptive placement and 6.5 months to reach planned foster-care, the study suggests that placement finding needs to begin very early. Many of these recommendations forcefully underwrite the main thrust of *Quality Protects*, with its emphasis on achieving stability and higher standards of welfare outcome for children in the public care.[69]

12

The Last Resort:
Child Protection, the Courts and the 1989 Children Act

Joan Hunt, Alison Macleod and Caroline Thomas

Published by The Stationery Office (1999)

The philosophy of the Children Act 1989 is that children are best cared for within their families of origin without recourse to the courts, and that statutory intervention is a 'last resort' to be used only when other avenues have been tried and there seems to be no other way of ensuring a child's safety. This project concentrated on Part IV of the Children Act, the section dealing with Care and Supervision Orders, and focused in particular on the use of compulsory intervention by local authorities in child protection cases and the way in which these cases were managed by the courts. As the project was commissioned early in the Department of Health's programme of research on the Children Act, it was able to compare a sample of child protection court cases from before and after the Act as well as to look at how key principles of the Act, such as the 'no order' principle, were being translated into practice in its first two years.

Study design

The research was carried out in urban areas within three different local authorities. Information was gathered from a detailed examination of court and local authority files (105 pre-Act and 83 post-Act cases); from interviews with practitioners involved in the post-Act cases, including social workers, guardians ad litem, lawyers and members of the judiciary; and from observing court hearings in a sub-sample of 30 post-Act cases. Another strand of the project, covered in Study 9, investigated the views of the parents involved in these cases.

> *Key findings*
>
> - Many aspects of the new court framework were working well.
>
> - The threshold for court involvement was higher after the Act. Families whose cases reached court had more serious problems, and the proportion of previously known and active cases was higher.
>
> - Options for supporting children within their families had been more thoroughly explored before applying for a court order.
>
> - The changes introduced by the Children Act were placing a heavy burden of risk assessment and management on practitioners.
>
> - Transferring control of case progress from the parties to the courts had not solved the problem of delay.
>
> - Care proceedings would have benefited from more ongoing contact between parties between hearings, rather than information being shared in court corridors.
>
> - The adversarial legal model was not well suited to the needs of care cases.

Thresholds for court intervention

This study was carried out in the early days of the Children Act implementation and when systems were still evolving. Already then, the Act appeared to be having a substantial impact on the compulsory protection of children and achieving many of its objectives in this area. Even before the Act the majority of child protection cases were handled without recourse to the courts, but afterwards the threshold of significant harm that triggered intervention was higher. The families subject to court procedures under the Children Act had more, and more serious, problems than those affected by previous legislation; the local authority was more likely to have explored alternative options for supporting children within their families before bringing care proceedings; and the applications were more clearly thought out and less challengeable. Fewer care proceedings were instigated in the wake of a crisis, and Emergency Protection Orders were not being used as a routine way to begin proceedings, as was sometimes the case with the former Place of Safety Orders. Comparing pre- and post-Act sample cases, the study found that post-Act the proportion of previously known and active cases was higher. Social work involvement was longer, and children were more likely to already be on the Child Protection Register and to have been registered for longer. More services were provided than before the Act, and the voluntary approach was more often persisted with in the face of difficulties.

Impact on practitioners

However, this was not achieved without cost. Social workers were frequently anxious and frustrated by the need to continue working with families on a voluntary basis beyond the point at which court action would previously have been taken to ensure a child's safety. Although there were no reports of serious injury to children as a result, the researchers concluded that in just over a quarter of the sample cases there was evidence of the children being harmed in less tangible ways through the postponement of court action. The changes introduced by the Children Act have placed a particularly heavy burden of risk assessment and management on practitioners, and the study underlined the need for additional training, a more structured evidence-based approach to case recording and good quality regular supervision of social workers. Whilst the research shows a great deal more could be done to prevent the need for care proceedings arising, once that point has been reached statutory intervention has to be perceived as a positive option, not simply the regrettable end of the road.

The courts

As well as looking at the decision-making processes within local authorities over child protection, the researchers also investigated how courts were handling such cases under the Children Act. Again, they found much that was working well. The new system of concurrent jurisdiction, whereby most orders can be made by any level of court, has meant that all child matters concerning the same family are now dealt with together. Transfers between court levels were working reasonably smoothly in the study areas. The new directions hearings were proving a useful innovation, if as yet of variable effectiveness, and there was widespread acceptance of the principle of transferring control of case progress from the parties to the courts. However, the latter had been less effective than anticipated in tackling delay. The Act appeared to have affected the attitude of professionals, so that they now identified delay as a problem to be addressed rather than tolerated or ignored. Despite this, attempts to speed up the legal process had been less successful, due in part to inadequate resources, increased use of experts and lack of court time, especially in the higher courts.

Care proceedings

The new court framework is described as operating surprisingly well, but the legal process, which is constructed on an episodic and adjudicative model, is seen as poorly adapted to the needs of care cases. Only a third of the care proceedings in the study were initiated with a clear end result in view. In most, what was sought was a legally protected space within which to assess and work towards a resolution of family difficulties. Care proceedings are also characteristically dynamic. During the average six-month period in the court process, well over three-quarters of the Children Act cases experienced some degree of change, for instance new information coming to light or relatives stepping forward to offer care. Three in five cases were resolved by the final hearing. The researchers offer a number of suggestions for remodelling the process (including a specialist, participatory family court and a short-term assessment and treatment order) as well as for making the existing system work more effectively. At the very least, they argue that there needs to be more contact between practitioners and more court involvement between hearings, with less business transacted at the last minute in court corridors.

Relevance now

Although the research was conducted in the early years of the Children Act, many of the issues highlighted continue to be topical, notably the continuing delay in court proceedings, difficulties around the use of compulsion, conflict about the proper domains of the courts and local authorities, and the arguments about the need for a specialist family court.

13

The Best-Laid Plans: Outcomes of Judicial Decisions in Child Protection Proceedings

Joan Hunt and Alison Macleod

Published by The Stationery Office (1999)

This research was a follow-up to the previous study (12), which addressed concerns that the plans made for children during court proceedings would be ignored or inadequately implemented by local authorities once the proceedings were over. It aimed to provide information on the likely outcomes of different types of court decisions and to show how far practice under the Children Act 1989 reflected the new framework for the relationship between courts, welfare agencies and families.

Study design

This study was commissioned as a 'fact-finding' exercise, which re-visited the cases of 131 of the children who had been involved in the care proceedings covered in Study 12. It compared the plans made for them by the courts with the reality of their situation between eighteen months and four years after the final hearing. The main source of information was a detailed examination of social services' case files on the children, supplemented by postal questionnaires and interviews with social workers, team managers, guardians ad litem and solicitors who had been involved at some point in the proceedings. The perspective of at least one of these practitioners was obtained for 90% of the children in the sample. Nineteen adults (from seventeen of the families) also agreed to be interviewed.

Key findings

- More than four in five care plans were both implemented and achieved.

- The main cause for concern was delay in achieving permanent substitute family placements and the subsequent breakdown rates.

- The most common plan was to return children to parental care. Just over a third of these cases subsequently broke down.

- Placement breakdown was most frequent for long-term care placements (60%) and least frequent for adoptive placements (none at the time the study ended).

- Around a half of the placement breakdowns were linked to a failure to provide services, especially therapy and direct work with children.

- Much delay is caused not by the courts but by the family-finding process. Closer liaison is needed between child protection workers and family-finding teams.

Outcomes

By the final hearing in the care proceedings, firm plans had been made for 120 of the 131 children in the original study. Parental care was the most common plan (47% of the children), followed by adoption (21%), long-term care (13%) and placement with relatives (12%). The high proportion of children who were expected to remain within their family network, and often with their parents, clearly reflects the Children Act emphasis on this principle.

There was little evidence to support the suspicion, which had been widespread among family justice practitioners in the original study,[12] that local authorities disregard the plans that have been agreed in court. There was not a single case in the whole sample in which no attempt was made to follow the general direction of the original firm plan. In addition, the majority of children were placed in accordance with the placement plan: only 14 of the 131 were not. However, by the end of the research, at least two and a half years after the conclusion of care proceedings, 16% of the children either remained unplaced or were facing a future that was again uncertain. Another 23% had had to wait for more than eighteen months before their placement was secured. The key issue appeared to be not whether local authorities implemented care plans, but how long it took for substitute placements to be found and the subsequent breakdown rates. Many of the children affected were very young, and thus particularly vulnerable to delay.

The type of placement most likely to break down was long-term care (60%) followed by parental and kinship placements (35% and 33%, respectively). All the adoptive placements were continuing at the end of the research period, although because they had taken longer to set up these had generally been tested over shorter periods of time.

Reducing the breakdown rate

The researchers analysed the data for clues to ways of reducing the breakdown rate. Testing a placement out in the course of proceedings did not seem to offer any protection against breakdown. Nor did greater use of orders necessarily help: in placements with relatives or parents those with the lowest level of legal protection had the lowest breakdown rates, and there were only a few cases of children placed with parents where it was suggested that highest levels of protection might have prevented breakdown. However, better provision of services could make a difference. Around a half of the placement breakdowns were linked to service failures, with long-term care placements suffering most severely, although changing circumstances were also a significant factor. A major deficiency was in the provision of therapy, and it is suggested that social workers could be well placed to take on some of this direct work with children, provided they are offered appropriate training and the time to engage in it.

Delay

Much of the concern about delay and its effects on children has concentrated on the actual legal process. This study suggests a need to broaden that focus to include what happens before and after the legal process is engaged. Analysis of the cases that took the longest before children were in a permanent placement revealed that relatively little of this time was occupied by the court proceedings themselves. Some of this delay could be reduced by paying more attention to the family-finding process. The research suggests that closer liaison is needed between child protection workers and family-finding teams, as well as an earlier start to the whole process, in order to maximise the chance of finding suitable carers for children who often have very complex needs.

The researchers make a number of recommendations for improving the quality of care plans and the way cases are managed post-proceeding, including better recording and information systems, greater involvement of independent officers in the reviewing process, closer liaison between child protection and family placement services and better support for placement with relatives. They also suggest changes in the orders available to the courts and a mechanism for providing feedback to the courts on the outcomes of cases.

Relevance now

The research has informed and is relevant to a number of current government initiatives – care planning, *Quality Protects*[69] and the new framework for assessment of children in need.[79] It also provides sound empirical data to inform the contemporary debate on the proper relationship between the court and local authorities.

Leaving Care in Partnership: Family Involvement with Care Leavers

Peter Marsh and Mark Peel
Published by The Stationery Office (1999)

This research built on earlier work (e.g. Study 3) into how local authorities were meeting their duty under section 24 of the Children Act 1989 to promote young people's welfare when they leave care. It focused on the important principle of partnership, which underpins the Act, by investigating how young people leaving care could be supported by social workers working more closely in partnership with the young person's family and other significant individuals in their lives.

Study design

The study involved 87 young people who were about to leave care and who were not going home but had some contact with their family. They were identified from a file review of all 160 young people leaving care in three different authorities (a county, a metropolitan district and a large city). The sample included 39 young men and 48 young women aged 16–18, around 14% of whom had a heritage other than white European. Around 21% lived in residential care, with a further 44% in foster care and 35% in semi-independent style accommodation. Social workers completed a questionnaire about the young person, partnership, family and family involvement. A sub-group of 43 young people were interviewed, as were 34 family members (nominated by the young people as their 'most important/influential' family member) and 22 social workers. The interviews covered family knowledge, desire for contact, perceived barriers to contact and the range of responsibilities felt and carried out. A further 21 interviews were carried out with a sample of the young people to see how their views may have changed over time, and a family tree graphic, developed for the project, was used to elicit information at each stage of the research.

Extended family involvement

This study found that although care leavers did appear to be receiving more support since the Children Act 1989, there was still very little active professional encouragement to extend the family involvement for these young people. Young people leaving care could often describe wide family networks, with an average of over twenty members, but there was not a great deal of active involvement. In addition to parents and grandparents, their networks included not only aunts, uncles, cousins and other relatives, but also individuals and groups who, though not kin, were seen by the young people as important and were classified as honorary family members, such as foster family. In comparison social workers offered a more limited picture of family networks, tending to overlook both the extended and honorary family members. 'Partnership' was interpreted by social workers as work with parents or people who acted as parents, and the opportunity for involving others who could play a significant role in supporting young people at this difficult time in their lives was often lost.

Key kin

An overwhelming majority of the young people (41 of the 43 in the interview group) were able to nominate one family member as the most important or influential person for them as they approached leaving care. In less than a quarter of the cases this was their natural mother, although it was mothers, if any family member, who were most likely to attend the review meetings. Social workers identified the same person as key kin for only 17 of the 41 care leavers. These key kin were of great importance to young people, and they were willing to play a central role if needed. The researchers suggest a model –

in the form of a target – of how young people could be supported by their families after care. At the centre are key kin. A second ring includes family members who, though willing to be involved in providing support, might not independently initiate it. A third ring includes family members who are known to the young person but are not likely to be involved in supporting them after care. Over time, the young people in this study developed a clear understanding of whom they might approach for what kind of help.

Preparation for independence

Young people about to leave residential units were more likely than other groups to have lost contact with one side (usually paternal) of their family, and young people of heritage other than white European tended to describe comparatively smaller family networks than other groups. Overall, young people leaving care were described by their social workers as 'poorly' prepared emotionally and only 'adequately' prepared practically for independence. They generally had infrequent contact (monthly or less) with their family, although the situation was better for young people living in semi-independent accommodation. Despite this, around half of the workers felt that their contact with young people would decrease after they left care. They expressed some confidence that family members were aware of the services for care leavers and would request additional services as and when required. However, the social workers' expectations of increased family support at this stage, both emotional and financial, seemed misplaced. Family members themselves were uncertain about the level of support and service young people should expect from the authority after leaving care, but they were hoping that workers would continue to offer care leavers a safety net of financial and practical help and would regularly keep an eye on them to ensure that they did not get into trouble.

Review meetings

Formal involvement and participation of family members in review meetings was not common. Forty-nine of the 75 reviews that were held before leaving care had no family member present, and in the rest it was usually the mother alone, unsupported by other relatives. Formal reviews did not seem to be providing a good basis for families to participate as partners in planning for leaving care, and a different style of planning meeting for leaving care could be more effective.

Overall, the study supported the view that partnership approaches to practice would be likely to improve the support available to young care leavers. The process of leaving care created a new opportunity for family members to create different relationships with young people. Past relationships with social services and/or young people may not be an accurate guide as to what is possible at this stage. Social workers could create greater opportunities for involving extended family, which, if sensitively done, would generally be welcomed by young people and family members and would help to provide the support that other young people generally receive at this stage in their lives.

Increasing family involvement

The researchers suggest a number of other ways of increasing family involvement and support when young people are leaving the care system, including seeking better information from the young people themselves about their family networks in order to build partnerships with those who are important to them, and producing information packs spelling out what happens after care and who is responsible for what. They also stress the importance of social workers giving priority to communication and understanding, beyond the building of formal agreements and contracts, when seeking to establish partnerships with family members, as the research showed that young people were concerned to avoid members of their family feeling forced or obliged to help them and wanted any help they were offered to be freely given.

Relevance now

The findings support the *Quality Protects* initiative to provide longer-term transitional arrangements for young people leaving the care system.[69] In particular, they highlight the importance of considering extended family in meeting the objective 'to maximise the number of young people leaving care after their sixteenth birthday who are still in touch with Social Services, or a known or approved contact, on their nineteenth birthday'. For many young people, if careful work is done listening to them and respecting their views, that contact could be extended family. The addition of a family tree to the Looking After Children records[67] would help to ensure that workers and young people know about extended family, and it would promote the important finding of this study that workers should try to ensure people have an active network of family on which they can rely as they move into adulthood.

From Care to Accommodation: Support, Protection and Control in Child Care Services

Jean Packman and Christopher Hall

Published by The Stationery Office (1998)

Section 20 of the Children Act 1989 replaced the old notion of voluntary care with a positive view of accommodation as a service that could be offered by local authorities to support families and children in need. Looking after children should be seen as a means of helping families, rather than as a last resort to be avoided wherever possible, and accommodation should be agreed on a voluntary basis in preference to using court orders to remove children from their homes. This study investigated how this new provision was being used, and how far the principles of working in partnership with parents and listening to children's wishes were being upheld.

Study design

The researchers revisited two local authorities in which research on admissions to care had been conducted ten years previously and were thus in a unique position to explore changes in practice in response to the Children Act. They started by charting the organisational and policy changes in the two authorities over the intervening decade and by selecting sample areas in each with similar sized populations and social characteristics. All admissions to accommodation in these areas over an eight-month period, between October 1992 and May 1993, were studied (177 in total), using interviews with social workers and a search of case files. Each case was followed up twice, six months and two years after admission. In order to look at the formal and informal processes of negotiation about the need for accommodation, the researchers interviewed 23 parents and 18 children or young people, and they also attended 29 planning meetings in the role of observer or minute-taker.

Key findings

- Court action was being avoided in favour of negotiated solutions.

- Accommodation was being used for a much broader and more challenging range of family problems than the old 'voluntary care'.

- When children were perceived as at risk, parents often felt that they had little choice but to agree to accommodation and that partnerships were 'enforced'.

- Accommodation continued to be viewed by many professionals as a last resort rather than as a support to families.

- Parents and young people were frequently present at meetings, but they often experienced these as difficult and uncomfortable occasions.

- Only 15% of co-operative arrangements had had to be replaced by a court order two years later.

- There was a high level of placement changes, especially for adolescents.

The use of accommodation

The 'no order' principle was having a considerable impact on practice. Accommodation was being used for a much broader and more challenging range of family problems than the old 'voluntary care'. A third of the children accommodated under section 20 had been or were currently on the Child Protection Register, compared to only 1% of those in voluntary care in the earlier study. In fact, the majority of children now being accommodated were those who would usually have entered care via the courts under the old legislation. The children and young people thought to be at risk and the 'difficult' adolescents together accounted for two-thirds of all those accommodated. The modern counterparts of the 'victims' and 'villains' described in an earlier study, *Who Needs Care?*,[94] were clearly now being accommodated on a voluntary basis.

True partnership?

However, one consequence of this was that the 'voluntary' nature of some section 20 accommodations was being compromised. A majority of both parents and social workers favoured the admission to accommodation, but their views did not always coincide. Agreement was most in evidence where the families were in crisis, through parental ill-health or absence or because of the strains of parenting a difficult child. But it could also be reached in more contentious cases. However, two other models of partnership operated. The first was when Social Services wanted the child to be accommodated and pressed reluctant parents into agreeing, through the implied or explicit threat of legal proceedings. These 'sham partnerships' were most common in situations where risk to the child was feared, and they illustrate the dilemma of holding on to genuine 'voluntariness' in such situations. The other model was when Social Services was the reluctant partner, forced into agreeing to accommodation by young people who wanted 'out' or by desperate parents who demanded that Social Services take on the responsibility. The professionals' reluctance often led to a family forcing their hand by creating a crisis, which resulted in an emergency admission rather than planned accommodation. Rather than a step-by-step planning at all stages of the accommodation process, as envisaged under the Children Act, planning in these cases only really happened *after* the child had left home.

A last resort

A related finding was that the re-framing of accommodation as a support for families was being undermined by the persistent view that any kind of public care should be seen as a last resort. There were differences between the two sample authorities in this respect, with two-thirds of all admissions to accommodation in one authority being emergencies compared to only one-third in the other. Heavy investment in alternatives to accommodation, such as family centres, seemed to bolster a last resort stance, as did a strong, centralised and specialised organisational structure. In the authority where more power was devolved to practitioners and their immediate managers, practice was more varied and attitudes to accommodation were less uniformly defensive.

Listening to parents and children

The researchers looked for evidence of an increased emphasis on involving parents and listening to children. They found that although parents and young people were frequently present at meetings, they often experienced these as uncomfortable and difficult occasions. Four types of meeting were identified: those where parents said little (either because they were silenced by criticism, or because the main purpose of the meeting was for professionals to talk among themselves); supportive dialogues; argumentative encounters; and family decisions (where most of the discussions and decisions were directed by the family). The most positive partnerships with parents generally occurred when neither child protection nor adolescent rebellion was a primary issue.

The child's voice was more likely to be heard once accommodation had been offered than in the negotiations leading up to it, and again formal meetings were not the most comfortable settings for young people to make their views known. Had they been listened to more, they might have provoked a re-consideration of the current policy of reducing residential care in favour of fostering. Some young people perceived children's homes as places that offered emotional space and comradeship with peers, and they compared them favourably with the difficulty of trying to fit into a stranger's domestic environment.

Two years on

The follow-up of accommodated children suggested that the 'no order' principle was working. Two years later only 15% of accommodations had been replaced by adoption, Care or Residence Orders. Most co-operative arrangements had been sustained, even where there were child protection concerns. However, repeat admissions had doubled since the 1980s, and there had been a disturbingly high level of placement changes, especially for adolescents. Over half of the children had more than one admission in the two follow-up years, and four out of five had entered the system more than once at some time during their childhood. This, in turn, meant more disruption, since only 10% had received regular respite in a single placement. Rather than 'drifting' in care for lack of any planning, a small number of young children were subjected to several *changes* of plan as the potential of family and friendship networks were exhaustively explored. The severity of many of the family problems that accommodation attempts to alleviate was emphasised by the whereabouts of the accommodated children two years on. While over half were living at home within their family network, a quarter were still (or again) in accommodation or care and the rest were either scattered among friends, living independently or in custody or else their whereabouts were unknown.

Relevance now

The study concludes that there have been some changes that bring practice closer in line with the principles of the Children Act, but it also raises issues that need to be addressed by local authorities in order to implement *Quality Protects* objectives.[69] Court action is increasingly being avoided in favour of negotiated solutions, and accommodation is being offered alongside other services as part of a 'package' to support families. There are increased efforts to involve parents and young people in the decision-making process, and progress has been made in placing siblings together, maintaining family contact, encouraging degrees of shared care and ensuring continuity of schooling. On the negative side, entrenched attitudes have been harder to change. Accommodation is still perceived by many social services staff as a last resort to be avoided if possible, an attitude that is often not shared by children and parents. The success of some measures, in particular the diversion of families and children away from the courts, presents tough challenges to the ideals of voluntarism and partnership that lie at the heart of the Act.

16 Play and Care Out of School

Pat Petrie, Gill Poland and Sue Wayne
Published by HMSO (1994)

Part X of the Children Act 1989 extended regulation of day care services to include those providing for school-aged children up to the age of 8. Local authorities were also obliged to provide out-of-school services where appropriate to children in need. Little was known about this disparate group of services, which could include playschemes, after-school clubs, adventure playgrounds, out-of-school centres and day camps. This study was, therefore, commissioned early on in the research programme to describe and classify the different types of provision and provide baseline data against which the impact of the Act could later be judged.

Study design

The first stage of the study was based on detailed case studies of fifteen diverse services in England and Wales, during which the researchers sought to understand the different values, goals, organisation and practice in each setting. Interviewers visited each service, interviewed managers, senior workers and other staff, and carried out systematic observations. This was followed by a postal survey of 120 out-of-school services in eighteen English and two Welsh local authorities, selected to include both day care and 'open-door' types of provision, and before- and after-school as well as holiday playschemes. Data was also collected at a later stage from two case studies of the local authority registration and inspection process.

A typology of services

The early stages of the work allowed the researchers to identify a number of dimensions along which out-of-school services could be categorised. These were grouped into characteristics of provision, practice and organisation. *Provision characteristics* included: who ran the service, who it was primarily aimed at (children, parents or both), its value base (such as promoting equality, retaining employees, facilitating children's play, commercial viability), whether it targeted a particular population or was universal, whether it was open-door (where children are free to come and go) or day care (where children remain until picked up by a responsible adult). The *organisational characteristics* included: the type of management structure, whether it was a simple service or part of more complex provision, how the service was financed, its premises (purpose-built or adapted), opening hours (before/after school, term time only, holiday only, open all year) and staffing (use of volunteers, qualifications required). *Practice characteristics* were based on the way the different services operated in their day-to-day practice and included whether the bias was towards play, amusement or work; whether the emphasis was on the individual child or on the group; whether a punitive, democratic or 'group control' approach was adopted to discipline; and how much importance was attached to health and safety considerations.

The fragmented child

Overall, it appeared that different out-of-school services were addressing themselves to particular aspects of a child's needs, rather than looking at the child as a whole. So the child might be seen as in need of protection; or as a customer of leisure and recreation; or as the offspring of employees who need child care in the interests of the employer, the labour market and female equality; or as a member of society with a claim on its recreational services.

Diversity of provision

A striking finding from this first stage of the study was the sheer diversity of out-of-school provision that local authorities were now required to register and inspect. The researchers next carried out a survey of the physical and other standards to be found in out-of-school services when they became subject to regulation under the Children Act. The local authority and the voluntary sector (largely local community groups) were found to account for most of the provision, 43% each, and the private sector for only 14%. The basic distinction between care and play services turned out to be less clear-cut in practice, as some day care services allowed children to leave without being collected, whilst some working parents used open-door services virtually as day care.

Quality of provision

The survey took place in the second half of 1992, when registration and inspection under the Children Act should already have taken place, but many services for school-age children had yet to be visited. The survey revealed many shortcomings in both day care and open-door provision. Although there were examples of good practice, in general standards left a great deal of room for improvement. Most staff had no formal qualifications for the work, over a third were students and over half of the services had no hygiene procedures or equal opportunities policy. Local authority officers were finding it difficult to carry out their new duties because of their inexperience with services for children over 5, the lack of resources to help provision improve and the transient nature of holiday playschemes. Some of these problems were beginning to be addressed, for instance through under-eights officers working more closely with play officers or local play associations to develop appropriate standards for play services, and through a government initiative to promote out-of-school care for the children of working parents. The study concluded that without a national policy and sufficient resources it would be difficult to develop and sustain high-quality play and day care services for school-aged children.

Relevance now

Expansion of out-of-school services is a key component of the National Childcare Strategy and has received significant additional funding through the New Opportunities Fund. The typology of services developed in this study should inform the child care audits and plans that Early Years Development and Childcare Partnerships are required to undertake as part of the Childcare Strategy. This study also underlines the need for local authorities to ensure that adequate training and support are available to those working in out-of-school services, especially those recruited under the New Deal, who may have little previous child care experience.

17 Out-of-school Services, Out-of-school Lives

Pat Petrie, Itohan Egharevba, Christine Oliver and Gill Poland
Published by The Stationery Office (2000)

This set of linked studies built on the exploratory work in Study 16. It focused on the use of out-of-school services by children and young people of different ages, by minority ethnic groups and by disabled children and explored the part played by these services in the lives of children and their parents.

Study design

The second set of out-of-school studies explored the perspectives of children and parents. It looked at families in general, but especially sought to understand the satisfactions and preferences on out-of-school services expressed by i) families of minority ethnic backgrounds, ii) families with a disabled child and iii) families with a child aged 10–13 years. The intention was to develop understandings of social disadvantage and exclusion as they relate to out-of-school services and of the ways in which different childhoods are socially constructed. Thirty-three out-of-school services and 93 families were included. Similar designs informed the three studies, including selecting equal numbers of services providing mainly for the group of children under consideration (exclusive services) and services provided for children in general (mainstream services). All the parents and most of the children were interviewed, using semi-structured interviews. Ethnographic fieldwork was carried out in all of the services. There was also a telephone survey of 187 parents about their use of and satisfaction with a further 30 play and care services.

Key findings

- Services mostly met the expressed needs of users, who were often very appreciative of what was on offer.

- Where dissatisfaction was expressed, this was more common among girls and children in the older age group (10–13).

- Parents with a disabled child were especially pleased with out-of-school services, as much for the play opportunities they offered children as for their function in providing respite care and reducing isolation for both parents and children.

- However, staff were often not properly trained or supported for work with disabled children, to the discomfort of staff and children alike.

- Attending a 'mainstream' or a 'targeted' service was not a prime consideration for the majority of users – although for families with an older child, age-appropriateness was often seen as important.

- Members of minority ethnic groups had few specific cultural requirements of the services. However, they were pleased to have the support of staff drawn from the same ethnic group as themselves and saw their presence both as a safeguard and as a means of cultural support for their child.

- Many staff in out-of-school services were unaware of racist behaviour, had no properly formulated means for dealing with it and did not always recognise the necessity of affirming the identity of children from minority ethnic communities.

Relevance now

Out-of-school services are an important form of support for families under stress and children in need. They are valued by families, but local authorities need to ensure that adequate training and support are available to ensure a high-quality service, and especially that staff are able to meet the needs of all the children in the community.

18

Making Progress:
Change and Development in Services to
Disabled Children under the Children Act 1989

Carol Robinson, Clive Weston and John Minkes
Published by the Norah Fry Research Centre, University of Bristol (1995)

The Children Act 1989 and subsequent *Guidance and Regulations* [49] gave local authorities a new framework for work with disabled children, defining them as 'children in need' and bringing them within mainstream child and family services for the first time. Key principles were that disabled children were children first and that services should be provided to give these children the opportunity to lead lives that are as normal as possible (Schedule 2). Services should be provided in partnership with other agencies; should take account of the race, culture, religion and language of the child and the family; and should listen to the views of the children themselves. This study assessed how far these changes were happening in two kinds of services for disabled children: day care for children under 5 and short-term accommodation in residential homes for children over 10.

Study design

This was an action research project in which the research team worked with service providers to help them evaluate the quality of their own provision. Assessment materials were developed to help providers to do this, including tools to enable disabled children to express their views about the service they received.* Two types of service for disabled children were studied: residential homes offering short-term accommodation, mostly run by Social Services; and specialist day care services for under-fives, run by a variety of statutory and voluntary agencies. Five projects of each type – situated in both rural and urban areas in England and Wales – were visited twice. The research team worked with staff in each service to assess its strengths and weaknesses, and for each evaluation a senior member of the local social services department worked alongside the researchers, acting as a co-evaluator and later supporting staff in developing action plans to improve their service. The initial evaluations took place over a three-day visit, which included interviews with managers, staff and parents; observation in each setting; and guided discussion with the children (aged 10+) using the residential homes. A set of goals was then agreed to develop the service in line with the Children Act, and a second evaluation took place a year later to assess progress.

* Assessment tools: 'Quality in day care services for under-fives' (Robinson, Weston and Minkes: The Stationery Office 1996); 'Quality in residential short-term care services' (Robinson, Weston and Minkes: The Stationery Office 1996); 'Observing for quality' (Weston, Minkes and Robinson: The Stationery Office 1996).

Impact of the Children Act

The researchers describe separately the main findings from the evaluations of short-term residential accommodation and day care for under-fives. They found that by the time of the second evaluation the residential homes had made progress in a number of areas related to the requirements of the Children Act. They had moved away from accepting children under 5, were emphasising family-based services for this age group and showed a marked improvement in the information provided for users and their families and friends. They were also better at planning for the transition to adult services, although many parents remained anxious about what would happen to their son or daughter once they reached school leaving age. Written guidance to staff on issues such as risk-taking, HIV and AIDS and sexuality had improved significantly between the first and second evaluations. Where there had been less progress was in areas that required action beyond the service itself, such as in salaries and conditions of service for residential care staff and the development of co-ordinated planning for children with disabilities. The extent to which local authorities supported and trained their residential care staff was very variable and was particularly lacking around cultural issues.

Consulting children

Few of the services in the study had found effective ways of directly consulting children about their wishes and feelings regarding short-term care arrangements, and this was a particular problem for children who were unable to speak. The researchers developed a number of tools to help children express their views, but they concluded that for some children systematic observation was likely to be the best way of judging their response. The children who participated in the study mostly seemed to be happy about their placement, but a significant minority were clearly not.

Day care services for under-fives

The day care services for under-fives were very varied in terms of their organisation and the needs of the children they catered for. All were set up as specialist services for children with disabilities and accepted children as referrals from professionals. Between the first and second evaluations most services drew up a written commitment to treat children as 'children first' and disabled second, in line with the principles of the Children Act, but in practice this was often limited by inappropriate buildings and facilities, and there was little effort to provide contact with non-disabled children. Apart from this, the standard of care was usually high, with the children being offered a wide range of stimulating and educational experiences. These standards were achieved despite, rather than because of, the provision of training opportunities. Voluntary day care services in particular had little access to training, including training on child protection.

Interagency working

The day care services studied generally had good relationships with parents, but relationships between professionals in different agencies were less satisfactory. This was the case both for the education assessment units, which would have liked a social worker to act as their link person with the social services department, and for the social services day nurseries, which reported little contact with the education service. Services run by the voluntary sector often felt that neither department shared important information with them, such as whether a child was on the Child Protection Register. Whilst there were some minor improvements between the first and second evaluations, this lack of co-operation between agencies remained a significant problem in developing the kind of provision for disabled children envisaged in the Children Act.

What worked

Taken together, a number of common findings emerged from the studies of both short-term care and day care services for disabled children. Firstly, the model of joint evaluation was judged a successful one, because the involvement of staff in setting their own goals and action plans gave them a greater commitment to improving quality. This was reflected in the fact that all the services made changes over the course of the project which brought their practice closer into line with the principles underlying the Children Act. Secondly, the research identified some common factors that seemed to help promote change in the right direction. These included support and relevant training for staff, especially front-line managers; involvement of staff in decision-making about the running and future direction of the service; positive feedback to staff from managers about the value of the service they provided; close involvement of a senior officer able to co-ordinate the process of change; and a willingness to involve parents and act on their comments about the service.

Constraints

A number of factors inhibited change. They included the climate of financial constraint and the uncertainty caused by continuing reorganisation of social services departments, a lack of co-ordination between agencies, the practice of employing large numbers of temporary or very part-time staff and lack of specific guidance, for instance on how to consult with disabled children or work effectively with other agencies. The researchers conclude that although resource constraints make meeting the principles of the Children Act more difficult, the factors that promote change do not always involve a great deal of extra finance or staff time. Rather, they are dependent upon good staff management and a willingness to share the decision-making process.

Relevance now

This study highlighted low levels of multi-agency working in relation to disabled children. Recent government initiatives indicate a growing awareness of the importance of sustained joint working for all children, as exemplified by the *Quality Protects* programme[69] and the Health Act 1999.

19

Family Centres and Bringing Up Young Children

Teresa Smith
Published by HMSO (1996)

Family centres gained 'official' recognition in Part III of the Children Act 1989 as part of the range of family support services local authorities are required to provide 'as appropriate' in their area, and as a key element in preventive provision to meet need. This study explored how family centres operate and whether they are an effective way of providing services for families with young children, from the point of view of those who use them.

Study design

The study was carried out between 1988 and 1992 in six family centres/ projects run or supported by the Children's Society. The main source of data was in-depth interviews with 125 parents (mainly mothers) of pre-school children, who were randomly selected from a list compiled by the researchers 'sitting on the door' for a week at each project and recording all users with pre-school children. The researchers also observed in the centres, interviewed staff and studied project records.

Key findings

- The family centres adopted different approaches, but all served highly disadvantaged areas.

- Parents using the centres had similar needs and aspirations, regardless of the family centre's approach.

- The level of need was high not only among users referred to the centres by social workers, but also among those attending by choice.

- Most users thought the family centres had had a positive impact on their lives and those of their children.

- The centres were least able to satisfy parents' needs for financial support and day care services.

- The two centres with an explicit focus on adult education were particularly successful in raising self-confidence among users.

- Family centres run on the neighbourhood and community development models were able to reach more families in need than those accessible only through social work referrals.

The centres

Two of the family centres worked largely with referred clients and offered direct counselling, access visits, play sessions and advice on parenting skills, budgeting and diet. Two were 'neighbourhood centres', which ran a range of activities (both 'open access' and 'closed'), offered space to other groups and facilities such as a telephone, photocopier or meeting room, and provided a listening ear and counselling where necessary. The remaining two operated with a 'community development' approach and were run by local organisations or hoped to move in that direction. They offered premises to other groups, provided facilities for the community to use, encouraged local people to identify needs and issues, and worked closely with local groups and other professionals rather than running the services directly. Although the focus and way of operating differed in the six centres, all were located in highly disadvantaged neighbourhoods with high levels of unemployment, low income, dependent children, lone-parent households and large families. One area had a high level of households of minority ethnic origin.

Parents' needs

Parents from the six centres talked about the same kind of issues to do with bringing up children: the importance of safe neighbourhoods, the difficulty of 'making ends meet', depression and health problems, difficulties of bringing up children on your own, the need for day care so people could go out to work, the importance of free time, their desire to learn about child development, the value of social contact, and the importance of support networks – friends, family, baby-sitting. People with the additional stresses of lone parenthood, or being a 'client' of Social Services, were found to have very similar priorities to other users. However, the client-focused centres gave less priority to these 'normal' needs of bringing up young children and more to monitoring and checking on families and children seen as vulnerable.

Parents' views

Most users thought the family centres had had a positive impact on their own lives and those of their children. They saw the family centres as a safe place to go, with welcoming staff. Ninety-seven per cent said they would recommend the centre to someone else, 86% said the centre had made a difference to them and 84% said the centre had made a difference to their children. Parents were most satisfied with the centres as somewhere for their children to mix with other children and have space to play, and as somewhere for themselves to talk to other adults and have some 'time off' from their children. Financial support (money to spend on their children) and day care were the two needs where there was the biggest gap between what mothers felt they needed and what the family centres were able to provide.

There were some differences in users' perceptions of the aims of the centres, depending on the type they attended. Parents at the client-focused centres were more likely to see the projects as checking on children of concern to Social Services and helping them to understand themselves and their children better, while users of the neighbourhood and community development types of centre were more likely to emphasise a sense of community, learning new skills and gaining confidence. The two centres with an explicit focus on adult education (one community development, the other neighbourhood) were particularly successful in raising self-confidence among users.

Referral or open access

A key finding was that the level of need was high not only among users referred to the centres by social workers, but also among those attending by choice. Referred families (16% of the sample) were slightly *more* disadvantaged than families using the centres on a 'drop in' or 'open access' basis, but lone parents (26% of the sample) were even *more* disadvantaged. Large numbers of children who were not necessarily considered 'at risk' or who were living in families referred to the centres by social workers were nevertheless growing up in very disadvantaged circumstances. The particular mix of open access and closed groups and services that neighbourhood and community development family centres could offer was particularly important in enabling them to respond flexibly to local needs and reach a large number of families. The study concludes that all three types of family centre helped users and their children, but that, given the high levels of disadvantage evident in many areas, centres that offer 'open access' and provide support for community resources are in the long run likely to benefit more families, as part of a neighbourhood-based strategy, than family centres accessible only through social work referrals.

Relevance now

The study provides evidence to support the provision of neighbourhood family centres in disadvantaged areas. They are able to meet a variety of needs and are popular with users, a finding confirmed in the SSI report *Getting Family Support Right*.[35] The provision of family support services in a non-stigmatising way forms a key policy in many government initiatives such as New Deal for Communities, Sure Start and Health/Education/Employment Action Zones, and this study suggests neighbourhood family centres could play an important part in strategic plans to implement such initiatives.

20 Young Children in Wales: An Evaluation of the Children Act 1989 for Day Care Services

June Statham

Published by the Thomas Coram Research Unit, Institute of Education, University of London (1996)

This study was commissioned by the Welsh Office and linked to Study 6 in England. It explored the implementation in Wales of the parts of the Children Act 1989 relating to day care and the regulation of services for children aged under 8 (Parts III and X). It had a particular focus on the provision of services in rural areas, on respect for children's language and culture and on partnership with the independent sector, all of which are mentioned in Volume 2 of the Children Act *Guidance and Regulations*.[47]

Study design

The research was carried out between 1992 and 1995 in all eight Welsh counties, before the re-organisation into 22 unitary authorities. It addressed the same issues and used similar methods to the day care project in England (Study 6), including interviews with key local authority officers soon after implementation and again two years later; analysis of documentation; a survey by bilingual interviewers of 200 child-minders, playgroups and day nurseries across Wales; interviews with representatives of voluntary and private child care organisations; and attendance at voluntary sector early years forums.

Key findings

- The Children Act gave day care services a higher profile and increased communication between agencies with young children.

- Progress with joint planning of children's services was slow, and there was little evidence of corporate strategic planning.

- Despite their important role in providing services in rural areas, voluntary organisations felt consulted rather than involved in planning.

- Resources for registration and inspection work were generally inadequate.

- Local authorities were concentrating on their statutory duty to register and inspect day care services at the expense of providing support and training.

- Welsh language issues were being addressed by day care providers, but issues of race and ethnicity were often seen as irrelevant.

Impact of the Children Act

The findings reinforced the conclusions of the English study. The Children Act had resulted in Welsh local authorities paying more attention to day care services and improving the information they collected about them. Communication between agencies concerned with young children had increased, but authorities had made little progress with corporate planning for children's services or joint commissioning. There was a more thorough system for regulating standards in day care, and the re-registration and annual inspection of day care services required by the Children Act were generally being carried out in a fair and flexible way, with the particular circumstances of small rural services being taken into account. However, resources for registration and inspection were generally inadequate. Local authorities were concentrating on their statutory duty to register and inspect, at the expense of their discretionary powers to provide training and support for independent day care providers.

Interagency working

Some findings of the study were of particular significance for Wales. Given the very low level of local authority day care (two of the eight authorities had no nurseries or family centres of their own), it was especially important for social services departments to find ways of involving voluntary and private services and other agencies in planning and developing day care provision. In rural areas, independent services were often the only ones available. Yet there was little evidence of joint strategic planning, and voluntary organisations often felt consulted rather than involved. A typical comment from the independent sector was: 'I still feel we're on the periphery, not really involved. We have a very good relationship [with the authority] at the ground level, but I don't feel we're involved above that.'

Language and culture

Definitions of need had an urban bias. Only one authority specifically mentioned rural deprivation as a criterion of need. The study found that Welsh language issues were being addressed by day care providers: over two-thirds of the playgroups and nurseries and a third of child-minders used at least some Welsh with the children in their care. However, little attention was being paid to equal opportunities issues and the need to help children develop positive attitudes towards cultural and racial differences, with many day care providers in Wales thinking this was irrelevant to them.

Like the study in England, the Welsh research concluded that the Children Act has led to some worthwhile improvements in day care services for children under 8, but that its impact has been limited by the continuing fragmentation and low priority of services for young children.

Relevance now

This study highlights the importance of finding appropriate ways of ensuring that voluntary organisations have a real say in the multi-agency groups that are increasingly planning and developing early years services, such as the Early Years Development and Childcare Partnerships[64] and the Sure Start initiative.[65] Many of the policy issues raised by this study are now being addressed by the National Childcare Strategy in Wales,[105] and changes to the regulation and inspection of day care services are taking place. The study highlights the importance of developing an integrated strategy that brings together the different strands of provision for young children and pays particular attention to the difficulties caused by rural isolation. This has begun to happen: *Building for the Future: Social Services White Paper for Wales* sets out the basic principles for such a strategy, and the National Assembly for Wales has committed it self to developing a Children and Young People's Strategy covering all public services to children and young people from pre-birth to age 18.[109]

21

Placed and Paid For: Supporting Families through Sponsored Day Care

June Statham, Jean Dillon and Peter Moss

Published by The Stationery Office (forthcoming)

Sponsored day care refers to the purchase of places by social workers and other professionals from independent providers such as child-minders, playgroups and private day nurseries. Guidance accompanying the Children Act 1989 encourages local authorities to use such services to help them fulfil their duty to support children in need. This study explored how and to what extent authorities were using this provision, and its effectiveness from the perspective of the different stakeholders.

Study design

The study had three parts. It began with a national mapping exercise based on a postal questionnaire to all English social services departments (response rate 83%) plus secondary analysis of government day care statistics and relevant local authority documentation. This was followed by visits to twelve authorities operating day care placement schemes, including interviews with key officers and a postal survey of day care providers who had accepted referred children. The final stage of the study involved case studies of the referral process in two authorities, focusing on individual families and including an assessment of the quality of care in sixteen child-minding placements.

Key findings

- Most local authorities purchase places in voluntary and private day care facilities, but for very few children.
- Nearly two-thirds of the authorities have targeted sponsored day care on families with a higher level of need since the Children Act.
- Sponsored day care is increasingly being offered on a part-time, short-term basis.
- Over half of the authorities experienced difficulty in recruiting enough suitable independent providers in the areas where they most needed them.
- Day care providers valued the satisfaction and challenge of providing a service for children in need, but many were critical of the poor support and training and inadequate remuneration they received.
- Parents were generally appreciative of the service, but many still had a high level of need after the service was withdrawn or the child moved on to school.
- The quality of care in the sponsored child-minding placements varied, but was on average better in the authority which provided more training and support.

The extent of sponsored day care

The mapping stage of the study demonstrated the difficulty of obtaining accurate information on the number of children provided with sponsored day care and the amount spent on this form of family support, especially when places were funded from locally managed section 17 budgets. Almost all the local authorities did purchase places in voluntary and private day care, but generally for very few children – nationally, around half a per cent of children under 5 at any one time. Sponsored places were used for children in need. Nearly two-thirds of the authorities reported that since the Children Act such places had been targeted on families with a higher level of need, and that single parents needing child care were no longer eligible. Less than a third of the authorities subsidised day care fees for families who were on low incomes but did not meet any other criteria of need. In some cases, stricter criteria for access to day care were being applied in order to free resources for broader family support measures, and because other initiatives such as the National Childcare Strategy were thought to be making day care more widely available.

The service

There was substantial variation in how placements were organised and day care providers recruited, with organised schemes more common for referrals to child-minders than for playgroups or private day nurseries. Day care advisers and under-eights officers played a key role in recommending suitable providers for social work referrals, but only a minority of authorities had an officer with specific responsibility for placing children in voluntary and private day care. Sponsored places were increasingly being offered on a part-time and short-term basis, often for two or three sessions a week for an initial maximum period of three or six months. The service was provided at times of particular difficulties or crisis, after which sponsorship would be withdrawn, rather than providing on-going support. However many of the families had ongoing, chronic needs, and both they and their children could have benefited from more extensive periods of day care support.

The providers

Over half of the authorities in the survey reported experiencing difficulty in recruiting enough suitable independent providers, mainly because of geographical issues (a shortage of services in deprived or rural areas), a lack of appropriately skilled providers to take children in need and poor rates of pay, especially for child-minders. The providers themselves could see both advantages and disadvantages in working in partnership with the local authority in this way. On the plus side, they valued the sense of satisfaction and challenge from providing a much-needed service to vulnerable children, and the opportunities for development offered by working alongside other professionals and learning new skills. On the other hand, only a third judged the level of training and support they were given as good, and there were many complaints about the lateness and inadequacy of local authority payments. Satisfaction was higher when authorities were able to offer a reasonable level of support and appropriate training, and this was often linked to having a designated officer and a formal scheme for matching children and providers.

The parents

Parents were generally appreciative of the service offered and most thought it had helped, although many still had a high level of need after the service was withdrawn or the child moved on to school. The case studies in the final stage of the study documented the considerable amount of work that local authority officers put into finding and setting up placements with child-minders. However, in both case study authorities, only half of the placements offered were taken up by parents. A number of these placements also finished prematurely.

Quality of care

On a widely used observation rating scale for family day care, the sponsored child-minders observed in the final stage of the study had ratings between 'minimal' and 'good'. None had an overall rating approaching 'excellent'. Although there were some very positive examples of good practice where child-minders supported both children and parents, there were also cases where vulnerable children did not appear to be receiving the high-quality care they needed. Quality was on average better in the authority where child-minders received more support and training from the local authority.

The study concluded that sponsored day care has an important role to play as part of a continuum of services for children in need, allowing local authorities to respond flexibly to a range of needs of children and parents, and to provide home-based care for younger children. However, concerns were raised about the lack of training and support for independent providers who take referred children, the inadequate monitoring of placements, and the difficulty local authorities often experienced in finding suitable services in the areas where they were most needed.

Relevance now

Supporting children and their families through services such as sponsored day care contributes towards meeting the objectives in *Quality Protects* and *Children First* of protecting children from abuse and neglect and improving the life chances of children in need.[69, 106] The findings from this study reinforce the importance of a strategic framework for Children's Services Planning which integrates different levels and types of support, so that short-term interventions offered to families at times of crisis are provided within a framework of universally available services. The study also demonstrates the need for better training and support for the social care workforce, which includes independent day care providers, and for funding (such as the start-up grants for new child-minders announced in June 2000) to encourage the development of services in the areas where they are most needed.

Family Support in Cases of Emotional Maltreatment and Neglect

June Thoburn, Jennifer Wilding and Jacqueline Watson
Published by The Stationery Office (2000)

This study investigated the relationship between children 'in need' and children 'in need of protection' because of concerns about neglect or emotional abuse. It builds on earlier research reported in *Child Protection: Messages from Research*, which found that a large majority of children referred because of child protection concerns were quickly filtered out of the system and received no protective or support services.[52] This was particularly marked for referrals for emotional maltreatment or neglect. The present study took a closer look at this type of referral, focusing on children aged under 8.

Study design

Information was gathered from three social services departments (two inner-city areas with ethnically diverse populations and a mainly rural county with a predominantly white population). In the first phase of the study, social services staff completed a monitoring form for every child referred over a period of 20–30 weeks in 1994–95, which yielded information on 712 children in 555 families. From these monitoring forms a sample of 180 families were selected for a more detailed study of their files. They comprised families with children referred because of concerns about neglect or emotional maltreatment, and a smaller comparison group who had requested or been referred for a family support service. A particular strength of this study is the inclusion of a substantial number of parents of minority ethnic origin. Of these 180 families, 122 agreed to be interviewed by the researchers and to allow health visitors or school nurses to complete a health record on their children. These families were interviewed eight to twelve months later, and updated information was collected from health professionals and social services' records. A final phase of the study involved group discussions with social workers and managers about how they reached decisions, as well as interviews with the social workers for eighteen of the families who received a longer-term service.

Key findings

- Just under half of the referrals of children under 8 involved child protection concerns and just over half did not.

- The most common reason for referral for emotional maltreatment or neglect was parents leaving their child alone, often because they were unable to afford child care.

- The general picture was of families struggling and not quite managing to cope with serious practical problems. Parents who were deliberately neglectful or cruel, or who were chronically incompetent, comprised only a small minority of those referred because of concerns about neglect or emotional abuse.

- Neglectful families referred to Social Services and those referred for or requesting a service had similar needs, but the former were less likely to receive a service.

- Even when a family had been referred without their consent for neglectful behaviour, they were quite likely to report satisfaction with Social Services provided some help had been delivered.

- Three years after implementation of the Children Act 1989, assessment was still based on risk rather than need, and opportunities were thus missed to provide services that might have prevented more serious problems developing.

Reasons for referral

Of all the referrals of children under 8 to social services departments, just under half involved child protection concerns and just over half did not, at least initially. Of those that did involve child protection concerns, only a third were concerned with allegations of possible physical or sexual abuse, whilst two-thirds were concerned with allegations of possible neglect, emotional maltreatment or other child protection concerns. There was considerable overlap in reasons for referral, demonstrating that concerns about children's care and safety cannot be neatly pigeon-holed into mutually exclusive categories.

The researchers obtained further details of the reasons for referral from social services' records for the 180 families in the interview sample. These showed that the most common reason for referral for emotional maltreatment or neglect was parents leaving their child alone, usually for short periods. These families often had working parents who were unable to afford child care. The next most common category was other physical neglect (such as inadequate care or nourishment), followed by children living in households where there was extreme spouse abuse. There were few referrals due to withholding of affection or emotional cruelty, and the general picture was of families who were struggling and not quite managing to cope with serious practical problems, rather than families of the 'high criticism, low warmth' type highlighted in previous research.[52] Through pressure of circumstances and in a family crisis, they had become caught up in a child protection system that was more attuned to assessing risk than to bringing out the best in parents struggling in adversity. A disproportionate number of refugee and recent immigrant families came into this group.

The response of Social Services

'Neglectful' families referred to Social Services and those referred for or requesting a service resembled each other more than they did families in general in the local population, and appeared to have similar needs. However, team leaders were found to respond differently depending on the type of referral. Referrals framed in terms of neglectful behaviour or emotional abuse were more likely to be steered away, not only from the formal child protection system, but also from the provision of services. The initial assessment of such referrals tended to be low-key and to concentrate on the risks rather than on the needs of children and parents. Three years after implementation of the Children Act, social workers and their managers were still essentially basing their practice and their systems for allocating resources on the actions of parents rather than on the actual or likely harm to, or impairment to the development of, the children. Opportunities were thus missed to provide services which might have prevented more serious problems developing.

The parents' views

The most important influence on parents' attitudes to the social services departments was whether or not they had received some help. Even when a family had been referred, without their consent, for neglectful behaviour, they were quite likely to report satisfaction with Social Services provided some help had been delivered. If social workers were able to look beyond the presenting incident, make some assessment of need and deliver some help, they were often able to overcome the parent's initial hostility. However, if parents were merely investigated and warned about the consequences of further incidents, they were usually left dissatisfied and angry.

Assessment

Given the large volume of cases that cross the threshold of social services departments concerning potential 'children in need', the researchers argue that there needs to be a better system for assessing referrals, based not so much on the reason for referral as on an assessment of whether the family will be able to meet the needs of their children without the provision of services. The following categories are suggested:

- cases that can be closed after a broad assessment of need, possibly with referral to a more appropriate service;

- cases that need a short piece of work or advocacy to put together a package of appropriate services to alleviate needs and risks;

- cases that need more extensive or intensive family support and/or therapeutic services; and

- cases that require the formal child protection system plus a package of practical and emotional support services.

The 'revolving door'

A small but significant number of the families in this study kept returning to Social Services again and again, in a 'revolving door' syndrome that was expensive for the authority and alienating for the family. For some, a short piece of intensive work or advocacy might have prevented problems later on. For others, access over a longer period of time to a less intensive service, such as a family centre, could have provided them with support at times when they needed it and thus avoided repeated referrals to Social Services. Knowing which families are likely to need such help requires social work expertise and highlights the important role of the duty social workers who process the initial referrals.

Relevance now

This study supports the development of the new framework for assessment of children, which looks holistically at the needs of children within their families and the communities in which they live. It supports an approach that attempts to strengthen parental capacity and is based on assessing the children's developmental needs. The findings reinforce the value of early intervention to support families and to make child care more affordable, for example through the Sure Start and National Childcare strategies. It reflects the view in the White Paper *Modernising Social Services* that social services departments have a part to play in supporting children in need and their families in the community.[74]

Services for Children in Need: From Policy to Practice

Jane Tunstill and Jane Aldgate
Published by The Stationery Office (2000)

This study was concerned with families who approach Social Services themselves for help, or who are referred by other agencies for services under section 17 of the Children Act 1989 rather than because of child protection concerns or because they are disabled. It looked at the circumstances and needs of these families and the support they were offered, from the perspective of parents, children and social workers.

Study design

The original intention of this study was to focus on services for children in their middle years (7–12), as most previous work had looked at support for families with younger children. However, the slow rate of sample identification required this plan to be modified, and the final design involved 93 children from seven local authorities (both urban and rural). Half were aged 7–12 and the rest either 0–6 or adolescents aged 13–16. Children referred because of child protection concerns or disabilities were excluded. Families were recruited with the help of social workers, who gave parents a brief written explanation of the study and details of how to enlist as a participant. No information was available on the number or characteristics of families who declined to participate. Data was collected from interviews with the main parent or carer at the time of referral and again six months later, between 1995 and 1997. Social workers also completed a questionnaire for each case, including information about the involvement of other agencies.

A major methodological problem for the researchers was that less than half of the authorities kept a record of all those who requested a service, so it was impossible to know the proportion of the study cases to total referrals. Defining what constituted a 'referral' also presented a challenge, since access to family support services (for instance those provided by family centres) is often deliberately open and informal in order to reduce stigma.

The families' needs

There was a high level of need among families approaching or referred to Social Services for support. Half of the families had housing problems, half had health problems and almost two-thirds had financial problems. Difficult parental relationships and reconstituted families were common. Over a third of the children had educational needs, especially children in families under stress. Families had often been struggling for a long time with a high level of need before approaching Social Services, and many had past histories of difficult births, post-natal problems, parenting problems and domestic violence. When interviewed by the researchers they often revealed higher levels of need than they had presented to Social Services, pointing to the need for assessment to be exploratory and open. For example, a parent who had gone to Social Services asking for practical help with housework and child care, after being injured in a car accident, turned out to be very concerned about her daughter's behavioural problems and relationship with her stepfather.

Children's behavioural problems and parents' emotional problems were associated. Social workers viewed almost half of the families as having problems related to family stability. There was an escalating spiral effect: family stress made children's behavioural problems worse and this in turn increased family stress.

The parents' views

The parents had various motives for approaching Social Services. The researchers categorise these as 'opting in' (families actively trying to solve their problems and seeing Social Services as one resource among others); 'welfare dependency' (relying on others to solve their problems) and 'no option' (where the involvement of Social Services was essential or inevitable because of the nature of their problems). One key finding was that for many of the parents in this study – none of whom were referred because of child protection concerns – Social Services was seen as a first rather than a last resort when help was needed. Just under half of the children and over two-thirds of the parents had positive views of Social Services, and there was great potential for working constructively with them to address their problems. Where parents did receive a service they were generally very appreciative and made good use of it. The benefits anticipated and obtained by families were stress relief, help with child development, improved family relationships and alleviation of practical problems.

Provision of services

Whether or not families received a service varied substantially, depending on the authority in which they lived. Overall, a third received no services, but those who were professionally referred had more chance of receiving them. Families in need because of social deprivation were not only refused services more often than those in other need categories but were also more likely to be offered a single service rather than a package including social work support. Once families got through the threshold of eligibility, the range of services available to support them was quite wide, including day care, family centres, out-of-school provision, youth clubs, befriending schemes and referral to other agencies such as education and mental health. Much of it was provided by voluntary organisations supported financially by the local authority. One gap was in services for children in the middle age group, 7 to 12-year-olds, who exhibited behavioural problems. If they behaved badly at school, they were likely to be excluded; if they behaved badly at home, there was little to help parents cope.

The most requested form of help by parents was social work support, yet this was the least likely to be met. What parents wanted was someone to share their problems, provide a listening ear and help them access the services they needed. Support did not have to involve material resources; it could mean direct casework with families or acting as an advocate on their behalf. Although social workers recognised the importance of this work, they were often unable to offer it because of the expectation that they focus on child protection.

The children's views

The children mostly wanted support, help with schooling and resolution of family conflict. Although around half of them felt involved by parents and Social Services, few took part in decision-making. Only a third knew why the approach or referral had been made.

Relevance now

The study demonstrates the overlapping nature of social deprivation, parental ill-health, parenting problems and children's needs. It reinforces the importance of taking a holistic view of a family's needs, and of agencies working together to provide a range of services, possibly through joint commissioning and budget arrangements as detailed in the Partnership in Action initiative. Access to such services needs to be simplified, perhaps using family centres and GP surgeries as well as social services area offices. The study also highlights the lack of services to support middle-age and older children, especially those with emotional and behavioural problems. More attention needs to be paid to the design and delivery of services for this age group, and to finding appropriate access points for older children to access support, such as school and youth services.

24 Looking After Children: Research into Practice

Harriet Ward (editor)
Published by HMSO (1995)

The Looking After Children (LAC) project was established by the Department of Health in 1987 to consider the question of outcomes in child care and to produce a series of practical instruments (the assessment and action records) to help social work practitioners to consider the quality of parenting offered to children looked after away from their families.[67] This study piloted the early LAC materials and investigated the issues surrounding their implementation by local authorities between the publication of the original materials in 1991 and the launch of the revised materials in 1995.

Study design

This study was a research and development project. It included a study of 204 children looked after in five local authorities, the purpose of which was to discover how acceptable the assessment and action records would be to social workers, carers and children, and whether they would be used on a regular basis. It also included a study of a community group of 379 children in 'ordinary' families, to discover whether the content of the records adequately reflected parents' concerns about the upbringing of their children, and an in-depth study of implementation in one of the participating authorities. The focus of the project was on testing and developing the assessment and action records, but it also provided information on the experience of looked after children in the participating authorities.

Key findings

- The areas assessed by the LAC materials did reflect the concerns of 'ordinary' parents.

- The materials were used more effectively when they were integrated into existing local authority assessment procedures and their use was supported by senior managers.

- Social workers found that the materials helped them to identify when important information about looked after children was missing.

- Children looked after by the authority were less likely than those living with their families to receive adequate health and education services.

The community study

Evidence suggested that the materials were neither as time-consuming to use nor as costly as some critics had anticipated, and that the benefits to be gained from using them increased over time and eventually justified the initial expenditure. Objections that the original records were not applicable to children with disabilities or from minority ethnic groups were upheld and were taken into account during the revision. The criticism that the questions asked were too middle class and too remote from the situation of disadvantaged children was found not to be justified.

Introducing the materials

Certain conditions were necessary to facilitate the introduction of new initiatives, such as the Looking After Children materials, into local authorities. The researchers found that social work practitioners were more likely to complete the records if the project had the unequivocal support of management, if there were clear attainable time-scales and if there was a specific requirement for all staff in a team or area office to take part. For the materials to be more widely used on a regular basis, they needed to be seen as part of an ongoing planning process for looked after children and to be integrated into existing local authority procedures rather than tacked on in addition.

Using the materials

Having established that practitioners could be persuaded to use the records, the research team next considered whether they were being completed correctly and used in the way in which it was intended. They found that almost all the primary 'quality of care' questions were answered. Social workers and carers were willing to examine the everyday details of children's experiences, and the materials frequently helped them to identify instances where important information about a child was unavailable. However, in some cases questions were ignored. For example, social workers did not always consider it necessary to answer questions on identity if a child was white, even though only a few of these refer to racial issues and the dimension covers many other areas that are relevant to all looked after children. The questions in the education section were also occasionally disregarded if the child was one of the 10% in the looked after group who was not attending school. When a looked after child was excluded from formal education, it appeared that there could be no one who took on responsibility for compensatory action.

ervices received by looked after children

looked after children were generally less likely than their peers in the commun-
o receive health and education services, despite the fact that the local
ority, in its capacity as a corporate parent, should be in a strong position
ure that the children for whom it is responsible benefit from the services
d by other agencies. This was partly because looked after children

moved more frequently (the most common experience was three placements *during the period that they had been looked after*, compared to one change of address *in their lives* for similar aged children in the community). However, the looked after children's poorer access to services also reflected inadequate co-operation and dialogue between the different organisations responsible for their care.

Relevance now

The revised Looking After Children materials were published in 1995, having addressed some of the issues raised by this study. A three-year implementation programme was undertaken, and all authorities in England and Wales are now expected to use the system. Further research has been undertaken: firstly to identify how the data collected on individual children could be aggregated and analysed on a routine basis in order to provide management information on looked after children; secondly to investigate how the LAC materials can be used to identify the needs of children in the community as well as those looked after by the authority. The LAC assessment and action records form the basis of the *Framework for the Assessment of Children in Need and Their Families*.[79]

Section II

B. Reports and studies

Alongside the Department of Health's commissioned research programme, the Social Services Inspectorate carried out a series of inspections and studies that addressed aspects of the Children Act 1989. The reports included here were published between 1992 and April 1999. They chart the ongoing process of putting the Act into practice, and the later reports provide an update on developments since some of the research projects were completed. The SSI reports are of two kinds, drawing on different sources of evidence:

- national or overview inspection reports, which addressed the topics covered by the Children Act programme; and

- short studies concerned with court orders, which explored issues arising as the Act was being implemented. These studies aimed to clarify policy and feed into the implementation process. They differ from SSI inspections by being focused on the experiences rather than the performance of authorities, and they differ from the research projects by being shorter term and less rigorous in their methodology.

The Secretaries of State for Health and Wales also produced a number of reports for parliament on progress in implementing the Children Act covering the period 1992–2000.

SSI inspection reports

25 Services to Disabled Children and their Families (1994)

Report of a national inspection of services to disabled children and their families, undertaken in four local authorities in January 1994. Aimed to establish the progress made in implementing the requirements of the Children Act 1989 in relation to disabled children.

- Progress has been slow and some aspects of the service were only just starting to receive attention.

- None of the four authorities was operating an effective register of disabled children.

- There was insufficient emphasis on an interagency approach and little evidence of effective co-ordination of assessments for disabled children under different legislation.

- Authorities with specialist children's disability workers had in general made better progress than those with generic workers.

- There was a lack of management information for planning.

- Mechanisms for consulting with parents, especially those from minority ethnic groups, needed to be more widely developed.

- More culturally sensitive services were needed.

- Despite a commitment to ascertaining the wishes of children, there was little support or guidance for staff on how to do this.

- Authorities needed to work more closely with the independent sector to provide services for disabled children and their families.

26 Inspection of Private and Voluntary Day Nurseries for Children under Eight (1994)

Assessment of the effect of the Children Act 1989 on the process of regulating voluntary and private children's day services, and how that process had influenced standards of care. Based on inspection of sixteen independent nurseries in four local authorities.

- The quality of care and co-operation with parents in the nurseries inspected was generally good. Regulation appeared to be having a positive impact on standards.

- Areas that could be improved included cultural sensitivity, awareness of child protection procedures and record keeping.

- Authorities needed to involve the independent sector more closely in planning services for children under 8.

27 Children in Need: Report of an SSI Inspection of Social Services Departments' Family Support Services 1993/1995 (1996)

Examination of the availability of family support services under section 17 of the Children Act 1989 in eight local authorities.

- All local authorities were committed to the key principles of the Children Act but were less successful in implementing them in practice.

- Social services departments tended to focus on children at risk rather than on family support.

- Management information systems were poor, and authorities often had little knowledge of the level and type of need in their area.

- Assessment, planning and review systems were not in place in most social services departments inspected.

- Most social services departments had some good services, but overall they had not been well thought out and were not making the most effective use of resources.

28 When Leaving Home is also Leaving Care (1997)

An inspection of leaving care and after-care services in nine social services departments in the first half of 1996, focusing on the experiences of young people.

- Found some good work on leaving care services and many examples of good practice, especially involving the voluntary sector.

- Specialist leaving care schemes led to young people being better supported, more likely to maintain contact and more confident about their needs.

- Young people valued the support of foster carers, but their role was often not formally recognised by the authority after the young person left care.

- Access to primary health care services was usually good, but there were problems in obtaining mental health services.

- Disabled young people experienced particular difficulties in moving from child to adult services.

- Poor information and monitoring systems hindered good planning. Authorities rarely tracked what happened to their care leavers.

29 The Education of Children Who Are Looked After by Local Authorities (1997)

Joint inspection by the SSI and the Office for Standards in Education (OFSTED) of the education received by the 1,607 children looked after in four local authorities. Based on records provided by social services departments and detailed inspection of 18 cases.

- There was widespeared underachievement among looked after children, especially in secondary schools.

- Liaison between social workers, carers and teachers was fragmented and patchy, and there was no co-ordinated approach to raising achievement.

- It was unclear who was responsible for overseeing the education of looked after children. Sometimes conscientious carers assumed this role and pressed for improvements, but this was not consistent.

- There was insufficient training available on how to meet the educational needs of looked after children.

30 Issues Emerging from Children and Families Overview Reports (1997)

Brings together the lessons from twelve overview reports by the SSI on services for children and families. Attempts to provide an overall assessment of the way in which four key Children Act principles have been implemented: promoting the welfare of the child; having regard to the child's wishes and feelings; working in partnership; and meeting children's specific needs:

- Found 'mainly an encouraging picture'.

- The four principles had not been fully translated into practice due partly to limited placement choice, but also to the lack of recording of children's wishes and feelings.

- The area requiring most work was that of meeting specific needs (with respect to race, religion, disability, etc.).

- There was a strong association between specialist teams and high user satisfaction, for example in work with children with disabilities, youth justice and leaving care services.

- Parents particularly valued working in partnership with family centres and preferred being assessed there.

- There had been significant improvements in child protection work between 1992 and 1996, including clearer time-scales and better multi-agency working.

- Management information systems were universally poor, making it difficult for authorities to know how far they had managed to re-focus services towards family support.

- Training was needed for social workers in the following key areas: direct work with children; working with ethnic minority families; communicating with children with special needs; assessment and record-keeping.

31 Responding to Families in Need: Inspection of Assessment, Planning and Decision-making in Family Support Services (1997)

Report of SSI inspection of the responses of eight social services departments to requests for services from children in need and their families.

- Found 'a very worrying picture'. Most social services departments were doing some things very well, but only one performed adequately against every standard.

- All authorities had established interagency Children's Services Planning arrangements, but in most authorities some partner agencies were not playing their full part.

- Child protection investigations and looked after children cases were prioritised over support to other families of children in need. There had been limited progress in refocusing children's services.

- Eligibility criteria for family support services were poorly developed and used to exclude people rather than to make services more widely available. Front-line staff were often making decisions about eligibility without adequate training.

- There was limited management information about the demand, quality, quantity and effectiveness of services or the outcomes for users.

- On the positive side, most social services departments were beginning to develop a wide range of services to support families, such as day care for under-fives, family centres and outreach work.

32 Someone Else's Children (1998)

Brings together the findings from two inspections of services for looked after children: one on the planning and decision-making for such children in ten authorities; the other on the safety of children looked after in seventeen authorities.

- Services for looked after children were very inconsistent. Staff did not always follow agreed procedures, and managers did not have systems in place to check on this.

- Relationships between social services departments and health authorities were extremely variable. There were particular problems in meeting the health needs of children with severe behavioural or psychiatric problems.

- There was a lack of placement choice, especially for children with specialised needs, and many children who required permanent placement had a long wait.

- A high proportion of looked after children were excluded from school, especially those living in residential care.

- Contracting arrangements with the independent sector were poorly developed compared to adult services, and authorities were not using contracts to ensure that they had access to a range of appropriate placements.

- There were some serious deficiencies in the vetting of the staff and volunteers who would have contact with looked after children.

33 Removing Barriers for Disabled Children: Inspection of Services for Disabled Children and their Families (1998)

Based on multidisciplinary inspections in eight authorities of the services for disabled children living in the local community with their families. Focused on the experience of the service users.

- Families of disabled children still faced many barriers when they tried to access social services. It was difficult for them to find out what services were available and support may only have been offered when a situation had reached crisis point.

- Parents had to 'tell their story' to a range of professionals in social services, health and education to receive all the support they needed.

- Most children and their families were assessed for existing services rather than receiving services to meet their assessed needs.

- However, when services were offered they were generally of good quality and much appreciated by families.

- Users were more satisfied and the service was of a better quality when specialist rather than generic workers were used.

- The goal of integration of services for disabled children and their families had not yet been achieved, but where multi-agency services existed they worked very well, especially in services for children under 8.

- Since the earlier inspection[25] authorities had made considerable progress in setting up registers of disabled children. These were not yet being widely used for planning purposes, but they did have an important function in the dissemination of information.

- Areas still needing development were joint working, direct work with children, making information accessible and 'joined-up thinking' on service planning.

34 Planning to Deliver: Inspection of Children's Services Planning (1998)

Inspected interagency planning arrangements for developing Children's Services Plans in eight local authorities between April and December 1998.

- Local authorities were struggling to get to grips with planning children's services, and there was little evidence of strategic planning.

- Most Children's Services Plans described what authorities were currently doing rather than acting as a tool for planning.

- Few plans contained information on costs, and there was little sharing of financial information between agencies.

- Most authorities still did not have a definition of children in need that was shared between agencies.

- There was little reference to performance or outcome measures.

- Consultation with users was often poor, although there was some good practice in relation to parents of disabled children, and comments or feedback on previous plans did not appear to be fed into the planning cycle.

35 Getting Family Support Right: Inspection of the Delivery of Family Support Services (1999)

Inspection of eight authorities between December 1997 and July 1998, after the policy drive to re-focus children's services. Examined three key family support services: community social work, child and adolescent mental health social work and family centres. Looked at the experience of over 2,000 families from the third month of service to a year on and studied 80 cases in detail. Whilst the 1997 report[31] looked at access to family support services, this one looked at those who actually received a service.

- Families were generally very satisfied with and appreciative of support services once they received them.

- Many families had not realised that such services were available, or that Social Services was an agency that could help them rather than take away their children.

- Social workers lacked the skills or training to undertake direct work with children and young people as a form of support.

- Family centres were rated highly as a form of family support. Parents liked them; they provided a range of services despite limited resources; and they were good at promoting the identify of black and minority ethnic and disabled children and at consulting with families.

- In a substantial minority of the cases studied, as many as 40% in some authorities, there were possible indicators of the abuse or neglect of children that were not being properly recognised or assessed.

- Twenty-five per cent of the children using services had parents with mental health needs, but relationships between child care and adult mental health social workers were often poor.

- There was insufficient understanding of the impact of emotional abuse on children.

SSI court orders and other studies

36 Court Orders Study (1992)

Examined the influences on local authority decision-making in 21 cases where there was a choice between providing services without recourse to court and seeking a court order to endorse service plans.

- The reasons for not seeking a court order were very varied, and no authority had a coherent list of key factors that could serve as a framework for risk assessment.

- Whether or not cases proceeded to court, all 21 families were provided with a significant level of services.

- There was a mistaken belief that the 'no order' principle of the Children Act 1989 could not be satisfied if parents were co-operating with the local authority.

- In almost all cases the local authorities judged with hindsight that they had made the right decision about whether or not to seek a court order, but were nevertheless pessimistic about the prognosis for the children involved.

37 Timetabling of Interim Care Orders Study (1994)

Investigation of the reasons for the length of proceedings in 25 cases involving applications for section 31 Care or Supervision Orders.

- Cases lasted an average of 33 weeks, with those ending in the county court lasting the longest and those in family proceedings courts taking the least time. Most cases involved at least one transfer of courts.

- The three factors contributing most to the length of proceedings were, in order: assessment by experts, complexity of the issues and lack of co-operation by parents.

- Less than half of the social workers involved in these cases felt like equal partners in the scheduling process, and nearly all felt they needed more help with writing statements for courts.

- Delay was not always negative. All guardians and most social workers agreed that all the study cases had involved purposeful delay.

38 Planning Long-term Placement Study (1994)

Exploration of 66 complex cases in four local authorities to evaluate social workers' claims that the Children Act 1989 had made it more difficult to make long-term care plans for these children.

- Found no evidence that under the Children Act it was more difficult to plan and achieve long-term placements for children who needed this approach.

- Many of these cases were very complex and would be difficult to manage under any legislation.

- Difficulties were often due to inadequacies in the assessment processes and procedures within local authorities and courts.

- Social services departments made great efforts to consult with parents about decisions concerning their child, but they were sometimes in danger of losing sight of the child's best interests.

- It was difficult to find enough long-term carers for children with special long-term needs.

39 Contact Orders Study (1994)

Follow-up to the previous study, exploring in more detail the contact arrangements made by courts in a small number of selected cases and drawing on discussions with local authority staff and guardians ad litem.

- The Children Act 1989 had resulted in courts and local authorities treating contact issues as an integral part of the care plan rather than as a separate issue.

- Contact plans were often complex, including full, half- and step-siblings as well as significant adults, and required a high level of service input and resources.

- Contact issues were frequently subject to prolonged legal argument, which delayed implementation of large parts of the care plan.

- Some local authority managers were concerned that children's needs were not being put first by allowing parents extensive opportunities to prove their suitability through access arrangements rather than seeking long-term substitute families for the children.

40 Residence Orders Study (1995)

Study of the experience in three local authorities of the new Residence Orders introduced by the Children Act 1989, based on discussions with local authority staff, guardians ad litem and other interested parties.

- There was great diversity in how these new orders were used, and they had yet to be widely taken up.

- Residence Orders were being made for children of all ages, but they seemed to be more easily made for children over the age of 6.

- Residence holders were predominantly grandparents and foster carers.

- Local authorities were cautious about the use of Residence Orders and mostly used them to confirm existing arrangements rather than introduce new ones.

- There was a need for clearer policies on issues such as payment to relatives.

- There was a need for more information and research on the outcomes of Residence Orders.

41 Care Planning and Court Orders Study (1998)

Description of the experiences of four local authorities in developing care plans and putting them into effect. Studied 28 cases in detail and summarised a range of judicial opinions on the use of care plans at court.

- In general, local authority legal staff, social workers, guardians and courts worked together well.

- Practitioners were committed to the principles of the Children Act 1989 and to keeping families together.

- Courts perceived plans as having improved in recent years and being more authoritative.

- Courts and legal staff supported the idea of a national care plan format, but social workers and managers were less sure.

- Social services departments needed to do more to monitor and review how far permanent placements were being achieved for children and to share these findings with the court.

Children Act Reports to Parliament

42 Children Act Report (1993)

The first report to Parliament by the Secretaries of State for Health and for Wales on the Children Act 1989. It was too early to gauge the success or otherwise of the Act, but the report found 'some encouraging trends as well as some early difficulties'.

On the positive side, one year on:

- There had been a drop in the number of children looked after by local authorities, and an increase in the proportion looked after through voluntary arrangements.

- All authorities had established systems to receive representations and complaints about services from children, parents and carers.

- All authorities had established properly managed panels of guardians ad litem to fulfil the new requirements of the Act, and early indications were that this was reducing delay in appointing guardians.

- Many authorities had gone to considerable lengths to publicise their services, in a variety of languages, and to bring them to the attention of those who may need them.

However, progress was less advanced in the following areas:

- Re-registering existing private and voluntary day care services for children under 8, and inspecting and registering those wanting to set up private children's homes.

- Ensuring all child protection cases were allocated to a social worker.

- Seeking out the extent of children in need and developing services to meet them.

- Working with voluntary bodies and independent agencies to develop services.

43 Children Act Report 1993 (1994)

The second report concentrated on particular aspects of children's services, including family support, looked after children, child protection and day care.

- Progress with implementing section 17 of the Children Act 1989 was slow. More family support services needed to be developed, and some authorities were finding it hard to move towards a more pro-active partnership role with families.

- The number of court orders was higher than the previous year, but still below the pre-Act level. The number of children looked after and on a child protection register continued to decline.

- The duty to review day care services for children under 8 had led to increased co-operation between local agencies and given a higher profile to such services, but the reviews were often weak on how proposals would be taken forward.

- There was still a high proportion of unallocated child protection cases, which could not be explained by social needs indicators, child protection registration rates or particular management arrangements.

- The report concluded that 'it is still too early to make a firm judgement, but it appears that overall the Act is working smoothly'.

44 The Children Act Report 1995–1999 (2000)

This is more comprehensive than previous reports and includes useful summaries of statistics and key messages from inspections. It presents information within the framework of the eight *Quality Protects* objectives and covers:

- secure attachment and stability;
- child protection;
- life chances of children in need;
- life chances of looked after children;
- life chances for care leavers;
- services for disabled children and their families;
- assessment and decision-making;
- resource planning;
- activity in the courts; and
- early years.

Section III

References

The references are listed under several headings. The first four headings refer to the studies themselves and the material that is summarised in Section II. The 24 studies are arranged in alphabetical order, according to the first author of each study. The SSI inspections, reports and court studies, Children Act Reports to Parliament, *Guidance and Regulations* and previous Department of Health overviews are all arranged in chronological order, starting with the earliest. The final section, containing a miscellany of relevant references, is arranged in alphabetical order. When there are many references with the same authorship, these are arranged chronologically.

1   The 24 Children Act studies

2   Social Services Inspectorate inspection reports

3   SSI court orders and other studies

4   Children Act Reports to Parliament

5   Children Act 1989 *Guidance and Regulations* and accompanying documentation

6   Previous Department of Health overviews

7   Other relevant publications

References

1 The 24 Children Act studies

1 Aldgate, J. and Tunstill, J. (1995) *Making Sense of Section 17: Implementing Services for Children in Need within the 1989 Children Act*, London: HMSO

2 Aldgate, J. and Bradley, M. (1999) *Supporting Families through Short-term Fostering*, London: The Stationery Office

3 Biehal, N., Clayden, J., Stein, M. and Wade, J. (1995) *Moving On: Young People and Leaving Care Schemes*, London: HMSO

4 Brandon, M., Thoburn, J., Lewis, A. and Way, A. (1999) *Safeguarding Children with the Children Act 1989*, London: The Stationery Office

5 Brophy, J. with Bates, P., Brown, L., Cohen, S., Radcliffe, P. and Wale, C. J. (1999) *Expert Evidence in Child Protection Litigation: Where Do We Go From Here?* London: The Stationery Office

6 Candappa, M., Bull, J., Cameron, C., Moss, P. and Owen, C. (1996) *Policy into Practice: Day Care Services for Children under Eight,* London: The Stationery Office

7 Cleaver, H. (2000) *Fostering Family Contact : A Study of Children, Parents and Foster Carers*, London: The Stationery Office

8 Colton, M., Drury, C. and Williams, M. (1995) *Children in Need: Family Support under the Children Act 1989*, Aldershot: Gower

9 Freeman, P. and Hunt, J. (1998) *Parental Perspectives on Care Proceedings*, London: The Stationery Office

10 Grimshaw, R. and Sinclair, R. (1997) *Planning to Care: Regulation, Procedure and Practice under the Children Act 1989*, London: National Children's Bureau

11 Harwin, J., Owen, M., Locke, R. and Forrester, D. (forthcoming) *Making Care Orders Work: A Study of Care Plans and their Implementation*, London: The Stationery Office

12 Hunt, J., Macleod, A. and Thomas, C. (1999) *The Last Resort: Child Protection, the Courts and the 1989 Children Act*, London: The Stationery Office

13 Hunt, J. and Macleod, A. (1999) *The Best-Laid Plans: Outcomes of Judicial Decisions in Child Protection Proceedings,* London: The Stationery Office

14 Marsh, P. and Peel, M. (1999) *Leaving Care in Partnership: Family Involvement with Care Leavers*, London: The Stationery Office

15 Packman, J. and Hall, C. (1998) *From Care to Accommodation: Support, Protection and Control in Child Care Services*, London: The Stationery Office

16 Petrie, P., Poland, G. and Wayne, S. (1994) *Play and Care Out of School*, London: HMSO

17 Petrie, P., Egharevba, I., Oliver, C. and Poland, G. (2000) *Out-of-school Services, Out-of-school Lives*, London: The Stationery Office

18 Robinson, C., Weston, C. and Minkes, J. (1995) *Making Progress: Change and Development in Services to Disabled Children under the Children Act 1989*, Bristol: Norah Fry Research Centre, University of Bristol

19 Smith, T. (1996) *Family Centres and Bringing Up Young Children*, London: HMSO

20 Statham, J. (1996) *Young Children in Wales: An Evaluation of the Children Act 1989 for Day Care Services*, London: Thomas Coram Research Unit

21 Statham, J., Dillon, J. and Moss, P. (forthcoming) *Placed and Paid For: Supporting Families through Sponsored Day Care*, London: The Stationery Office

22 Thoburn, J., Wilding, J. and Watson, J. (2000) *Family Support in Cases of Emotional Maltreatment and Neglect*, London: The Stationery Office

23 Tunstill, J. and Aldgate, J. (2000) *Services for Children in Need: From Policy to Practice*, London: The Stationery Office

24 Ward, H. (ed.) (1995) *Looking After Children: Research into Practice*, London: HMSO

2 Social Services Inspectorate inspections reports

25 Social Services Inspectorate (1994) *Services to Disabled Children and their Families*, London: HMSO

26 Social Services Inspectorate (1994) *Inspection of Private and Voluntary Day Nurseries for Children under Eight*, London: HMSO

27 Social Services Inspectorate (1996) *Children in Need: Report of an SSI Inspection of Social Services Departments' Family Support Services 1993/95*, London: Department of Health

28 Social Services Inspectorate (1997) *When Leaving Home is also Leaving Care*, London: The Stationery Office

29 Social Services Inspectorate (1997) *The Education of Children Who Are Looked After by Local Authorities*, London: The Stationery Office

30 Social Services Inspectorate (1997) *Issues Emerging from Children and Families Overview Reports*, London: The Stationery Office

31 Social Services Inspectorate (1997) *Responding to Families in Need: Inspection of Assessment, Planning and Decision-making in Family Support Services*, London: The Stationery Office

32 Social Services Inspectorate (1998) *Someone Else's Children*, London: The Stationery Office

33 Social Services Inspectorate (1998) *Removing Barriers for Disabled Children: Inspection of Services for Disabled Children and their Families*, London: The Stationery Office

34 Social Services Inspectorate (1998) *Planning to Deliver: Inspection of Children's Services Planning*, London: The Stationery Office

35 Social Services Inspectorate (1999) *Getting Family Support Right: Inspection of the Delivery of Family Support Services*, London: The Stationery Office

3 SSI court orders and other studies

36 Department of Health (1992) *Court Orders Study*, London: HMSO

37 Department of Health (1994) *Timetabling of Interim Care Orders Study*, London: HMSO

38 Department of Health (1994) *Planning Long-term Placement Study*, London: HMSO

39 Department of Health (1994) *Contact Orders Study*, London: HMSO

40 Department of Health (1995) *Residence Orders Study*, London: HMSO

41 Department of Health (1998) *Care Planning and Court Orders Study*, London: Department of Health

4 Children Act Reports to Parliament

42 Department of Health (1993) *Children Act Report 1992: A Report by the Secretaries of State for Health for England and for Wales on the Children Act 1989 in Pursuance of their Duties under Section 83(6) of the Act*, Cm 2144, London: HMSO

43 Department of Health (1994) *Children Act Report 1993: A Report by the Secretaries of State for Health for England and for Wales on the Children Act 1989 in Pursuance of their Duties under Section 83(6) of the Act*, Cm 2584, London: HMSO

44 Department of Health (2000) *The Children Act Report 1995–1999: A Report by the Secretaries of State for Health, the Secretary of State for Education and Employment and the Lord Chancellor on the Children Act 1989 in Pursuance of their Duties under Section 83(6) of the Act*, Cm 4579, London: The Stationery Office

5 Children Act 1989 *Guidance and Regulations* and accompanying documentation

45 Department of Health (1989) *An Introduction to the Children Act 1989*, London: HMSO

46 Department of Health (1990) *The Care of Children: Principles and Practice in Regulations and Guidance*, London: HMSO

47 Department of Health (1991) *The Children Act 1989: Guidance and Regulations, Volume 2: Family Support, Day Care and Educational Provision for Young Children*, London: HMSO

48 Department of Health (1991) *The Children Act 1989: Guidance and Regulations, Volume 3: Family Placements*, London: HMSO

49 Department of Health (1991) *The Children Act 1989: Guidance and Regulations, Volumes 1–9*, London: HMSO

6 Previous Department of Health overviews

50 Department of Health and Social Security (1985) *Social Work Decisions in Child Care*, London: HMSO

51 Department of Health (1991) *Patterns and Outcomes in Child Placement: Messages from Current Research and their Implications*, London: HMSO

52 Department of Health (1995) *Child Protection: Messages from Research*, London: HMSO

53 Department of Health (1996) *Focus on Teenagers: Research into Practice*, London: HMSO

54 Department of Health (1998) *Caring for Children Away from Home: Messages from Research*, Chichester: Wiley

55 Department of Health (1999) *Adoption Now: Messages from Research*, Chichester: Wiley

7 Other relevant publications

56 Aldgate, J. (1980) 'Factors influencing children's length of stay in care', in Triseliotis, J. (ed.) *New Developments in Foster Care and Adoption*, London: Routledge and Kegan Paul, pp. 29–40

57 Aldgate, J. and Colman, R. (1999) *The Post-Qualifying Award in Child Care: A Conceptual Framework*, Report to the Department of Health

58 Audit Commission (1994) *Seen But Not Heard: Co-ordinating Community Child Health and Social Services for Children in Need*, London: HMSO

59 Booth, Dame M. (1996) *Avoiding Delay in Children Act Cases*, London: Lord Chancellor's Office

60 Bradshaw, J. (1990) *Child Poverty and Deprivation in the UK*, London: National Children's Bureau

61 Brophy, J., Wale, C. and Bates, P. (1999) *Myths and Practices: A National Survey of the Use of Experts in Child Care Proceedings*, London: British Agencies for Adoption and Fostering

62 Butler-Sloss, Lord Justice E. (1988) *Report of the Inquiry into Child Abuse in Cleveland 1987*, London: HMSO

63 Cleaver, H. and Freeman, P. (1995) *Parental Perspectives in Cases of Suspected Child Abuse*, London: HMSO

64 Department for Education and Employment (1998) *Meeting the Childcare Challenge*, Sudbury: DfEE Publications

65 Department for Education and Employment (1999) *Sure Start: Making a Difference for Children and Families,* Sudbury: DfEE Publications

66 Department for Education and Employment and Department of Health (2000) *Guidance on the Education of Children and Young People in the Public Care,* London: Department of Health

67 Department of Health (1995) *Looking After Children: Trial Pack of Planning and Review Forms and Assessment and Action Records (Revised),* London: HMSO

68 Department of Health (1996) *Refocusing Children's Services: Conference Proceedings, 26 September 1996,* London: Department of Health

69 Department of Health (1998) *Quality Protects Circular: Transforming Children's Services,* Local Authority Circular (LAC(98) 28)

70 Department of Health (1999) *Care Plans and Care Proceedings under the Children Act 1989,* Local Authority Circular (LAC(99) 29)

71 Department of Health (1998) *Partnership in Action: New Opportunities for Joint Working between Health and Social Services: A Discussion Paper,* London: Department of Health

72 Department of Health (1999) *Audit of Looking After Children Records,* London: Department of Health

73 Department of Health (1999) *The Government's Objectives for Children's Social Services,* London: Department of Health

74 Department of Health (1999) *Modernising Social Services,* Cm 4169, London: Department of Health

75 Department of Health (2000) *Children Looked After By Local Authorities: Year Ending 31 March 1999. England,* A/F 99/12, London: Department of Health

76 Department of Health (2000) *Assessing Children in Need and Their Families: Practice Guidance,* London: The Stationery Office

77 Department of Health (2000) *New Children's Services Planning Guidance Working Draft 16 March,* London: Department of Health

78 Department of Health and Department for Education and Employment (1996) *Children's Services Planning Guidance,* London: Department of Health

79 Department of Health, Department for Education and Employment and Home Office (2000) *Framework for the Assessment of Children in Need and Their Families,* London: The Stationery Office

80 Department of Health, Home Office and Department for Education and Employment (1999) *Working Together to Safeguard Children: A Guide to Inter-agency Working to Safeguard and Promote the Welfare of Children,* London: The Stationery Office; and National Assembly for Wales (2000), *Working Together to Safeguard Children: A Guide to Inter-agency Working to Safeguard and Promote the Welfare of Children,* Cardiff: National Assembly for Wales

81 Department of Health and Social Services Inspectorate (1995) *The Challenge of Child Protection: Practice Guide,* London: HMSO

82 Department of Health and Social Services Inspectorate (1998) *Social Services: Facing the Future. The Seventh Annual Report of the Chief Inspector, Social Services Inspectorate 1997/8,* London: Department of Health

83 Department of Health and Social Security (1983) *Code of Practice: Access to Children in Care,* London: HMSO

84 Department of Health and Social Security (1985) *Review of Child Care Law: Report to Ministers of an Interdepartmental Working Party,* London: HMSO

85 Department of Health and Social Security (1987) *The Law on Child Care and Family Services,* London: HMSO

86 Hansard, House of Lords, 6 December 1988, 2nd reading, Col. 488

87 Hardiker, P. (1998) 'Children still in need indeed: prevention across five decades', in Stevenson, O. (ed.) *Child Welfare in the UK,* Oxford: Blackwell Scientific, pp. 42–61

88 House of Commons Social Services Committee (1984) *Report of the Social Services Committee on Children in Care,* London: HMSO

89 House of Commons Health Committee (1998) *Report of the Committee on Health in Relation to Children Looked After by the Local Authority*, London: The Stationery Office

90 Law Commission (1988) *Family Review of Child Care Law: Guardianship and Custody*, Report No. 172, London: HMSO

91 Monkton, Lord W. (1945), *Report on the Circumstances which led to the boarding out of Denis and Terence O'Neill at Bank Farm, Ministerley, and the Steps taken to Supervise their Welfare*, Cmd 6636, London: HMSO

92 National Assembly for Wales (2000) *Framework for the Assessment of Children in Need in Their Families: Consultation Draft (March 2000)*, Cardiff: National Assembly for Wales

93 Nicholson, D. and Ward, H. (1999) *Looking After Children: Good Parenting, Good Outcomes. Report of an Audit of Implementation in 11 Local Authorities in Wales*, Loughborough: University of Loughborough

94 Packman, J. with Randall, J. and Jacques, N. (1986) *Who Needs Care?* Oxford: Blackwell

95 Robinson, C. and Macadam, M. (1995) *Balancing the Act: The Impact of the Children Act 1989 on Family Link Services for Children with Disabilities*, London: National Children's Bureau

96 Seebohm, F. (1968) *Report of the Committee on Local Authority and Allied Personal Social Services*, London: HMSO

97 Sinclair, R. and Carr-Hill, R. (1997) *The Categorisation of Children in Need*, London: National Children's Bureau

98 Stevenson, O. (ed.) (1998) *Child Welfare in the UK*, Oxford: Blackwell Scientific

99 Thoburn, J., Murdoch, A. and O'Brien, A. (1986) *Permanence in Child Care*, Oxford: Basil Blackwell

100 United Nations (1989) *United Nations Convention on the Rights of the Child*, Geneva: United Nations

101 United Nations (1990) *World Summit for Children*, Report of conference proceedings, September 1990, New York: United Nations

102 Utting, D. (1995) *Family and Parenthood: Supporting Families, Preventing Breakdown*, York: Joseph Rowntree Foundation

103 Utting, Sir W. (1997) *People Like Us: The Report of the Review of the Safeguards for Children Living Away from Home*, London: The Stationery Office

104 Welsh Office (1996) *Children's Services Planning*, Circular 20/96, Cardiff: Welsh Office

105 Welsh Office (1999) *The National Childcare Strategy in Wales*, Cardiff: Welsh Office

106 Welsh Office (1999) *The Children First Programme in Wales: Transforming Children's Services*, Circular 20/99, Cardiff: Welsh Office

107 Welsh Office (1999) *Sure Start: A Programme to Increase Opportunity for Very Young Children in Wales*, Circular 21/99, Cardiff: Welsh Office

108 Welsh Office (1999) *Children and Youth Partnership Fund for Wales*, Circular 22/99, Cardiff: Welsh Office

109 Welsh Office (1999) *Building for the Future: Social Services White Paper for Wales*, Cardiff: Welsh Office

110 Welsh Office (1999) *Social Services Statistics Wales 1999*, Cardiff: Welsh Office

Index

Index by Mary Norris